FOOD and NUTRITION

FOOD and NUTRITION
Customs and Culture

Paul Fieldhouse

CHAPMAN AND HALL
LONDON • NEW YORK • TOKYO • MELBOURNE • MADRAS

UK	Chapman and Hall, 2–6 Boundary Row, London SE1 8HN
USA	Chapman and Hall, 29 West 35th Street, New York NY10001
JAPAN	Chapman and Hall Japan, Thomson Publishing Japan, Hirakawacho Nemoto Building, 7F, 1-7-11 Hirakawa-cho, Chiyoda-ku, Tokyo 102
AUSTRALIA	Chapman and Hall Australia, Thomas Nelson Australia, 102 Dodds Street, South Melbourne, Victoria 3205
INDIA	Chapman and Hall India, R. Seshadri, 32 Second Main Road, CIT East, Madras 600 035

First edition 1986
Reprinted 1988, 1991

© 1986 Paul Fieldhouse

Printed and bound in Great Britain by
Mackays of Chatham PLC, Chatham, Kent

ISBN 0 7099 1042 8 (HB)
    0 412 38470 1 (PB)

British Library Cataloguing in Publication Data

Fieldhouse, Paul
    Food and nutrition: customs and culture.
    1. Food habits
    I. Title
    394.1'2   GT2860

    ISBN 0–7099–1042–8
    ISBN 0–412–38470–1 Pbk

Library of Congress Cataloging-in-Publication Data

Fieldhouse, Paul.
    Food and Nutrition.

    Includes bibliographies.
    1. Food habits.   2. Nutrition.   I. Title.
    GT2850.F52   1985   394.1   85–21276
    ISBN 0–7099–1042–8
    ISBN 0–412–38470–1 (pbk.)

CONTENTS

List of Tables
List of Figures
Preface
Acknowledgements

TABLES AND FIGURES

Tables

Figures

As someone who was trained in the clinical scientific tradition, it took me several years to start to appreciate that food was more than a collection of nutrients, and that most people did not make their choices of what to eat on the biologically rational basis of nutritional composition. This realisation helped to bring me to an understanding of why people didn´t always eat what (I believed) was good for them, and why the patients I had seen in hospital as often as not had failed to follow the dietary advice I had so confidently given.

When I entered the field of health education I quickly discovered the famous WHO definition of health as being a state of complete physical, mental and social well-being, and not merely the absence of disease. Health was a triangle - and I had been guilty of virtually ignoring two sides of that triangle. As I became involved in practical nutrition education initiatives the deficiencies of the ´physical side´ only approach became more and more apparent. The children whom I saw in schools knew exactly what to say when asked to describe a nutritious diet: they could recite the food guide and list rich sources of vitamins and minerals; but none of this intellectual knowledge was reflected in their own actual eating habits. Yet nutrition education continued to focus on rote learning of nutrition information and food values. The situation in higher education did not seem to be much different. The curriculum focused on physiological and biochemical aspects of nutrition, whilst acknowledging only peripherally - if at all - the non-biological meanings of food. This, I think, was a result of a pervading medical model of nutrition which was disease-prevention rather than health-promotion orientated. Within this context it should not perhaps have been surprising that courses in sociology and psychology were seen by many students as being largely irrelevant.

When I went to teach in Canada, a country where multiculturalism flourishes, the importance of comprehending social meanings of food and food-related behaviours was driven home even more forceably. In Britain there had been some recent interest in developing nutrition education materials suitable for use with Asian groups - a recognition of the obvious cultural differences which existed in food patterns and preferences. In Canada I had, in one class, students whose parents came from Germany, the Ukraine, Iceland, Malaya, Nigeria, Scotland, Norway, the USA...the list seemed endless. Although the majority of these students were ´Canadians´ they had grown up with quite different ideas of what constituted normal eating habits, what foods were acceptable on what occasions, what foods represented security, love, hospitality.... and so on. I was fortunate to be able to teach a course which dealt solely with the diversity of ethnic food habits and the cultural basis of food choice. It was from that experience that the idea for this book emerged, in which I have tried to cover a broad range of topics in sufficient detail to provide a basic appreciation of the non-biological reasons for food choice. If, as nutritionists, we gain only a small understanding of the role of food in society, we may be better able to put into perspective our own concerns for the metabolic adequacy of diets.

Eating to Live
Human beings the world over share a common need to meet certain fundamental conditions for survival. One of these needs is the securing of an adequate diet which will provide energy and the various nutrients necessary for metabolic functioning. Whilst the fact of this commonality may be so obvious as to hardly merit comment, it gives rise to an equally true but less readily appreciated observation. The range of human nutritional requirements is fairly narrow, but the ways in which these similar requirements are met are hugely diverse. Vastly differing dietary patterns, utilising thousands of different foodstuffs and combinations of foodstuffs are capable of achieving the same end - that of survival. It is also apparent that the body is able to call upon certain compensatory mechanisms to ensure short-term survival when nutritional needs are not being met. Biological adaptations have been described which act to conserve precious energy and body nutrient stores during periods of fasting or starvation; similarly, metabolic adjustments help to ensure successful outcome to pregnancy even where the mother is not optimally nourished. These are biological mechanisms; there are also culturally learnt adaptations designed to enhance survival prospects under adverse circumstances. Techniques of delaying or displacing hunger, for example, are important in societies where food shortages are common occurrences.
     The variety of substances which are consumed as food by various peoples of the world is truly

remarkable; though for any given cultural group the list of acceptable foodstuffs is usually severely curtailed. The traditional Inuit diet consisted almost entirely of meat and fish; in many developing countries today, a single type of grain forms the bulk of what is eaten every day. In contrast, some N. American Indian tribes traditionally ate over a hundred kinds of seeds, roots and nuts. In Europe and North America, meat comes mostly from beef, pork, lamb and chicken; but for the Dusan of Northern Borneo snake, gibbon, anteater, mouse and rat, are all acceptable protein sources. South American Indians eat monkeys, iguanas, grubs, bees and head lice, whilst the Aborigines of Australasia relish insects. Fluids too come in a variety of forms: water, fruit juices, milk and blood; tea, coffee, cocoa, beer and wine. Non-food substances are regularly consumed; clay-eating practices amongst Mississippi Blacks: rotted wood consumption by the Vedda of Sri Lanka: pebble-eating by the Guiana of South America - are examples. Sometimes humans learn to consume and to prefer substances which are intrinsically unpalatable. Coffee and chili are flavours which have become widely desired despite the bitter and burning sensations they evoke. Rotted food is appreciated by the Dusan of Northern Borneo, who allow meat to spoil to liquefaction before consuming it with rice. The Vietnamese create sauces from putrified materials; sophisticated Europeans hang game birds until they are ´ripe´.

Eating as a social experience
Whilst the task of delineating ´What is eaten´ is a far from simple one it is as nothing compared to addressing the question of ´Why is it eaten?´. Food has always been much more than a source of body nourishment; it has played a major part in the social life, both religious and secular, of human groups. The following list drawing on the work of Bass, Wakefield & Kolassa (1979) indicates some of the diverse uses of foods in society, and includes both biological and cultural functions. Food is used to:
1. Satisfy hunger and nourish the body
2. Initiate and maintain personal and business relationships
3. Demonstrate the nature and extent of relationships
4. Provide a focus for communal activities
5. Express love and caring
6. Express individuality

7. Proclaim the separateness of a group
8. Demonstrate belongingness to a group
9. Cope with psychological or emotional stress
10. Reward or punish
11. Signify social status
12. Bolster self-esteem and gain recognition
13. Wield political and economic power
14. Prevent, diagnose and treat physical illness
15. Prevent, diagnose and treat psychological
    illness
16. Symbolise emotional experiences
17. Display piety
18. Represent security
19. Express moral sentiments
20. Signify wealth.

This book is largely devoted to a discussion of the social meanings and cultural uses of food in ancient and contemporary societies throughout the world and many of the above themes are taken up in the ensuing pages. Chapter 1 introduces the topic of bioculture and outlines conceptual models of food choice and ways of studying food habits. Chapter 2 explores food ideology - the concept of ´what is food?´, and looks at various classification systems for foods and food habits. Chapters 3 and 4 are devoted to social and religious meanings of foods, the latter including a discussion of food cultism. Chapter 5 deals with food myths and superstitions, and the topic of taboos and prohibitions is specifically illustrated with the examples of ´The Sacred Cow´ and of ´Cannibalism´. Chapter 6 examines individual food choice from a psycho-cultural perspective.
     Whilst economic and political factors play a significant part in shaping food choice they act for the most part at the level of availability rather than acceptability. For this reason I have viewed them as being beyond the scope of the present volume except for the short discussion of politics and personal ethics in Chapter 4. My remarks concerning food guides and my somewhat sympathetic treatment of food cultism may not find universal favour, critical as they are of conventional wisdom, but I hope that students are at least faced with the challenge of having to think through the issues before taking up positions on one side or the other. The simple but central message repeated throughout the book and supported by a variety of examples from different cultures and ages, is that eating is not and never has been a merely biological activity. Probably most people including my professional nutritionist colleagues would agree with this assertion; my hope

is that this knowledge can be taken off the shelf of intellectual ideas and incorporated into teaching and, ultimately, the way in which nutritionists and dietitians deal with communities and with patients.

For the reader who is neither nutritionist nor student, but who picks up the book through a general interest in food and people, my hope is that they will enjoy the feast. The multi-course menu, of potlatches, hunger strikes, festivals, sacrifices, taboos, and dinner parties, should provide sustenance enough, but if attention wanes, then remember - there´s always the coffee pot and the biscuit tin...

REFERENCE

Bass, M.A., L.M. Wakefield, and K.M. Kolasa. Community Nutrition and Individual Food Behaviour. Burgess Publ., Minn. 1979

ACKNOWLEDGEMENTS

I gratefully acknowledge the following permissions to reprint excerpts of published material. G.F. Stickley Company and Dr V. Herbert for ´16 Tips to spot the quack´ from ´Nutrition Cultism´. Copyright Victor Herbert 1980-81. ´Food Avoidances amongst Women of Tamilnad´ from Ferro-Luzzi G.E., Ecology of Food and Nutrition 3:7-15, 1974; Reprinted by permission of the publishers; Copyright Gordon and Breach Science Publishers Inc. ´List of Useful Tags to Apply When Judging the Credibility of Nutritional Information´. Reprinted by permission from Nutrition: Concepts and Controversies, Second Edition by Eva May Hamilton and Eleanor Whitney; Copyright 1978, 1982 by West Publishing Company. All rights reserved. Page 10.
I would also like to thank Professor Reverend Vincent Eriksson for his helpful comments on Chapter 4 ´Religion´. Mr Tim Hardwick of Croom Helm Ltd. has been more than patient with the process of transatlantic communications involved in preparing this book and has provided many valuable suggestions. Finally I must thank my wife, Corinne Eisenbraun, for her continuing support and encouragement during the preparation of the text, and for her contributions to proofreading . Nevertheless responsibility for errors and omissions rests with the author who remains conscious of the debt owed to the many authors whose work has been drawn on in this volume.

Chapter 1

BIOCULTURAL PERSPECTIVES ON NUTRITION

> In no area of biology is the relationship with
> the social sciences more inclusive or critical
> than in the nutritional sciences.
> Richard Barnes (1968)

FOOD AND CULTURE

Even a cursory glance through the scientific
literature, or a modicum of reflective thought is
enough to produce ready agreement with the idea that
culture is a major determinant of what we eat.
Whilst it is easily seen that the direct
consequences of food intake are biological - food
meets the energy and nutrient needs of the body, it
is also apparent that the nature of that food intake
is shaped by social, religious, economic, and
political processes (Sanjur 1982, p18). Recognition
of the fact that food intake is a response to both
biological and cultural stimuli and that eating
fulfils both biological and social needs, leads
inescapably to the conclusion that the study of
nutrition is a biocultural issue par excellence.
Human foodways - a term which includes as well as
food choice - methods of eating, preparation, number
of meals per day, time of eating and the size of
portions eaten, are an integrated part of a coherent
cultural pattern in which each custom and practice
has a part to play. Food habits come into being and
are maintained because they are effective, practical
and meaningful behaviours in a particular culture.
They are a product of everyday environmental forces

1

acting within the context of historical conditioning
- a melding of new ideas and imperatives with old
traditions.

When we use the term ´culture´ in everyday
speech, we often employ it as a convenient shorthand
for an ill-defined entity which we might better
describe as ´way of life´. We are vaguely aware that
our culture is what makes us similar to some other
people and yet different from the vast majority of
people in the world. It is a kind of social
heritage. Moreover, we usually distinguish this
usage of the word from the artistic vision of
´culture´, and from the notion of ´culture´ as that
which is refined, sophisticated and highbrow. It
nevertheless defies precise definition.
Anthropologists too, have disagreed about the
meaning of ´culture´. Although many different
attempts at formulations have been made over the
years, Tylor´s early definition is still useful;
culture is ´that complex whole which includes
knowledge, belief, art, morals, law, customs, and
any other capabilities and habits acquired by man as
a member of society´ (Tylor 1871). And indeed, it is
complex, being the sum total of a group´s learned,
shared behaviour, unique in that it is shared
through time. The terms ´culture´ and ´society´ are
sometimes used interchangeably; whilst it is true
that there can be no culture apart from society,
they are nevertheless not the same thing. Culture
describes patterns of behaviour; society refers to
the people who participate in the culture and thus
give it concrete expression. Although there is great
diversity between cultures, a number of
characteristics applicable to all cultures may be
identified (Foster 1962).

1. Culture is a LEARNED experience; it is
acquired by man. It is not biologically determined
and therefore can be modified or unlearned. (This is
important for the nutrition educator to note).
Culture is a group phenomenon, not an individual
one; it is transmitted from one generation to the
next, and in the absence of socialisation processes
would not be continued. It may be transmitted
formally or informally, by verbal instruction or by
non-verbal cues and through personal example.

2. Culture INVOLVES CHANGE; each generation,
although it learns the culture it is born into, is
never exactly the same as its predecessor. Learning
is incomplete. Food habits are part of a dynamic
process; whilst they are basically stable and

2

predictable, they are paradoxically, at the same time undergoing constant and continuous change. Culture is not static; it preserves traditions but also builds in mechanisms for change. Though the elements of food behaviour remain the same, the manner in which they are carried out is modified from generation to generation (Bass, Wakefield & Kolassa 1979, p4).

3. Every culture RESISTS CHANGE; food habits, though far from fixed, are resistant to change.

4. We are on the whole, UNCONSCIOUS of our culture. It is internalised so that most of our routine behaviours are done unthinkingly, simply because ´that´s how they are done´. We may even be unaware that there are rules governing many aspects of our behaviour. ´Because man internalises his cultural traditions, they become an inseparable part of him; few people realise to what extent they are both the beneficiaries and the victims of the cultural traditions in which they were raised.´ (Gifft et al 1972, p11).

5. Culture has a VALUE SYSTEM. Amongst the substances accepted as food by a culture, some are labelled ´good´ and some ´bad´. ´Bad´ foods are sometimes highly desired - as in the case of empty calorie ´junk foods´. The ambivalence of attitudes to good and bad foods in many Northern cultures is explored further in Chapter 3.

In addition to the above universals, Foster also points out that a culture contains symbols that are understood by the group, emphasises specific activities, and provides for interaction between people in a socially acceptable manner (Foster 1962). The ´success´ of a culture may be judged by the extent to which it meets the needs of its members (Bass, et al 1979, p7). If there is a widespread failure of culturally sanctioned behaviour patterns to meet the needs of people, then the cultural ´norms´ which dictate acceptable behaviour may be overthrown. Food riots and antisocial behaviour during food shortages are consequences of the inadequacy of established social mechanisms in dealing with abnormal situations. The complex food system of modern industrialised nations removes most people from a direct role in food production and puts them at the mercy of an intricate food distribution network. There is a danger that this system cannot meet the food needs of all segments of the population, as evidenced by increasing numbers of reports of malnutrition in

´affluent´ commmunities, and the appearance of ´food
banks´ and other forms of food relief in ostensibly
rich Northern cities. [1] If abnormal situations
become common enough, there will be pressure for
changes in cultural patterns to accomodate the new
reality. Another instance in which cultural norms
may be over-ridden is when necessity dictates.
Cannibalism is looked upon with revulsion by
Judeao-Christian societies, but is tolerated when
circumstances make it the only hope of survival.
        The five universal attributes of culture
identified above, are now further discussed
specifically as they apply to food habits.

SOCIALISATION AND ACQUISITION OF FOOD HABITS

Culture is LEARNED. Food habits are acquired early
in life and once established are likely to be
long-lasting and resistant to change. Hence the
importance of developing sound nutritional practices
in childhood. Socialisation describes the process by
which culturally valued norms of behaviour are
passed on from generation to generation. It is a
life-long process; natural functions, such as
eating, become socialised as the growing child is
conditioned by customs and traditions. (Some authors
distinguish between socialisation - the transmission
of culture, and enculturation - transmission of a
specific culture. For a scholarly discussion, see
Williams (1973).) The early acquisition of food
habits and the implications of this process for
nutrition education has been discussed elsewhere
(Fieldhouse 1983). This earlier discussion
concentrated on the learning of nutritional values;
of equal importance is the concurrent learning of
social values attached to food and food events.
Figure 1.1 depicts the socialisation process as
applied to food habits.
        Primary socialisation occurs mainly through the
agency of the immediate family. Food is one of the
basic mediums through which adult attitudes and
sentiments are communicated to the child; indeed,
the mother receives her definition for the child in
association with feeding experiences (Fathauer
1960). The infant and young child are dependent on
adults for what they get to eat; they have little
choice in the matter other than through the refusal
to eat at all. Appropriate or desired behaviour is

Figure 1.1 Socialisation and the acquisition of food habits

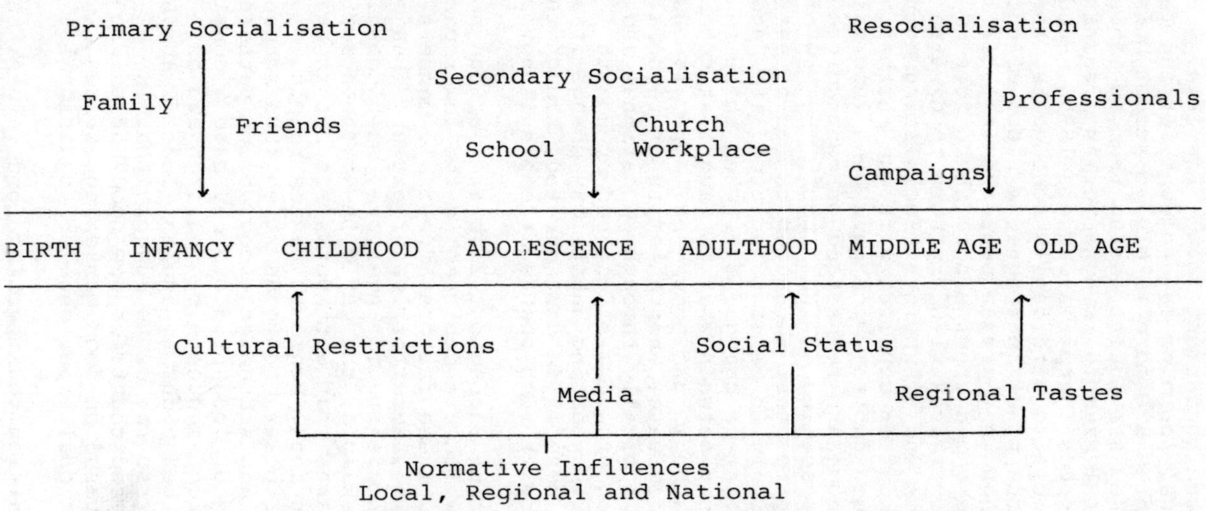

Primary Socialisation

Family   Friends

Secondary Socialisation

School   Church
          Workplace

Resocialisation

          Professionals

          Campaigns

BIRTH INFANCY CHILDHOOD ADOLESCENCE ADULTHOOD MIDDLE AGE OLD AGE

Cultural Restrictions

          Media   Social Status

                                    Regional Tastes

Normative Influences
Local, Regional and National

Resocialisation refers to change and is thus more of a consideration in adult life as indicated in the diagram. It can however apply at any time throughout the life span. Similarly, normative influences are always present though they may be more or less powerful at different times of life.

reinforced whilst deviant or undesired behaviour is sanctioned. Thus the child learns through a system of reward and punishment (q.v). Low level observational learning may account for the fact that young children are more likely to accept unfamiliar foods if they see adults eating them, which suggests that parental example is a factor in ´learning to like´ new foods (Harper & Sanders 1975). Foods become associated with family sentiments, thereby acquiring the power to trigger a flood of childhood memories when they are encountered in later life.

As the child grows older, the circle of influence increases with exposure to diverse experiencies and viewpoints. Socialising agencies may complement or conflict with one another. For example, food habits which have been informally learnt at home are reinforced or contradicted in the more formal setting of the school. The Law of Primacy implies that those habits learnt earliest are most likely to persist in later life, and to be most resistant to change; thus when there is a conflict, say between what is taught at school and what is taught in the home, the latter is most likely to dominate. When attempts at resocialisation are made - typically through educational and intervention programmes designed by health professionals - eating habits may change if a sufficient benefit is demonstrated, though the failure rate of such change attempts is notoriously high.

Operating throughout life are various normative influence which are depicted in the lower part of figure 1.1. These factors affect all members of the society to a greater or lesser extent. Thus cultural restrictions define for everyone, what constitutes food; for example, the child in Northern society quickly learns that earthworms are not regarded as being human food. Regional tastes result in selective exposure to foods which then shapes preference and subsequent food choice patterns. Advertising of food products may have a considerable impact on food requests by children and on purchasing behaviour by adults. Indeed, Abrahamsson (1979) goes so far as to suggest that in industrialised countries new food habits are developed based on food marketing strategies rather than on rational experience or traditional practices.

In addition to imparting food values, the socialisaton process teaches the social, cultural

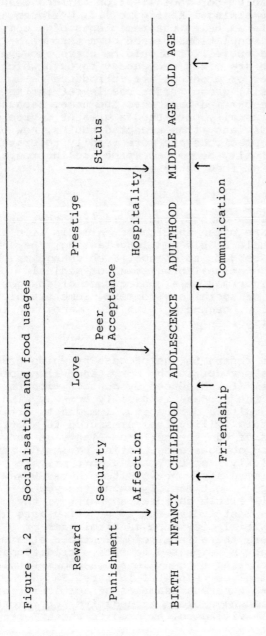

Figure 1.2   Socialisation and food usages

Whilst the learning of various social meanings of food is a continuous process, particular values or usages may be emphasised at different stages of the life span. The role of food in friendship and communication may be considered to be a 'normative' meaning, operating most of the time.

and psychological meanings and uses of food. A
parallel paradigm for socialisation of food meanings
might look something like figure 1.2. Children are
portrayed here as being the recipients of a complex
code of food regulations passed down through
socialising agencies. It should be noted, however,
that children are often the agency through which new
food practices or products are introduced to a
family or social group. Practices learnt in the
school may be carried back into the home. Because
children are usually permitted a greater degree of
latitude in deviancy from accepted habits, new or
strange food practices are more readily tolerated
and may eventually become accepted and incorporated
into mainstream food behaviour.

CHANGE

Culture involves change, and it is true that whilst
food habits are often inculcated early in life and
are on the whole stable and long-lasting, they are
nevertheless subject to change. Such change may be
induced by educational programmes or medical
intervention, or may be a consequence of changes in
the physical or social environment. Some examples
are given below, beginning with the phenomenon known
as acculturation.

Acculturation
Acculturation refers to the process by which groups
and individuals adapt to the norms and values of an
alien culture. It is induced by contact with foreign
cultures and the process is usually two-way with,
however, one culture dominating. Immigrants arriving
in a new cultural milieu feel pressured to adopt the
outward signs of the new culture - language and
clothing being obvious ones. Eating habits do not
change so quickly, for they are a more private
affair, not immediately obvious to others. However,
they do change - most rapidly among the young - and
where there is little cultural support for the old
ways. Thus an East Indian family settling into a
British industrial city such as Birmingham or
Bradford, where there is already a stable ethnic
community might be expected to retain traditional
practices much longer than Vietnamese Boat-People
who find themselves relocated in rural Saskatchewan.
     There are numerous examples of acculturation
processes which have produced negative nutritional
effects. Inuit villagers, exposed to White North

8

American culture brought about in recent years by
oil-field exploration in the Arctic, have suffered
an erosion of their traditional lifestyles. From
being a basically hunting-and-gathering culture,
they have become more and more dependent on prepared
foods sold in stores. This process began when
fur-traders began to infiltrate remote areas and
when trading posts were established. Game became
less available, and hunting was made easier with the
introduction of firearms. As permanent White
communities grew up, Native peoples were more and
more influenced by the cultural values of the
outsiders. Eating the White Man's food was a source
of prestige. Today we see extensive examples of
malnutrition where traditional food habits have been
abandoned in favour of a limited diet of largely
empty-calorie foods. A good example of the effects
of the acculturation process is provided by
Schaefer's description of two Inuit communities –
one exposed to urban values and the other retaining
a more traditional lifestyle (Schaefer, Timmermans,
Eaton & Matthews 1980). A comparison of Arctic Bay,
a small Eastern Arctic settlement following largely
traditional practices, with Inuvik, an urbanised
Western Arctic centre established during the oil
boom of the 1950's, revealed a pattern of ill-health
in Inuvik Native peoples similar to that seen in
industrialised North America – and which was not
prevalent in the more isolated community of Arctic
Bay.
    Another example is furnished by the Dene
(Chipewyan) Indians of Northern Canada, who were
traditionally a hunting and fishing society. With
the development of the fur-trading economy, fishing
and hunting became intensified and food resources
were consequently depleted. As the Indians settled
in permanent communities they developed increasing
reliance on staples of the White traders, bought at
the local store (Schaefer & Steckle 1980). Berkes
and Farkas (1978) discuss the impact of
socio-economic changes on the traditional diets of
Cree Indians from Eastern James Bay. They recommend
a rejuvenation of traditional food habits as well as
an increase in the quality of store-bought food in
order to preserve adequate standards of nutrition.
    In a different time and place, an example of
acculturation leaving a permanent mark on food
usages is seen in the language of food itself. The
English names of ox, cow, calf, pig, sheep, boar,
and deer are used to describe living animals; when

9

these animals are cooked and served at table they
bear the French names of beef, veal, pork, bacon,
mutton, brawn and venison. This difference is often
attributed to the fact that in Medieval times the
lower classes were responsible for keeping the
animals, whilst the upper classes did most of the
actual meat-eating. The influence of the Norman
conquest in England resulted in adoption of French
manners and customs particularly amongst the
aristocratic classes, and hence the use of French
food names at table. Vestiges of this manifestation
of social distinction may be seen in modern
high-status restaurants, where the menu is
ostentatiously written or printed in French.

Changing cultural patterns

Dietary changes do not necessarily have to be
externally induced. Shifts in cultural patterns and
values within a society inevitably affect or are
reflected in dietary practices. Sanjur summarises
recent trends in the U.S. which have had just such
effects (Sanjur 1982, p65-66). One outstanding shift
is the continuing change in family structure. The
traditional extended family system is rapidly
disappearing, and with it the concept of set meal
times to be eaten in the company of specified family
members. The nuclear family, consisting of mother,
father and children is a more flexible, mobile unit
in which, as Sanjur says, eating ´can be and is an
individual non-scheduled event´. The nuclear family
itself may represent a diminishing proportion of
households as one-parent families, and other live-in
arrangements become more common. When single parents
and married women take employment outside the home -
through economic necessity or for reasons of
self-actualisation, other family members become more
responsible for their own diets.

   Conservation of food and energy resources is an
issue which is gaining increasing attention amongst
those who give thought to ecological concerns.
Together with a growing emphasis on non-material
expressions of the meaning of one´s life, away from
consumption of material goods and services, this has
spurred an increased emphasis on home production in
the form of family gardens as a source of food. As
the inner cities become revitalised, gardens spring
up on waste lots, in tiny backyards and even on
rooftops.

   Increased preoccupation with health and
physical fitness gives rise to weight-consciousness,

ever-changing fad diets, and planned
calorie-controlled regimes by the thousand. North
Americans are continually bombarded with messages
exhorting them to seek ultimate fitness, and part
and parcel of this quest is the search for ´health
foods´ - whether they come from organic gardens or
the shelves of ´health stores´ which thrive on
massive sales of diet supplements and pills.

Whilst the United States has opted for a
´melting pot´ policy, and Canada has stressed the
´cultural mosaic´ approach, in both countries there
is a tremendous mix of ethnic groups, each with its
own particular foodways. Acculturation of
minorities, accompanied by an increased interest in
cultural heritage and self-identity has promoted the
popularity of ethnic foods as American ´staples´.
The shopping malls of North America are enlivened
with an endless selection of cafes and fast-food
outlets selling such favourites as tacos, pyroghies,
chow mein, patties, pizzas and the ubiquitous
burgers. Here is a good example of the two-way
nature of acculturation.

Sanjur discusses some of these trends in
greater detail, and they are also addressed at
various points in this book. A major facet of social
change in the last few decades has been in the
communications industry. In a comparatively short
time members of industrialised societies have
progressed from being dependent on occasional
printed material and oral reporting as sources of
information, to a point where they have
instantaneous access to news of worldwide events,
distributed by a complex and technologically
sophisticated communications system. The channels
through which this rapid communication is effected
are often collectively known as the ´mass media´;
T.V., radio, newspapers and magazines are the main
channels, with T.V. being predominant. The ubiquity
of the television set in the homes of industrialised
nations has turned it into a powerful means of
disseminating information. Not surprisingly, those
with something to sell have identified television
advertising as a potent tool.

MASS MEDIA, ADVERTISING AND FOOD HABITS

The role of the mass media in shaping food habits is
a controversial one. As it is generally accepted
that an impersonal communication channel is most

11

effective in conveying information rather than in
active persuasion, some would claim that mass media
impact is limited simply to making people aware of
what is available. This view would suggest that a
television advertisement only affects those who are
already predisposed to buy the product and does not
induce a desire for previously unwanted items.
Advertising may indeed influence choice of
brand-name or specific commodity within an already
desired category of items. Thus if I intend to buy a
car and I see an advertisement for a recent model,
then I may be inclined to examine that model for
possible purchase. Similarly, if I intend to
purchase a cake mix or a can of soup, ads may push
particular brands to the forefront of my mind, so
that when actual purchases are made these brands are
likely to be selected. However, if I have no desire
to eat canned soups, then no amount of advertising
is going to persuade me to buy that product. This
line of thought reflects the belief that mass media
advertising can do no more than provide information
- and that information alone is an insufficient
motivation for action. The latter is certainly true;
but there are those who would maintain that
advertising does do more than provide information.
    Meyers (1963) credited advertising with the
ability to induce action. Certainly advertisers,
being prepared to pour millions of pounds or dollars
into short television commercials, believe that this
technique does sell products. The audience for such
advertisements is extremely large, and several
studies in the U.S. have revealed that a substantial
number of people derive their nutrition information
from seeing and reading ads. (Fox et al 1970, Sanjur
& Scona 1971, Emmons & Hayes 1973). Hanssen (1980)
says of advertising that it ´...persuades us that
the right taste for a food is the result of some
particular concept designed by marketing men,
created by food technologists and produced in
beautiful factories, with sales potential as the
guiding light, rather than nutritional
consequences.´ In a similar vein, the People´s Food
Commission reported the words of C.W. Post, founder
of General Foods. ´You can´t just manufacture
cereal. You´ve got to get it halfway down the
customer´s throat through advertising. Then they´ve
got to swallow it´ (People´s Food Commission 1980,
p60). Advocates of food advertising claim that it
stimulates competition and keeps prices down;
opponents maintain that the huge sums spent on ads

inevitably increase the price of a product.
Nutritional concerns are raised because many of the
products most heavily advertised are low in
nutritional value. The commercial promotion of food
products does not, on the whole, focus on the
nutritional value of a product or the contribution
it makes to physiological well-being. Rather,
advertising appeals utilise the symbolic meanings of
foods, so that what is being sold is not just a
product, but a lifestyle, a dream, an emotional
fulfilment (Figure 1.3).

Figure 1.3 Marketing Appeals in Food Advertising

The food itself: Convenience
                          Newness
                          Naturalness
                          Traditional
                          Nutritional value

Economics: Cost
                          Value for money
                          'Specials'
                          Economy packs

Food as a means to   Status value
something else   Endorsement by personalities
                          Popularity
                          Ideal mother/wife
                          Sexual attraction
                          Fitness and slimness
                          Reward
                          Success

In middle class America most individuals seem
to be attempting to satisfy their love or
esteem needs. If advertising at all reflects
the American need structure, this becomes
evident from a casual perusal of present day
ads. Seldom does one see an advertising message
like 'Crispy crackers fill your stomach fuller
than other products'. More typically one sees:
'Serve Crispy crackers with exotic cheeses and
impress your friends'.
(Kassarjian & Robertson 1968)

Of particular concern is the role of mass media
advertising in the formation of children's food

habits. Many ads are specifically targeted at children and feature confectionery, soft drinks and snack foods. Their intent is to persuade the child to put pressure on the mother to buy brand name products. Young children may not be able to distinguish between adverts and programmes, and certainly do not have the sophistication to descry fact from fiction. Older children can, especially if guided, recognise the essentially unreal nature of adverts. The amount of research in this area is limited - possibly by the difficulties inherent in assessing the diffuse impact of mass media channels. However it is evident that children are exposed to a large amount of food advertising and that the products advertised are often inimical to long-term healthly eating habits.

IMPACT OF FOOD INNOVATIONS ON SOCIETY

Food is an integral part of culture; food usages are prescribed by explicit and implicit rules. Just as social trends can produce changing food habits, so when changes in food usages occur, there may result widespread, and unexpected changes in other aspects of society. An outstanding example of this, studied over a period of several generations, is the adoption of wet rice cultivation by the Tanala tribe of Madagascar (Linton 1933, Broom and Selznick 1955).

Dry rice cultivation was practised by the Tanala, who planted in cleared jungle areas near to a village. After one or two crops the land was abandoned until the jungle overran it again; another spot was cut and burned and the village moved to the new spot. There was communal ownership of territory; joint families being the chief units of organisation. Joint family members worked as a group and they owned the crops from the land they cleared. The head of the joint family divided the crop amongst the households; there was little variation in wealth between families. Game belonged to whoever caught it.

Wet rice cultivation was adopted from a neighbouring tribe; it was done on relatively small plots by single households. Unlike with dry cultivation, the land was in continuous cultivation. The idea of exclusive ownership developed, and because there was only a limited amount of land, a landholder and a landless class developed. Those who held wet rice land no longer had to be involved in

14

joint family efforts in jungle clearing, and they
did not want villages to be moved. The landless
people continued dry rice cultivation and had to
move into the jungle too far to return to their
village at night. Thus they began to develop
separate household organisation. Other changes
emerged - in the kinship and marriage system,
warfare, slavery - and in the growth of a
centralised authority with autocratic control.

Rogers and Shoemaker (1971) use this as an
example of the dangers of being too eager to
introduce apparently benefical nutritional
innovations without being aware of the potential
social ramifications.

Resistance To Change
Although change is inevitable, and is indeed
essential to the well-being of a society, it is true
that resistance to change is often widespread and
difficult to overcome. The introduction of a new
idea or practice may be termed an innovation; it
usually originates from an external source. Whether
the innovation is accepted or not, and the speed at
which it diffuses throughout a society is dependent
on a variety of factors associated both with the
nature of the innovation and the nature of the
society into which it is introduced. Five
characteristics of innovations may be identified and
briefly discussed in relation to food habits; these
are, relative advantage, compatibility, complexity,
trialability and observability.

The greater the perceived relative advantage of
an innovation, the more rapid its rate of adoption.
Obviously a proposed change must be seen to have
more advantages than drawbacks, unless it is to be
enforced rather than being a matter of voluntary
adoption. Compatability is the degree to which an
innovation is perceived as being consistent with the
existing values and needs of society members. In the
field of nutritional health many examples of
incompatability could be cited. For example; the
promotion of beef as a good protein source in school
classes of Hindu children; the advocacy of margarine
as a source of vitamin D for Indian immigrants; the
promotion of citrus fruit to the elderly - many of
whom believe these foods are ´acid´ and will harm
them. The adoption of an incompatible innovation
requires the prior adoption of a new belief or value
system. Complexity is the degree to which an
innovation is perceived as being difficult to
understand and use. Those innovations which require

15

little effort from the recipient will be adopted
more rapidly than those demanding new skills and
understanding. Where little effort is combined with
much gain ready adoption may be expected, as in the
case of an ulcer patient directed to forgo fried
foods. Trialability is the degree to which an
innovation may be experimented with on a limited
basis. A trialable innovation represents less risk
to the individual or group which is considering it.
Substituting artificial sweetener for sugar is
eminently trialable, whilst fluoridation is not.
Observability is the degree to which the results of
an innovation are visible to others. The easier it
is for an individual to see the results of an
innovation, the more likely he is to adopt it
permanently. Many ´desirable´ health behaviours do
not have observable effects because they are, in
essence, preventive actions. Thus it is very
difficult to demonstrate the potential benefits of a
particular dietary pattern in preventing coronary
heart disease or gastro-intestinal disorders.

The rate of adoption of an innovation by a
social group is usually measured by the length of
time required for a certain percentage of the group
to adopt the innovation. Members of the group are
often classified as; innovators, early adopters,
early majority, late majority and laggards. Social
systems typified by modern, rather than traditional
norms exhibit faster rates of adoption. According to
Rogers and Shoemaker (1971, p33), a social system
with modern norms is more change-orientated,
technologically developed, scientific, rational,
cosmopolite and empathic. This suggests that not
only will food innovations be more readily accepted
in industrialised countries, but also that they will
have most impact amongst the higher socio-economic
groups of a society. In the U.K. it has been well
recognised that the modern trend to breast-feeding
is most marked amongst women from social classes I
and II - the same groups who led the move to bottle
feeding forty years ago.

OUR ´UNCONSCIOUS´ CULTURE

As a result of socialisation processes, many of our
everyday decisions become ´routinised´; that is they
are performed as a matter of habit, without
conscious deliberation. We understand that cereals
are proper breakfast foods, and that milk is good to
drink, without having to be reminded every day. More

fundamentally, we know what is and what is not food; we may deliberate over a choice between carrots and cauliflower - but not between chicken and snake. Some nutrition educators argue that the creation of sound nutrition routines, which are internalised during the period of primary socialisation, holds out the greatest promise of success for long term nutritional health.

Values
The value system of a culture shapes the way in which foods are used. Hsu (1975) defined contemporary U.S. values as being those of: achievement, success, activity, work, humanitarianism, efficiency, democracy and individualism - all springing from a core value of self-reliance. A total culture is composed of many parts or subsystems, and each of these has an impact on individual food behaviour. Sometimes the interaction of subsystems may give rise to conflicting values. Bass et al (p9-11) identify the following subsystems in contemporary North America: ideological; technological; economic; educational; political; family; mass media. Some of the value implications these have for food behaviour are listed in Figure 1:4.
    Acculturation of minority groups is made more difficult where values conflict. Native peoples have had to adjust to the values of the dominant culture in North America - and have experienced differing degrees of success. Harris (1982) points out that Euro-Canadians tend to use their own value system to judge Native Canadians and that this results in a less than empathic attitude. Unless there is a willingness and sensitivity to recognise and accept differences in cultural values, problems in co-existence and communication will persist. Figure 1:5 shows a comparison of Native and Euro-Canadian values.

NUTRITIONAL ANTHROPOLOGY

    Applied nutritional anthropology may be defined, in one sense, as the application of anthropological data and methods to the solving of the cultural aspects of human nutrition problems...or as the study of the interrelationships between diet and culture and their mutual influence upon one another. (Freedman R. 1977, p1)

17

Figure 1.4 Impact of cultural subsystems on food values

Ideological	Man has the right to control the earth's resources to his own ends. It is good to feed the poor and underprivileged
Technological	Man can solve world food problems through the application of ever more sophisticated technology Greater energy inputs are needed to produce food
Economic	Food is treated as a commodity with a specific monetary value Food supply and distribution occurs independently of actual human need
Education	Food knowledge, beliefs and attitudes are transmitted from one generation to the next Research efforts are directed to improving the food supply
Political	Government regulations affect production, trade, distribution, safety and quality of food.
Family	Each family member directly influences the food habits of the others. Changes in the diet of one family member has repercussions for the rest of the family.
Mass Media	Food habits are shaped by a powerful socialising agency Food products are promoted selectively on a non-nutritional basis

18

Figure 1.5   A Comparison of Euro-Canadian and Native Values

EURO-CANADIAN (Urban-industrial)	INDIAN, METIS, INUIT (Tribal-traditional)
1. Mastery over nature – (Intensive resource use)	Harmony with nature (Extensive resources use)
2. Future orientation	Present orientation
3. Scientific explanations	Explanations of natural phenomena through mythology & supernatural
4. Aspiration – achieve higher than father	Follow in ways of old people – accept as is
5. Competition for survival	Cooperation for group survival
6. Individuality & collegiality	Group
7. Aggression	Submission
8. Work to get ahead	Work to satisfy present need
9. Sharing – impersonal	Sharing – personal
10. Clock-watching – precision	Time always with us – imprecision
11. Action – attack a problem	Patience – wait for problem to disappear
12. Nuclear family	Extended family
13. Materialistic (static)	Non-materialistic (nomadic)
14. Democracy	Hereditary leadership or temporary leaders
15. Appropriate behaviour codes (group)	Mamasis (individual)
16. Work out conflicts	Repress conflicts
17. Formal rules of proper conduct	Ethic of non-interference

Source: Sealy, D.B. and N. McDonald. 'The Health Care Professional in a Native Community.' Unpublished manuscript, Winnipeg 1979. Cited in Harris (1982).

19

Anthropologists have tended to view food practices simply as an element of the set of customs which makes up a culture, without being concerned about the impact of these practices on health. Nutritionists, on the other hand have focused on the health effects and have not been greatly concerned with cultural values regarding food (Krondl & Boxen 1975). Anthropological reports have traditionally been qualitative in nature; nutritionists have favoured quantitative approaches, describing the dietary habits and nutritional status of populations in statistical terms. A marriage of these two approaches promises fruitful research efforts within the emerging discipline known as nutritional anthropology.

Early American studies on food habits were carried out in the 1920s and 1930s, culminating in the formation of the U.S National Research Council Committee on Food Habits. Kurt Lewin and Margaret Mead were prominent names in the early history of this committee whose work included the production of a handbook which was, in effect, a procedure manual for gathering data (Committee on Food Habits 1945). The principles espoused forty years ago are still sound. For example, the handbook advises that in attempting to change misconceptions about food and diet, one should challenge as few beliefs as possible and subtly work to weaken the grip of these beliefs before attempting to replace them with ´scientific truths´. Zealous planners and field workers need to be constantly reminded of the ´fools rush in´ syndrome.

Success in designing programmes to influence food patterns was enhanced by the realisation that nutritional practices are largely determined by basic customs which are, in turn, interrelated with other aspects of social organisation - such as basic economy. In regard to this particular parameter, Freedman gives case history examples of change attempts - some of which were successes and some failures. For example, he cites Cassel´s studies of the Polela Zulus of Natal; initial efforts to promote use of eggs and milk amongst the Polela were resisted due to complex kinship rules and practical economics. Subsequently, beliefs regarding eggs were identified: (1) to eat an egg which would later hatch was uneconomical; (2) eating eggs was a sign of greed; (3) eating eggs made young girls lascivious. By taking measures to increase the productivity of the hens, the first of these

barriers was overcome; further persuasion and
education resulted in a weakening of the other, less
important rationales, and eventually in the adoption
of egg-eating (Freedman 1977). The case of milk
taboos is discussed later (q.v. Food and Sex).
     In Chile, powdered milk introduced at health
clinics was provided free to needy families. It was
initially rejected as it was suspected to be of poor
quality or to be harmful, but a small charge made it
quite acceptable (Freedman p 12). (A similar
phenomenon is sometimes seen in Britain, in health
clinics which offer slimming programmes and free
dietary advice. The ´free´ service is judged to be
inferior to the programmes of commercial slimming
organisations. Underlying this is the attitude that
´you get what you pay for´, even though most people
are at least aware that they have already indirectly
paid for the service through their taxes.) Many more
examples in the nutritional and anthropological
literature attest to the importance of understanding
cultural values and norms if nutrition innovations
are to be successfully introduced.

Food habit research
Food habit researchers use a variety of approaches
to gather information. The method employed reflects
on the viewpoint of the researcher and colours the
results or the interpretations drawn from results.
Thus it is often difficult to compare findings of
different studies and it is also easy to find
conficting interpretations of the same cultural
phenomena. Grivetti and Pangborn (1973) have
summarised the most popular methodologies as
follows:
1. Environmentalism.   Causal relationships are
sought between culture, health and the environment.
This approach has been largely abandoned as it
treats humans as passive creatures taking whatever
diet is offered by the environment. Numerous
examples throughout this book will show that simple
availability is not a good basis from which to
predict food habits.
2. Cultural ecology.   The interaction of humans
with their environment is stressed in this approach;
culture is not defined solely by the environment,
but rather, there is mutual effect. Some authors
have identified a cultural response to limited food
supplies (Thompson 1949), whilst others suggest that
food availability predicates an evolving social
structure (Steward 1955). Thus it is posited that

21

physical and geographical conditions lead to certain
types of food getting and agricultural systems,
which in turn lead to types of social organisation
and rituals calculated to improve food production
(Back 1976, p30). Whilst ecologists can explain the
nutritive value of a particular cultural practice, a
statement of causality or origin cannot be derived
from that explanation - a weakness which critics are
quick to exploit. Some of the more attractive
cultural ecology theories, propounded by Marvin
Harris, are discussed in detail in later chapters.
3. Regionalism. Instead of focusing on specific
societies, some researchers have dealt with food
production and consumption trends on a large-scale
geographical or, even, world-wide basis.
4. Culture-History. An analysis of archaeological,
linguistic, historical and oral tradition data is
used to trace the origins and spread of dietary
practices. The work of Simoons, which is extensively
discussed in Chapters 3 and 4, is an outstanding
example of the use of this approach.
5. Functionalism. Food is seen as a vehicle for
social communication. Food habits satisfy particular
social needs and stabilise social relationships.
Maslow´s hierarchy of human needs (discussed below)
and Lewin´s channel theory are examples of
conceptual theories derived from this premise. Using
this approach, researchers have often been able to
identify reasons for apparently irrational
behaviours and for rejection of attempts to change
existing food habits. One practical drawback is the
need for long-term participant studies.
6. Quantitative approaches. Attempts to quantify
cultural data are a reaction to the usual
descriptive anthropological accounts obtained of
food habits. Computer simulations and
multidimensional scaling techniques are becoming
increasingly common tools used to analyse food
selection behaviour and to predict dietary
acceptance of food items. Whilst some may agree with
the sentiment that when you can measure something
and express it in numbers then you know what you are
talking about, critics argue that human behaviour is
not susceptible to such treatment.
7. Clinical approaches. Recognition is given to
the fact that traditional diets and dietary
practices may be nutritionally adequate when the
value of indigenous foods is fully appreciated. By
gaining an understanding of the total culture,
nutritionists are less likely to propose changes

which are unnecessary or impractical.

Grivetti and Pangborn comment on the short-comings of each of these approaches and argue that no single one provides all the information necessary for a full understanding of food habits. A fusion or combination of approaches, and collaboration between researchers working in multi-disciplinary teams would be of immense value. Cattle (1976) also condemns what she calls 'nutritional particularism'. She says that it has hindered interdisciplinary co-operation, and has resulted in the generation of discrete and disconnected units of information; furthermore, the conclusions offered by particularistic research are: 'usually low-level or "localised" generalisations which can be characterised as repetitive and unexciting' (Cattle, p37). The problems which Cattle identifies centre around three underlying attitudes in scholarly endeavour. These are: Western standards and cultural bias; institutional and disciplinary rivalries; research versus application. As an alternative to particularism she proposes an adaptive model which embraces biological, evolutionary, ecological and sociocultural processes (op cit p41). Many other authors also stress the need to integrate socio-cultural and biologic approaches to the study of nutrition (See for example, Pelto & Jerome 1978). New research techniques are needed which will make it possible to relate data from one field to the other.

FOOD CHOICE MODELS

Obviously, the selection of foods by human groups is influenced by a myriad of factors. The answer to the question 'why does one eat what one eats?' is indeed a complex one. Most people would probably feel that they are fairly free to choose their own diets - and most people would be surprised to learn the constraints that are in fact operating in limiting their choices. Various models of food choice processes have been proposed over the years. Some have emphasised environment, others have concentrated on internal motivation. Each has contributed to an understanding of the factors which shape our food choices, whilst at the same time leaving many questions unanswered. Indeed, it seems unlikely that the plethora of factors which impinge on food choice can be codified in a single paradigm.

23

Sanjur (1982) describes some of the major
theoretical frameworks which have been used in the
study of food habits. Briefly, these are:
  1. The multidimensional code. In this approach,
the dietary patterns of people are described as
being functions of food consumption, preference and
ideology, and of sociocultural parameters. Sanjur
claims that this model highlights the
interrelatedness of the dimensions studied (Sanjur
p26).
  2. Environmentalist model. Food habits are seen
as being a function of the home and school
environments. The model focuses on the knowledge and
motivations of the child. Lund and Burk (1969)
developed this approach to study the way in which
children's food habits are patterned. Whilst the
model again emphasises the interrelatedness of
factors affecting food consumption, it omits
considerations of food availability and peer
influence.
  3. Ecological model. Food habits are viewed as
being a result of the interaction of objective and
subjective forces in an economic setting. Objective
forces include physical and technological
availability; cultural and psycho-social factors
form the subjective component. This model, proposed
by Wenkam (1969), makes clear the fact that any
given food may have different meanings to members of
the same society and it is not possible to
generalise this meaning when change efforts are
contemplated.
  4. Motivational model. Food habits satisfy
social needs; food is symbolic of human values and
relationships. The conceptual framework derived from
these premises is commonly known as the channel
theory and was first propounded by Kurt Lewin in the
1940's (Lewin 1943). He proposed that food moved
step by step through 'channels' until it ended up on
the table, where it would be eaten by one or other
family member. Each of the channels was controlled
by a person, whom Lewin called the 'gatekeeper';
this person had to be identified in any change
efforts. Four decades ago, Lewin was able to
consider the housewife as being the gatekeeper of
family food intake. With changes in family
structures, work opportunities, and social roles,
this can no longer be considered to be the case -
though Sanjur (p46) points out that it still holds
in traditional rural societies. The number of
channels and the number of steps within a channel

24

varies for different foods and in different cultural
contexts; entrance into and movement through food
channels is governed by values such as taste,
health, social status and cost. These values
interact, and actual food choice is thus a complex
decision based on motivations of which the consumer
may not even be aware.

Another motivational framework which finds
support amongst the functionalist school of thought
was described by Abraham Maslow, when he applied his
well-known 'human needs' model to food usage (Maslow
1970). This is discussed in some detail below as it
yields valuable insights into the biocultural nature
of food needs.

Hierarchy of Human Needs
Maslow classified human needs in terms of
physiological and social parameters; he deduced that
some needs are more basic than others and was thus
able to construct a hierarchy of these needs (Figure
1.6). He suggested that at least minimum
satisfaction of one need is necessary before a
person can move up to seek satisfaction of the next
higher need. Above this minimum level of
satisfaction, needs may be met to a greater or
lesser extent, and progress to the next level is
still possible. Eckstein (1980) explains the
implications of the hierarchy in terms of food. At
the survival level, literally anything will do as
food; safety or security needs are concerned with
dividing substances into food or poison categories;
at the love-belongingness level, food is categorised
as acceptable/non-acceptable; esteem needs define
food on an economic basis (inexpensive = low
quality); and at the self-actualisation stage, items
are accepted or rejected as a symbol of personal
identity.

Figure 1.6 Maslow's Hierarchy of Human Needs

                    SELF ACTUALISATION
                    SELF ESTEEM
                    BELONGINGNESS - LOVE
                    SAFETY-SECURITY
                    SURVIVAL

25

Survival
At the base of the hierarchy are survival needs. No
matter what cultural variations exist in food usages,
there is one universal imperative; food is fundamental
for individual survival.

> When a person is truly hungry, his or her need
> for food dominates their entire being. In the
> extremities of hunger, one thinks only of oneself
> - having forgotten even family and loved ones. It
> is useless to ask people to think of anything
> else until their hunger is satisfied - at least
> to the extent that they are again physically
> comfortable.
> (Lowenberg et al 1979, p 128)

Maslow himself says: 'For the man who is extremely and
dangerously hungry, no other interests exist, but
food. He dreams food, he remembers food, he thinks
food; he emotes only about food, he perceives only
food, and he wants only food' (Maslow 1943). The
deliberate denial of this need, for example, during
hunger strikes (see below) is a demonstration of a
powerful commitment to an idea. A case history of what
happens when a group of civilised people are thrust
back into a state of survival, is provided by an
account of the blockade mounted around Leningrad
during World War II.

The Siege of Leningrad. In September 1941 German air
attacks commenced on the city of Leningrad, whilst
ground troops formed a barricade around the city,
marking the beginning of a 900-day siege. The people
of Leningrad trapped in the blockade were to
experience incredible hardships and deprivations -
including a drastic reduction of food supplies. Over
2.8 million people were trapped in the city, and they
had somehow to be fed. Near the beginning of the
siege, the major food-containing warehouse was
destroyed, and with it a large part of the city's
supply of meat, sugar, butter and grain. Food
rationing, which had been imposed earlier in the year,
became much more severe and widespread hoarding of
food occurred. By November of 1941, deaths from
starvation began to be commonplace. Desperate people
searched for alternative sources of nourishment,
consuming hitherto taboo foods such as dogs, cats and
birds. Celluloses such as tree bark and sawdust were
added to flour as extenders.

People began to stuff their stomachs with
substitutes. They tore the wallpaper from the
walls and scraped off the paste, which was
supposed to have been made with potato flour.
Some ate the paper. It had nourishment they
thought, because it was made from wood. Later
they chewed the plaster - just to fill their
stomachs.
(Salisbury 1969, p376)

As the siege continued, normal codes of
behaviour were increasingly flouted; murder for food
or for ration cards became an everyday event.
Rumours circulated that human flesh was being used
in sausages. Food lines grew, and police were
authorised to shoot food criminals on the spot.
Small amounts of food reached the city across frozen
Lake Lagoda, but not until the Spring was there any
real relief - when natural greenery provided a
source of food. The following year was not so severe
due to the reduced number of people to be fed and
partial breaks in the blockade - though bombing
raids continued to ravage the city. Estimates
suggest that between .6 and 1.0 million people died
of starvation during the siege.

Security
Once survival needs are assured, people begin to
worry about food security: that is not just ´will we
eat today?´ but also ´what will we eat next week?´
Security needs can be met through storage of food;
hoarding of food during a shortage reflects anxiety
about this need. The excessive storage of food
beyond immediate future needs is common amongst
families in affluent societies, and may be
interpreted as a form of insecurity. It is also
possible to view some cases of obesity as the result
of a security response; parents who have lived
through hard times, when food was scarce or
rationed, are determined that their offspring will
not be similarly deprived, and so overfeed and force
food on them.

Love-belongingness
When physiological and safety needs are fulfilled,
we can progress to meeting love, belongingness and
affection needs. Food is frequently used to meet
such needs, as evidenced by the use of foods as
rewards or gifts, or to show membership of a
particular socio-cultural group. ´Traditionally,

27

American women have expressed love of family through
careful selection, preparation, and service of
meals. Accordingly, disparaging remarks about food
are tabooed as bad manners. At the same time, a
compliment expresses love in a socially acceptable
way.´ (Eckstein 1980, p239). Social uses of food are
further discussed in Chapter 3.

Self-Esteem
Self-esteem is next in the hierarchy. Pride in food
preparation may be reflective of this. Lowenberg et
al (1979) cite as an example, ´best cook´ contests.
People enjoy being praised for the quality of the
foods they prepare. Food manufacturers have been
quick to exploit this need, as evidenced by
advertisements which depict a housewife (usually)
receiving praise for her cooking, by virtue of
having used a particular product. Success is what is
important, so tried and tested recipes are preferred
over new or exotic dishes.

Preparation of food has long been used as an
expression of individual creativity. Historically,
there have always been plaudits for good chefs..a
tradition that is continued undiminished in many
parts of the modern world. According to Lowenberg et
al (op cit, p31) the Ancient Greeks considered a new
dish to be as important as a new poem, and the
creativity of master cooks was greatly celebrated.
The elaborate feasts of Roman nobles attested to
their partiality to exotic foods and the status
attached to these lavish banquets led to outlandish
excesses. Much praise was given for unusual and
complicated ways of preparing food. Tannahill refers
to Petronius´s satirical description of Trimalchio´s
feast: ´..guests were offered a hare tricked out
with wings like a Pegasus, a wild sow with its belly
full of live thrushes, quinces stuck with thorns to
look like sea urchins, roast pork carved into models
of fish, songbirds and a goose.´ (Tannahill 1973,
p94).

Chefs who can create beautiful and delicious
foods are well rewarded in modern society. Recent
years have seen a revival in the art of food
preparation exemplified by an obsession with cook
books, magazines, and TV chefs. Highly popular,
often glossy, magazines stress creativity in
cooking, and the majority of their space is devoted
to elaborate and aesthetically pleasing dishes.
Undoubtedly the appeal is also related to status

28

needs, as discussed in Chapter 3. TV chefs command
huge viewing audiences and in some instances have
practically attained the status of cult figures.
    We have seen that food is commonly used as an
expression of maternal love. MacKenzie (1974)
suggests that cooking can be a substitute for
maternal creativity. When an older woman loses her
traditional role of homemaker and child-raiser, she
needs a new indicator of her talents with which to
maintain her self-esteem.

Self-Actualisation

Whilst self-esteem is bolstered through the praise
received for the successful preparation of a
sure-fire recipe, self-actualisation is expressed by
the innovative use of foods, new recipes, and food
experimentation. It only occurs if a person has
self-confidence and is not afraid of failure.
Self-actualisers dare to be different. Food becomes
a personal trademark - a source of personal
satisfaction and achievement.

    The lower rungs of the hierarchy thus represent
predominantly biological needs, whilst the upper
rungs are social in nature. Lowenberg et al (1979)
contend that most people, under normal
circumstances, try to climb the ladder - and that
slipping down the ladder signifies a disaster
situation. Such may be the case when famine strikes.
However, what are we to say of instances where
individuals actively choose to put themselves back
at the survival level of the hierarchy? For example,
the back-to-the-land movement, prominent in the
1960s, saw many people deliberately choosing a
simpler lifestyle in which much of their time and
energy was devoted to producing enough food just to
feed themselves. Is this a case of 'slipping down
the ladder'? I think not; rather it represents a
form of self-actualisation which, paradoxically,
resembles the survival stage. Here may be a lesson
in the dangers of drawing conclusions based on
appearances without understanding origins. Another
example where self-actualisation seemingly reverses
the needs hierarchy is found in the case of hunger
strikes.

Hunger Strikes. As has been noted, the drive to
obtain food for survival is a fundamental human
instinct. When starvation threatens, social

behaviour deteriorates as each individual selfishly
pursues the quest for food. Because this drive is so
powerful it is all the more astonishing to learn of
people who deliberately choose to deny themselves
food to the point of death. Such action reflects an
iron resolve and often stems from an unshakeable
belief in certain lauded principles. Thus hunger
strikes represent the actions of committed men and
women who are willing to die to focus attention on
their ideological concerns.

Mahatma Gandhi, that foremost champion of human
rights, understood the power of self-starvation in
drawing attention to his ideas. He made extensive
use of hunger strikes - or fasts - which proved to
be a potent weapon against the British, and later in
reconciling Hindus and Moslems in India. His first
public fast was a response to the situation of
deadlock between mill-workers and mill-owners at
Ahmedabad. Gandhi fasted to keep the mill-workers
loyal to their pledge to stay on strike until the
owners gave in to their demands; however his action
also put direct pressure on the mill-owners to
capitulate, as they did not wish to bear
responsibility for Gandhi´s death. Three days later
they accepted arbitration (Fischer 1950, p156).
Gandhi did not fast for personal gain but in order
to promote an idea...in this case, the idea of
arbitration. In September of 1924 Gandhi fasted in
the cause of Hindu-Moslem unity. He had no wish to
die, but his fast was dictated by his duty to the
brotherhood of man. He fasted in the home of a
Moslem, thus focusing wide attention on the sight of
a Hindu entrusting himself to a Moslem. Finally, in
1948, he fasted again in the name of Indian unity -
restoring peace to the strife torn city of Delhi. A
full account of this and other Gandhian fasts can be
found in Fischer´s book (Fischer 1950).

The use of hunger strikes in attempts to draw
attention to political causes is seen in the case of
Irish Republican Army prisoners in Northern Ireland.
The Manchester Guardian of December 21, 1980
reported that there were 39 hunger strikers in the
gaols of Northern Ireland. The leading seven
strikers in the Maze prison in Belfast were in poor
health and determined to die if their demands were
not met; one of them was losing his eyesight because
of a vitamin deficiency; he refused all treatment.
The strikers were seeking special status for
Republican prisoners. One of the prisoners received
a letter from the widow of the policeman he was

convicted of murdering, forgiving him. She said:
´after they die they (the hunger strikers) will be
forgotten, just as those policemen and soldiers who
died are forgotten after a while, except by those
who loved them.´ (Guardian , Dec 21 1980).
     The strikers did not attract public sympathy in
the way that Gandhi did. However there was concern
by the British Government that deaths should be
avoided if possible - though at the same time the
Government resolved not to give in to what it called
´Blackmail´, and indeed several hunger strikers
subsequently starved to death.

A FOOD SELECTION PARADIGM

De Garine (1972) suggests that in order to
investigate socio-cultural aspects of food habits,
three different parameters have to be measured.
First of all come techniques - of food production,
storage, distribution, processing and meal
preparation. Secondly there is the actual food
consumption - including such variables as seasonal
fluctuation and status of family members. Finally,
attention must be paid to food ideology - how people
think about food and its particular meanings and
values. These parameters have been incorporated in
different ways in the various food choice models
described above. A different approach is taken by
Krondl and Boxen (1975), who propose a model in
which energy is a major determinant of nutritional
behaviour. They point out that the diversity of
foods available increases along with the growing
sophistication of societies, and hypothesise that
this is a function of more intense energy inputs.
Thus in primitive society food resources were
dependent on a combination of solar energy and man´s
energy. Agricultural societies could add to these
auxiliary energy sources in the form of wind, water
and animal power. Industrial societies could further
supplement inputs with fossil fuels, hydropower and
atomic energy. Increased supplies of energy altered
the nature of available food resources by permitting
transportation, preservation and technological
processing - and thus indirectly influenced
nutrition behaviour. At the same time, the authors
suggest that decreases in energy required for
survival functions has had the effect of largely
replacing internal cues to hunger by culturally
conditioned external cues. They thus recognise the
role of food resources (what they call utility

stimuli) and of cultural values (non-utility
stimuli) on food behaviour, but posit energy as the
underlying determinant.
    Whichever model of food choice one opts for,
one inevitably accepts certain suppositions,
prejudices and omissions. Understanding what these
limitations are increases the usefulness of the
models as tools for study of the real world. The
framework presented below recognises that there are
clusters of influences which can be grouped together
for convenience of study, and which operate at
different stages of the food choice process. It does
not claim that a particular factor operates
exclusively at one level or that all the factors
identified have equal importance for all human
groups. The framework is built around the twin
concepts of AVAILABILITY and ACCEPTABILITY Figure
1.7b lists some of the components of the factors
identified in Figure 1.7a.

Figure 1.7a   Food Selection Paradigm

AVAILABILITY

CULTURE   ECONOMICS

ACCEPTABILITY

                              SOCIO-PSYCHOLOGICAL
RELIGION   FACTORS

                INDIVIDUAL
                CHOICE

    Human diets are governed first by what men can
get from the environment; given a choice they then
eat what their ancestors ate before them (May 1957).

Figure 1.7b   Elements of food selection

AVAILABILITY

Physical	Political	Economic
Land availability	Agricultural policies	Price
Water availability	Subsidies	Farm costs
Climate	Business controls	Marketing costs
Type of soil	Legislation	Packaging
Pest & plant control	Distribution	Processing
Transportation	Welfare programmes	Transport
Storage facilities	Rationing	Storage
	Nutrition policies and guidelines	Consumer demand
	Government sponsored research activities	Income
	Trade and aid policies tariffs and quotas	Patterns of expenditure

Figure 1.7b ctd. Elements of food selection

	ACCEPTABILITY	
Cultural & Religious	Individual choice	Socio-Psychological
Ideology	Preference	Prestige
Cuisine	Taste	Status
Myths	Therapeutic needs	Friendship
Superstitions	Personality	Communication
Taboos	Beliefs	Reward & punishment
Ritual	Personal values	Emotions
Morals		
Doctrine		
Prohibitions		

What food is available is a matter of geographical
and climatic factors, combined with various
influences which determine food transportation and
distribution capabilities and policies. Hence
physical and political parameters as well as
economic ones are of importance here. From the
universe of foods which are available or potentially
available for human consumption, the selection is
made for economic, cultural, socio-psychological and
religious reasons. It is these stages in the food
choice process that are the main concern of this
book. Individual or personal factors come into play
after all the other conditions of acceptability have
been met. It is in this realm, that individual free
choice may truly be said to occur, though even here
several conditioning factors are immediately
apparent, such as physiological status and
therapeutic needs. Internal factors, including
values, attitudes and beliefs about food, and food
preferences are largely shaped during the early
socialisation period. [For a discussion of
decision-making processes in relaton to personal
health behaviour, see Becker 1974, Fieldhouse 1982.]
The illusion that we choose freely what we eat is
perhaps a comforting one, and one which fits into
the ´free will´ philosophic tradition cherished by
millions of people. The truth is that food habits
are shaped to a considerable extent by a combination
of objective and subjective factors, many of which
are beyond individual control.

SUMMARY

The interrelationship of food habits with other
elements of cultural behaviour and with
environmental forces emphasises the futility of
treating food choices as being intellectual
decisions made on rational nutritional grounds
alone. Attempts to change food habits in order to
improve nutritional status may be thwarted by
failure to understand cultural needs. Where dietary
changes are introduced there is the probability that
other aspects of social life will also be affected.
A corollary to this is that changes in dietary
behaviour may be brought about, not by direct
modification of food habits, but by alteration or
manipulation of the material or non-material
culture.

As an example of the interaction and interdependence of cultural, biological and environmental variables, Cravioto´s work on low weight gain is illustrative. In a society characterised by technological backwardness, low income and little purchasing power is a reality for the non-privileged sections of the population. No surplus money is available to invest in hygiene or environmental sanitation as a consequence of which, disease is perpetuated. Concepts of the role of food in disease (such as ´food makes too much work for the sick stomach´) lead to restriction of food to sick infants and ultimately to low weight gain and malnutrition. Paradigms such as this are useful in so far as they show that what we tend to think of as purely nutritional problems, do in fact have complex aetiologies. Food usages, which produce the ultimate physical effects of malnutrition, are products of cultural and environmental conditions.

In studying food habits, researchers have developed a number of distinct methodological approaches and have devised several theoretical frameworks in attempts to unify their findings. Food choice models, some of which have been described, are useful in identifying elements of food choice behaviour, but are necessarily incomplete. In the following chapters, discussions focus on those elements of food selection which pertain to ´acceptability´ rather than ´availability´ as defined in figure 1.7 above. In doing so, a conscious decision has been made to largely avoid political and economic factors - recognising that these operate mostly at the level of macro-availability. However, political and economic considerations may certainly influence individual choices, and are addressed at appropriate points throughout the book.

REFERENCES

Abrahamsson, L. ´The Mother´s Choice of Food for Herself and Her Baby.´ In G.Blix (ed.), The Mother-Child Dyad: Dietary Aspects. Symposium of the Swedish Nutrition Foundation XIV, Almqvist & Wiksells, Uppsala 1979
Back, K.W. ´Food, Sex and Theory.´ In T.K. Fitzgerald (ed.), Nutrition and Anthropology in Action. Van Gorcum, Amsterdam 1977

Barnes, R.H. ´The Inseparability of Nutrition from the Social and Biological Sciences.´ Nutrition et Dieta , 10:1, 1968

Bass, M.A., L.M. Wakefield, and K.M. Kolassa. Community Nutrition and Individual Food Behavior. Burgess Publ., Minn. 1979

Becker, M.H. ´The Health Belief Model and Personal Health Behavior.´ Health Education Monograph. 2 (4):328-473, 1974

Berkes, F. and C.S. Farkas. ´Eastern James Bay Cree Indians: Changing Patterns of Wild Food Use and Nutrition.´ Ecol. Food & Nutr. , 7:155-172, 1978

Broom, L. and P. Selznick. Sociology. Harper & Row, New York 1955

Cattle, D.J. ´An Alternative to Nutritional Particularism.´ In T.K. Fitzgerald (ed.), Nutrition and Anthropology in Action. Van Gorcum, Amsterdam 1977

Committee on Food Habits Manual for the Study of Food Habits. NRC Bull. 111, NAS, Washington D.C. 1945

Cravioto, J. ´The Ecologic Approach to the Study of Nutrition and Mental Development.´ In W.M. Moore et al (eds.), Malnutrition, Environment and Behavior. U.S.D.H.E.W. Publ. 72-26, Washington D.C. 1972

De Garine, I. ´The Social and Cultural Background of Food Habits in Developing Countries (Traditional Societies).´ In G. Blix (ed.), Symposium on Food Cultism and Nutritional Quackery. Swedish Nutrition Foundation, Almqvist & Wiksells, Uppsala 1970

Eckstein, E.F. Food, People and Nutrition. AVI, Westport 1980

Emmons, L., and M. Hayes. ´Nutrition Knowledge of Mothers and Children.´ J. Nutr. Ed. , 5:134, 1973

Fathauer, G.H. ´Food Habits - an Anthropologist´s View.´ J. Am. Diet. Ass. , 37:335-338, 1960

Fieldhouse, P. ´Nutrition and Education of the School Child.´ World Rev. Nutr. & Diet. , 40:83-112, 1982

Fieldhouse, P. ´Behavioural Aspects of the Decision to Breastfeed.´ Can. J. Home Ec. , 32 (2):88-93, 1983

Fischer, L. The Life of Mahatma Gandhi. Harper & Row, New York 1950

Foster, G. Traditional Cultures and the Impact of Technological Change. Harper & Row, New York 1962

Fox, H.M., B.A. Fryer, G.L. Lamkin, V.M. Vivian, and E.S. Eppright. 'Family Environment.' J. Home Ec. , 62:241, 1970

Freedman, R.L. 'Nutritional Anthropology: An Overview.' In T.K. Fitzgerald (ed.), Nutrition and Anthropology in Action. Van Gorcum, Amsterdam 1977

Gifft, H.H., M.B. Washbon, and G.G. Harrison. Nutrition, Behaviour and Change. Prentice Hall, New Jersey 1972

Grivetti, L.E., and R.M. Pangborn. 'Food Habit Research: A Review of Approaches and Methods.' J. Nutr. Ed. , 5:204-7, 1973

Hanssen, M. Food and Health. G.C. Birch and K.T. Parker (eds.), Applied Science Publ., 1980

Harper, L.V. and K.M. Sanders. 'The Effect of Adult's Eating on Young Children's Acceptance of Unfamiliar Foods.' J. Exp. Child Psychol. , 20:206-14, 1975

Harris, K. 'Values and Viewpoints.' O.N.E. Newsletter , 3(4), 1982

Hsu, F. 'American Core Value and National Character.' In J.P. Spradley and M.A. Rynkiewich (eds.), The Nacirema. Little, Brown & Co., Boston 1975

Kassarjian, H.H., and T.S. Robertson. Perspectives in Consumer Behaviour. Scott Foresman, Glenview, Ill. 1968 (Cited in Lowenberg et al 1979, p200).

Krondl, M.M., and G.G. Boxen. 'Nutrition Behaviour, Food Resources, and Energy.' In M. Arnott (ed.), Gastronomy: The Anthropology of Food and Food Habits. Mouton Publ., The Hague 1975

Lewin, K. 'Forces Behind Food Habits and Methods of Change.' In The Problem of Changing Food Habits. Nat. Ac. Sci. Bull., 108, Washington D.C. 1943

Linton, R. The Tanala: A Hill Tribe of Madagascar. Anthropological Series Vol. XXII, Field Museum of Natural History, Chicago 1933

Lowenberg, M.E., E.N. Todhunter, E.D. Wilson, J.R. Savage, and J.L. Lubawski. Food and People. J. Wiley & Sons, New York 1979

Lund, L.A., and M.C. Burk. A Multidisciplinary Analysis of Children's Food Consumption Behavior. Agricultural Experimental Station Monograph, University of Minnesota, Minn. 1969

Manchester Guardian Weekly, Dec. 21 1980

Maslow, A.H. Motivation and Personality. Harper &
    Row, New York 1970

Maslow, A.H. 'A Theory of Human Motivation.'
    Psychol. Rev. , 50:370-396, 1943

May, J.M. 'The Geography of Food and Cooking.' Int.
    Record. Med. , 170:231, 1957

McKenzie, J. 'The Impact of Economic and Social
    Status on Food Choice.' Proc. Nutr. Soc. , 33
    (1):67-74, 1974

Meyers, L. Jr. 'Relation of Personality to
    Perception of Television Advertising Messages.'
    In L. Arons and M.A. May (eds.), Television
    and Human Behaviour. Appleton-Century-Crofts,
    New York 1963

Pelto, G.H., and N.W. Jerome. 'Intracultural
    Diversity and Nutritional Anthropology.' In
    M.H. Logan and E.E. Hunt (eds.), Health and
    the Human Condition: Perspectives on Medical
    Anthropology. Duxbury Pr., N. Scituate, Mass.
    1978

Peoples Food Commission. The Land of Milk and
    Money. Between The Lines, Kitchener Ont. 1980

Rogers, E.M. and F.F. Shoemaker. Communication of
    Innovations. Free Pr., USA 1971

Salisbury, H.E. The 900 days - The Siege of
    Leningrad. Harper & Row, New York 1969

Sanjur, D., and A. Scoma. 'Food Habits of Low-Income
    Children in Northern New York.' J. Nutr. Ed. ,
    2 (3), 1971

Sanjur, D. Social and Cultural Perspectives in
    Nutrition. Prentice Hall, New Jersey 1982

Schaefer, O., and J. Steckle. Dietary Habits of
    Native populations , Science Advisory Board of
    the Northwest Territories, 1980

Schaefer, O., J.F.W Timmermans, R.D.P. Eaton, and
    A.R. Matthews. 'General and Nutritional Health
    in Two Eskimo Populations at Different Stages
    of Acculturation.' Canadian Journal of Public
    Health , 71 (6):397-405, 1980

Sellitz, C., M. Jahoda, M. Deutsch, and S.W. Cook.
    Research Methods in Social Relations. Holt,
    Rinehart & Winston, New York 1966

Steward, J.H. Theory of Culture Change. The
    Methodology of Multilinear Evolution.
    University of Illinois Pr. Urbana, 1955

Tannahill, R. Food in History. Stein & Day, New
    York 1973

Thompson, L. ´The Relations of Men, Animals and
     Plants in an Island Community.´ Amer.
     Anthropol. , 51:253, 1949
Tylor, E.B. Primitive Culture: Researches into the
     Development of Mythology, Philosophy, Religion,
     Language, Art and Custom. J. Murray, London
     1871
Wenkam, N.S. ´Cultural Determinants of Nutritional
     Behavior.´ Nutrition Program News , U.S.D.A.
     (July-Aug.) 1969
Williams, B.J. Evolution and Human Origins: an
     Introduction to Physical Anthropology. Harper,
     New York 1973

Chapter 2

FOOD IDEOLOGY

ETHNOCENTRISM

Ethnocentrism is how one feels about oneself
compared to outsiders; it describes the belief that
one's own patterns of behaviour are preferable to
those of all other cultures. Because they are taught
the values of the culture in which they grow up
people tend to view their own patterns of behaviour
as being right, normal and best. As a corollary to
this, foreign cultures are viewed as being wrong or
irrational or misguided. Some degree of
ethnocentrism is virtually inescapable, so engrained
are such attitudes, though exposure to other
cultures can broaden tolerance and aid in an
understanding of how other peoples live.

Food habits are an integral part of cultural
behaviour and are often closely identified with
particular groups - sometimes in a derogatory or
mocking way. So, the French are ´Frogs´, the Germans
are ´Krauts´, the Italians are ´Spaghetti eaters´
and the British, ´Limeys´. The word ´Eskimo´ is an
Indian word meaning ´eaters of raw flesh´, and was
originally used to express the revulsion of one
group toward the food habits of another. Eskimos
refer to themselves as ´Inuit´, which literally
means ´real people´ - and is itself a linguistic
example of ethnocentrism, implying as it does that
members of other societies are not ´real people´.
The Toupouri of Northern Cameroon eat ritually the
rotting legs of beef and for that are mocked by
their neighbours, the Moussey, who are in return
derided by the Toupouri for their habit of using the
juice of centipedes in sauces. Food ridicule can be
considered as one of the criteria determing the
boundaries of a culture (de Garine 1976). Exposure
to unfamiliar food habits is almost guaranteed to

41

bring ethnocentrism to the fore. At a recent
informal supper I attended in Alberta - the beef
capital of Canada - lamb was served (albeit in the
form of ´lamb-burgers´). Most of the people present
took some convincing even to try this strange meat;
those who did were surprised to find it to be quite
acceptable. One confirmed lamb-eater, an Irishman,
was mercilessly teased (or ridiculed) for his
preference, and the attitude of the group was summed
up by one member who asked why anyone should want to
eat lamb when there was beef available.

Sometimes people will quite happily eat a food
until they discover what it is that they are eating,
when they suddenly become quite ill. Thus it is the
idea of what is food, as much as the food itself,
which evokes both physiological and psychological
feelings. Ogden Nash capures this feeling perfectly
in one of his poems entitled ´Experiment
Degustatory´. After overcoming initial feelings of
disgust, the hero of the poem discovers that
rattlesnake meat tastes just like chicken;
unfortunately he is subsequently unable to face the
thought of eating chicken - because it tastes like
rattlesnake meat! (Nash 1965). Probably everyone has
had this kind of experiences at one time or another,
albeit with less exotic delicacies than rattlesnake
meat. The feelings aroused by the sudden knowledge
that one is eating octopus rather than fish or that
the tasty jugged hare on one´s plate is actually
guinea pig can cause one to pause in mid-bite, or to
make a hurried dash for the bathroom. The actual
flavour of the food is irrelevant, for we don´t even
have to taste a food to label it as unacceptable or
disgusting; our culture tells us what is fit to eat,
and our ethnocentricity ensures that we obey.

Cultural Relativism
Cultural relativism is an approach to understanding
cultures which attempts to avoid the worst excesses
of ethnocentrism. In this conceptual framework
cultural practices must be examined within the
context of the indigenous cultural group; if they
are not dysfunctional within that group then they
must be accepted as ´normal´, no matter how
different they be from our own familiar practices.
Cultural relativism in effect says that there aren´t
really any universal standards of behaviour - a
view, which if taken to its extreme, also has
certain weaknesses. For example, most cultures have
sanctions against indiscriminate killing and other

42

persistent anti-social behaviour. Nevertheless, the
ability to set aside one's own cultural biases and
preferences helps significantly in understanding the
food practices and values of other societies. If we
appreciate this then we may not be quite so ready to
dismiss as irrational the Sacred Cow taboo of
Hinduism, or to reject as disgusting the eating of
insects and grubs. We may also realise that our own
food practices could seem irrational or disgusting
from the vantage point of another culture. What, for
example, are we to make of a 'pet-loving' society
which spends huge amounts of money on food for
animals which have no economic value, or the
sportsman who hangs game birds until they begin to
rot?

FOOD IDEOLOGY

Just as there are political ideologies, which
express beliefs concerning how people ought to
behave in social relationships, so there are food
ideologies which explain how they are to conduct
themselves with regard to eating behaviour. Food
ideology is the sum of the attitudes, beliefs and
customs and taboos affecting the diet of a given
group. It is what people think of as food; what
effect they think food will have on their health and
what they think is suitable for different ages and
groups (Eckstein 1980). Sometimes, the most
surprising items emerge as food. Was it Ogden Nash's
'Pioneer who first thought of trying to eat
artichokes? (Nash 1965); whoever decided that raw
oysters or rotting game were delicacies? And who was
persistent enough to entrench red-hot chili peppers
as a firm favourite in the diet? The very idea of
'acquired taste' indicates that there are foods
which are not intrinsically appealing and which we
have to actively learn to enjoy.
    Whilst it seems that some unusual dietary
choices have been made by various groups, it is also
true that of all of the animal and vegetable
substances which could serve as human food, only a
few are selected for actual consumption; that is,
certain potential foodstuffs are rejected because
they are not acceptable. What is deemed to be
acceptable constitutes an important part of the
cultural stability of a society and is passed on
from generation to generation via the socialisation
process. An idea of how we quickly categorise foods
according to ethnocentric rules of acceptability can

be gained by asking yourself the following question.
´Would I eat these foodstuffs?´

* Cereals. (wheat?...corn?...millet?)
* Fruit   (apple? lime? mango?)
* Milk   (cow´s? goat´s? sheep´s?)
* Meat   (Beef?..pork?..horse?..dog?..raw meat?)
* Insects
* Grubs

All of the above are potential foodstuffs.
Millet, a staple in many African countries is
rejected as ´bird seed´ in richer countries. Milk
evokes feelings of disgust in some societies.
Meat-eaters will eat only certain kinds of meat.
Westerners may be revolted at the thought of eating
insects. The point is that no social group
classifies as food all the potential food-stuffs
which are available. Moreover, where there is more
than sufficient food available for survival, choices
are made, which are assertions of identity (Back
1976, p 30). In the same ecological environment with
similar technological resources at their disposal,
different societies will make different choices
among the available resources. For example in
Senegal, the Serer and Wolof tribes use all parts of
the baobob tree - yet 4000km away in climatically
similar Chad, only the fruit is used (de Garine
1976).

Jerome (1969) says that people communicate who
they are through their uses of food. Basic cultural
themes expressed in the U.S., he says, are those of
individualism, democracy, capitalism, pluralism,
industrialism, leisure and youthfulness. The
thousands of products available in the modern
supermarket provide an oppportunity for each person
to express individual choices, albeit ones which are
usually but a minor variation on a theme. Why else
should there be a market for dozens of breakfast
cereals, differing little in composition and
nutritional value? Capitalist and industrialist
motives provide incentives for ever new and
´improved´ products - often only cosmetically
different from the old, but evangelically advertised
and eagerly consumed by a public who have been
taught that new is better. Such appeals show signs
of weakening as consumer movements begin to educate
people to make their own value decisions instead of
passively accepting advertiser´s promotions. The
value of leisure is expressed through the ever
increasing use of restaurants for eating out, and

the popularity of convenience or 'fast' foods.
Pluralism reflects the nature of U.S. society,
composed as it is of a tremendous variety of ethnic
groups. Despite a tendency towards cultural
homogeneity, expressed in the 'melting pot'
syndrome, and illustrated in the food world by the
ubiquitous fast-food outlets, North American cuisine
derives from diverse cultural inputs. The value of
youthfulness, exhibited particularly through the
medium of so-called 'health' foods and dietary
supplements, is discussed at length in Chapter 4.
Gifft, Harrison and Washbon, writing in 1972,
explained that these values were being evidenced by
the emergence of several major trends; an increase
in variety of products available, especially of
canned and frozen foods and other convenience
products; an increase in the frequency of eating
away from home, and an increase in the status value
of meat. In the decade or so since then, there has
been a slowing down or even reversal of some of
these trends, with a return to emphasising
simplicity, naturalness and home production.

FOOD CATEGORISATION

In every society, there are rules - usually
unwritten - which specify what is food and what is
not. Within the larger classification of 'food',
subgroups or categories of foodstuffs are identified
according to nutritional value, cultural usage,
emotional importance, or a combination thereof. In
fact, there are numerous ways of classifying or
categorising foods and food usages. Sometimes the
classifications have an obvious rational basis;
some, with less apparent rationality, have grown out
of coherent folk-medicine systems; yet others are a
result of mere fancy or caprice. Many of these
reflect the rational needs or ethnocentric views of
the classifiers; and it may be difficult to justify
their existence in reality.
        Eckstein (1980) uses the concept of 'food or
poison?' to divide what is eaten from what is not.
Whatever is not defined as food is automatically
poison - an idea which suggests that the adage, 'one
man's meat is another man's poison' is literally
true. There are several perspectives from which the
food/poison classification can be made. Eckstein
lists the following, of which most are discussed in
later chapters, as listed below.

45

* Physiological definitions
* Emotional/psychological definitions (Chapter 6)
* Socio-cultural definitions (Chapters 3,4)
* Health-related definitions (Chapter 4)
* Economic definitions   (Chapter 3)
* Aesthetic definitions   (Chapter 6)
* Sub-group definitions   (Chapter 4)

(In addition, the general topic of food avoidances and aversions is considered in Chapter 5).

Once we have differentiated ´food´ from ´poison´ we proceed to assign values based on a variety of possible criteria. Perhaps the categorisation with which we are most familiar as nutritionists, and which we seek to perpetuate through formal instruction, is the one in which foods are classified according to nutritional value. This is the basis for food guides such as the Basic Four in the U.S., Canada´s Food Guide, and the Food Groups of the U.K. In each case, the categories are designed to facilitate the choice of nutritionally balanced diets within the framework of normal cultural eating patterns. Usually, a food group includes a selection of foodstuffs rich in a particular nutrient or nutrients; by combining foods from each group, a wide spectrum of nutrients are obtained, thus ensuring nutritional adequacy. Food groups are basically a nutritionists´ teaching tool and do not seem to reflect the way in which people actually do classify their own foods. Although students are taught, and eagerly take up, the use of food guides, few of them can honestly say that that is how they choose their own food intake.

As we have seen, eating is a biocultural activity. One of the weaknesses of the ´Food Groups´ approach resides in the fact that it is predicated solely on biological needs. Other classification systems recognise the interaction between biological and cultural factors. For example; Bass, Wakefield & Kolassa (1979, p21) suggest that people classify food according to: (1) its actual use by the body; (2) its actual use in society; (3) its perceived use by the body and in society. Taking the example of potatoes they ennumerate uses as: (1) a source of energy and minerals for the body; (2) a food for snacks and meals; (3) perceived as ´fattening´ and a filler food for meals. The authors do not elaborate on this classification or demonstrate how it might be used in practice, though it seems to suggest a multi-stage process whereby a particular food is

46

judged to be appropriate or non-appropriate by a series of criteria. Let's say we were considering choosing an egg for breakfast; first of all it is a good source of protein; secondly, it is an appropriate food for this meal; lastly, it is judged to give us a good start to the day (Witness the British Egg Marketing Board's 'Go to work on an egg' slogan). The egg is therefore accepted.

Schutz, Rucker & Russell (1975) went one step further by allowing people to express their own judgements about foods, and as a result found four common food-use factors: utilitarian, casual, satiating and social. They also reported consumer classifications of actual foods as falling into five main categories.

1. High calorie treats. Cakes and pies figured prominently in this category of foods considered appropriate for social occasions. Snacks such as celery or carrot sticks were for when eating alone; they were more 'everyday'.

2. Speciality meal items: only to be served in particular circumstances, and definitely not everyday foods. Some foods placed in this category (eg Chili) are everyday foods for other ethnic groups.

3. Common meal items: were foods served at the dinner meal and seen to be suitable for all occasions and all ages. Meats ranked high in this category.

4. Refreshing foods: such as milk and orange juice were regarded as suitable for serving cold - though not as an entree. They were thought to be nutritious and easy to digest.

5. Inexpensive filling foods: were often high calorie, but lacked the social function or prestige of foods in category 1. Thus, bread, potato chips (crisps), chocolate bars and peanut butter appeared in this category. They were regarded as being unsuitable when weight loss was desired.

Although the actual categories were created by the authors on the basis of consumer responses, and are thus the product of scientific interpretation, it is interesting to note that a biological basis for classification is less readily discernable than in the previous systems. Nor is this particularly surprising. The majority of people in Northern countries, even those with extensive schooling, do not have a firm grasp of the nutritional value of foodstuffs. What they do understand, is the cultural meaning and usage of food - and people make decisions based on what they know. Thus whilst those educated in nutritional principles can appreciate the scientific rationality of food groups, those without such training follow other indicators. The verity and utility of classifications such as that of Schutz et al may certainly be questioned, but they at least merit further study as potential 'popular' tools for teaching sound nutrition.

In the developing South, nutritional analysis as a basis for food choice is even less of a likelihood. Foods are assigned values according to their functional role as well as their perceived nutritional and non-nutritional effects. Derek Jelliffe, who is noted for his cross-cultural studies in nutrition, offers the following 'world-wide' classification system; cultural superfoods, prestige foods, body-image foods, sympathetic magic foods, physiologic group foods (Jelliffe 1967). Cultural superfoods are the dominant staple foods of a society. Much effort is expended in producing and preparing them and they are often involved in the religious rituals and the mythology of the society. Prestige foods are those reserved for important occasions or for important people. They are characterised by relative scarcity and high price. Body-image foods are those which contribute to good health by maintaining a balance in the body. Yin-yang, hot-cold are examples of systems which embody this idea. In Western culture we hold the idea of fattening and slimming foods. Sympathetic magic foods are those which are believed to have special properties which are imparted to those who eat them. Physiological group foods are foods restricted to persons of a particular age, sex or physiological condition. (Examples of such restrictions are given in Chapter 5).

As in the food selection paradigm presented in Chapter 1, the contribution of religion, economics, and socio-cultural factors in shaping food behaviour is clearly shown by this classification. The food group approach, already criticised above, is again found lacking as it addresses only one (c) of Jelliffe's categories. Part of the problem is that the purpose of food categorisation is often a descriptive one - to reveal how foods are assigned value in a society, whereas for the nutritionist or dietitian concerned with promoting healthy eating habits, prescriptive categories are obviously more attractive - to advise on how food choices should be made. One approach which goes some way toward addressing both these needs comes from the early work of Passim and Bennett (1943), and is still useful today when considering strategies of dietary change. Dietary intake is divided into three categories of core, secondary and peripheral items in order to distinguish the frequency of consumption and the importance given to various foods.

1. CORE FOODS are universal, regular, staple, important and consistently used foods. Most members of the society will use these foods, which form the mainstay of the diet. Resistance to dietary modification will be greatest with reference to these core items. Examples would be cereal staples; large portions of meat in Northern cultures; milk, potatoes and bread.

2. SECONDARY FOODS are in widespread but not universal use; they may be thought of as supporting actors, playing differing roles in the diet. They are of less emotional importance to most people, and include recently introduced, and store-bought foods. Changes in respect of secondary items are more readily accepted. Most fruits and vegetables probably fall into this category, as do items such as cake mixes and tinned soups.

3. PERIPHERAL FOODS are least common and are infrequently consumed. They may be new foods or items only included through economic necessity. Their use is characteristic of individuals, and they are most amenable to change with the least of emotional resistance. Oysters and offal (sweetbreads) might be two very different examples of items in this category. Of course, what are peripheral foods for most people might be of greater importance to the few.

Analysis of a patient's diet in terms of core, secondary and peripheral foods would provide the wary dietitian with an indication of where dietary modifications could be most readily made - and where resistance might be anticipated. Such analyses could also add to our understanding of the phenomenon of non-compliance with dietary regimes.

Another prescriptive system of food classification which is in widespread use, and which is employed by lay rather than professional actors, is that of 'Hot and Cold'. Because it is a popular concept in folk-medicine and because it represents an alternative way of assessing food values, the hot and cold theory is discussed at some length below.

Hot and Cold
Classification of food into two divisions labelled
hot and cold, is common throughout the world. The
hot/cold theory of balance probably diffused from
Eastern to Western cultures, arising in Classical
Greece and spreading via Arabian merchants and
Spanish explorers to become entrenched in the folk
medicine of diverse cultures. Today, such beliefs
are held strongly by Latin Americans and are also
common in India and China. Interpretation of the
hot/cold system becomes problematical when it is
seen that: (a) classification does not seem to
correspond to physical properties of the foods; (b)
the same foods are classified differently in
different cultures; (c) a food may be classified
differently by individuals within a culture.
    Sanjur (1982) gives an account of hot/cold
dichotomies in Latin American folk medicine. The
Latin American system, originating in Greece, was
transferred to the New World at the time of the
Spanish conquests. Greek humoral theory held that
there were four bodily elements each of which had
particular characteristics: blood - hot and wet;
phlegm - cold and wet; black bile - cold and dry;
yellow bile - hot and dry. Medical practice
consisted of understanding the normal mixture of
humours or complexion of a person, the complexion of
their illness and the method of restoring harmony in
the body. The Spaniards established medical teaching
at the University of Mexico in 1580 where they
taught the principles of humoral medicine. Because
of the relative isolation of the region, these ideas
persisted for longer than in Europe, and became
firmly embedded in traditional medicine. In
addition, Sanjur says: ´A large component of present
day Latin American folk medicine relies on the
concept of emotional experiences - shame, fear,
anger, envy - as causes of illness, and probably
survives from pre-Conquest belief´ (op cit p151).
    A basic notion in hot/cold dichotomies is that
health is a temperate condition and that a balance
between hot and cold elements must be maintained.
Disease results from an imbalance (Ingham 1970).
Although the body as a whole is temperate specific
parts of it may vary in degree of hotness or
coldness; intestines and stomach are hot, mouth and
throat are cold. Blood is hot, milk is cold. Most
groups practising this lore agree that an excess of

cold is more dangerous than an excess of hot; hot
foods are easier to digest because the stomach is
hot, whilst cold foods have to be heated by the
stomach before they can be digested. Food mixtures
and combinations should produce an overall temperate
effect, and so meals are to be carefully constructed
to avoid extremes. Hot/cold properties of foods are
not always constant. Molony (1975) discusses Mexican
hot/cold valences, pointing out that they are based
on perceived qualities of foods; how a plant was
grown, what an animal ate, how a food was cooked,
how foods were combined. Chickens are hot if they
eat a lot of raw corn; maize corn is hot, because
plants need little water - becoming cold if boiled
in water. (Andeans also believe that exposure to
water changes the temperature rating of foods.
Usually, the effect of cooking is to moderate
ratings.) The hot/cold concept is stronger in Latin
America than it ever was in Spain. Therefore, says
Sanjur (op cit), it must serve some useful function
as a basis for preventive and curative folk
medicine. Indeed, pellagra - which is a cold
illness, is treated by giving hot foods, including
peanuts, which are high in niacin, the B-vitamin
which is deficient in the diet of pellagrins. With
this example, Logan (1972) points out how modern
medicine can take advantage of traditional belief
systems by building on current accepted practices.

As the humoral theory travelled and spread, it
inevitably took on different aspects. Asian beliefs
regarding hot and cold are contradictory; for whilst
eggs are perceived as cooling foods in Thailand,
they are hot in Bangladesh (Lindenbaum 1977).
Katona-Apte (1977), describing food habits in
Tamilnad, says hot and cold classifications vary
even with individuals. In Hindu society, raw foods
are ´hot´ and therefore purer than cooked foods
which are ´cold´ - a dichotomy which has
repercussons within the caste system, where it
delimits food preparation and sharing practices
(Hasan 1971. See also Chapter 4). In Bangladesh, in
direct contrast to Mexican beliefs, hot foods are
thought to be difficult to digest, and a weak person
must limit consumption of them. ´Hot´ honey and
mustard are given to newborns to provide strength,
and to keep infants free of colds.

Chinese practice should also be briefly
mentioned. The concept of yin and yang pervades all
aspects of traditional Chinese life. Qualities of
yin and yang must be balanced to produce harmony.

51

´Almost universally, oily and fried food, pepper-hot
flavouring, fatty meat and oily plant foods are
"hot", whereas most water plants, crustaceans and
certain beans are "cold".´ (Sanjur 1982, p277).
Yeung and his colleagues (1973) reported that
Chinese people in Canada continued to balance hot
and cold in daily meals. The yang element is
stronger in men and so they should avoid too many
yang foods; similarly, women should avoid an
overabundance of yin foods.

In all cultures practising hot/cold
classifications, the hot/cold concept is closely
tied to the reproductive cycle. Imbalances must be
particularly avoided by menstruating, pregnant and
lactating women. Except where specified the
following details relate to Latin American practice.
A woman is warm during menstruation and must avoid
cold foods - which cause cramps. Infertility is
caused by a cold womb and is cured by heating it
with tea made from hot herbs. Pregnancy is warm and
cold foods are avoided because of increased
vulnerability to cold at this time. Bolivian
peasants too, prohibit cold foods during pregnancy
and lactation (de Esquef 1972). For the Chinese, too
many cold foods are avoided in pregnancy for fear of
abortion. Puerto Rican women, studied by Harwood
(1971) considered pregnancy to be a hot state, and
they avoided hot foods and medications in order to
prevent babies from being born with a rash or a red
skin. Some women would avoid vitamin and iron
supplements which were also considered to be hot.

At birth, the foetus takes a great deal of
warmth from the mother, leaving her doubly
vulnerable, and so a post-partum woman is warmly
wrapped and avoids cold foods. Latin American women
refer to the forty days following childbirth as ´la
cuerenta´ or ´la dieta´. Hot foods are prescribed to
diminish post-partum bleeding; whilst in Chinese
tradition hot foods are recommended post-partum to
stimulate blood and prevent anaemia. For several
days after childbirth Bangladeshi women must not eat
meat, eggs, fish or hot curries - which would cause
indigestion; rather they are expected to keep mainly
to rice, bread, tea and cumin seed (Lindenbaum 1977,
p144).

During lactation, heat is believed to increase
the supply of milk whilst cold diminishes it. Too
much warmth within the mother may displace cold and
concentrate it in the breast causing the milk to
curdle and become indigestible. The implications of

this are that when a second pregnancy is diagnosed -
and pregnancy is a hot condition - the nursing child
should be immediately weaned, in order to forestall
problems of curdled milk. As in the case of food
withdrawal because of sickness, cessation of breast
feeding without adequate substitutes for breast milk
may give rise to malnutrition (Sanjur 1974).

Ramanamurthy (1969) has provided some
preliminary evidence that hot and cold dietaries may
produce physiological effects in the body. In his,
albeit limited, studies he found that hot foods
increased acidity of urine and decreased nitrogen
retention. An example of physiological consequences
of food classification is found in the Indian
ranking of animal milks in terms of their ´heating´
effects. In India, animal milk is generally
considered to be heating, and therefore a danger to
infant health if undiluted. Consequent dilution with
water may give rise to problems of malnutrition if
the mixture is too thin to provide adequate protein
and energy. Further, when a child develops infective
diarrhoea - a hot illness - hot foods such as milk
are withdrawn completely and the diet changes to one
of cool foods such as barley water, a practice which
may contribute to development of kwashiorkor.
However it is also true that carbohydrate
intolerance is frequently associated with diarrhoea;
high carbohydrate loads aggravate the problem and
their removal from the diet may actually be
beneficial. [In addition, malabsorption syndrome,
related to decreased levels of intestinal lactase is
not uncommon in Asia]. Buffalo´s milk, cow´s milk
and goat´s milk are ranked in a descending order of
heat and are consequently diluted more or less to
make them suitable for infant feeding. The different
´heats´ match the differing lactose contents of the
milks; thus those milks with higher lactose
concentrations - and which are therefore more likely
to cause problems of intestinal malabsorption - are
diluted more (McCracken 1971).

Examples presented above show that practical
consequences of the various hot/cold classification
systems can be, in terms of conventional nutritional
wisdom, both positive and negative. There are two
lessons here for the student of nutrition. The first
is that a lack of understanding of traditional food
classifications creates barriers to well-intentioned
attempts to introduce changes in food habits. This
is true not only in respect of the hot/cold
ideology, but in all instances where cultural codes

53

differ. The second lesson, perhaps more heartening
to the would-be change agent, is that sound
nutritional practices may, with care, be developed
and reinforced within the context of existing
traditional systems. Concepts of health and
nutrition must be viewed in their cultural context
and food habits should not be automatically labelled
good or poor on the basis of modern scientific
premises or rationale (Sanjur 1982, p149). As
Jelliffe and Bennett commented with regard to infant
feeding, practices may be functionally classified as
beneficial, neutral, unclassifiable or harmful. Only
the latter should be subject to intervention through
friendly persuasion; there is no justification for
change for change´s sake (Jelliffe & Bennett 1961).

CUISINE

> A fine sauce will make even an elephant or a
> grandfather palatable.
> De La Reyniere (1968)

Cuisine is a term commonly used to denote a style of
cooking with distinctive foods, preparation methods
and/or techniques of eating. A national cuisine is
what is, or what is thought of as, the normal or
typical food of a particular country; precisely
because it is ´normal´ it is not thought of as an
expression of individuality, but rather as an aspect
of group identity. Thus when someone refers to
French cuisine, or Italian cuisine; to haute
cuisine; to Cantonese or Szechuan cuisine, we have
an immediate idea of what kinds of foods and dishes
are being described. Sometimes though, our ideas of
foreign cuisines can be quite misleading, formed, as
they often are, from cook books, travelogues and
local restaurant interpretations of classic dishes.
Stereotypes are thus created and perpetuated and we
may be quite surprised on actually visiting, say
Italy, to discover that not everyone eats pizza and
spaghetti all the time. Some commentators suggest
that the cuisine of a society reflects its
predominant characteristics. Thus, Italian foods are
earthy, English foods are robust, Japanese foods are
aesthetically presented (Martin-Ibanez, cited in
Lowenberg et al, 1979, p120).
     Often it is difficult to define a native
cuisine; what, for example, is ´Canadian food´? As
in the United States, so in Canada cuisine has been
influenced not only by available native plants and

54

techniques but also by the many cultural groups who have immigrated to the New World over the past three hundred years. Practices which are now considered to be the epitome of American ways were in fact introduced by settlers from other lands. ´As American as apple pie´? - the apple pie was bought from England; barbecued steaks? - a technique introduced by Spaniards - who in turn learnt it from Caribbean natives. North American cuisine is indeed cosmopolitan; there is a willingness to borrow from other cultures that results in a tendency toward easy acceptance of new products and techniques. Most large cities offer a wide variety of ´ethnic´ restaurants, making it easy for urban dwellers to sample a dozen exotic cuisines with no more effort than a short car drive. Both the genuine ethnic dish and Americanised versions thereof are readily available, so when someone suggests ´let´s eat out´, the reply is: ´do you fancy Italian, Greek or Chinese´ ...or Vietnamese or Indian or Japanese? Probably the single major distinguishing feature of the North American diet is the emphasis placed on meat. In summer, the air of parks and gardens is filled with the smell of large slabs of meat being ritualistically barbecued, whilst for those with less ambition there are the ubiquitous steak houses and burger joints offering a hundred and one variations on the basic hamburger. Accounts of the cuisines of over one hundred ethnic groups in Canada are included in Barer-Stein´s comprehensive study. Her book also includes valuable background information on topics such as special occasions and home life and facilities (Barer-Stein 1979).

Farb & Armelagos (1980, p191) suggest that cuisine consists of four components: foods chosen for use, preparation methods, flavour principles and rules governing meal behaviour. Flavour principles are discussed in Chapter 6; the other components are considered at more length below.

Foods chosen for use

In a sense, the whole of this book is devoted to the question of what foods are chosen for use by different cultural groups. Considered here are those foods which assume central importance in the diet by virtue of being staple crops, and which constitute the bulk of what is eaten. Heisler (1981) provides a detailed account of the origins and importance of the world´s major staples. Because of their dietary pre-eminence, such foods may come to have special

55

ceremonial or supernatural properties associated
with them; they are sometimes called ´cultural
superfoods´. The word for the important staple may
come to stand for food in general, and may take on
extensive symbolic significance. Thus the Lord´s
prayer asks: ´Give us this day our daily bread´;
bread is referred to as ´the staff of life´; ´bread´
is used as a slang term for money - the basic means
of subsistence in our Northern societies.

Balfet (1976) explores the central role of
bread in some Mediterranean cultures. It may be made
with herbs, seeds and seasonings; eggs, cheeses, fat
or bits of meat may be mixed with the dough - as in
pizza. It is frequently served as a sandwich. Bread
is never thrown away but given great respect, while
the leaven is regarded as having hidden power.
Sorghum and millet, the chief cereals of Yemen are
mixed in a bread which is an indispensable part of a
meal (Bornstein-Johanssen 1976). Bread is used as a
utensil to scoop up other foods. The tortilla of
Latin America and the Chupatti of India are
flatbreads fulfilling a similar function. The
breadfruit, a native plant of Tahiti is used as a
bread throughout the West Indies. Captain Bligh´s
famous ill-fated voyage on the Bounty was in fact a
botanical expedition to transport breadfruit from
Tahiti to the West Indies where British planters
thought it would provide the answer to feeding their
plantation slaves cheaply. News of the breadfruit
had spread via tales of early South Seas explorers.
Howard (1953) quotes an extract from a report by a
British seaman named William Dampier.

> The breadfruit (as we call it) grows on a large
> tree, as big and high as our largest apple
> trees: It hath a spreading head, full of
> branches and dark leaves. The fruit grows on
> the boughs like apples; it is as big as a penny
> loaf when wheat is at five shillings the
> bushel, it is of a round shape, and hath a
> thick tough rind. When the fruit is ripe it is
> yellow and soft, and the taste is sweet and
> pleasant. The natives at Guam use it for bread.
> They gather it, when full-grown, while it is
> green and hard; then they bake it in an oven,
> which scorcheth the rind and makes it black;
> but they scrape off the outside black crust,
> and there remains a tender thin crust; and the
> inside is soft, tender, and white like the
> crumb of penny loaf.

Despite his first failure occasioned by mutiny, Bligh later made a second voyage on which he was able to accomplish his mission, and was rewarded with a gold medal and election as a Fellow of the Royal Society (Howard, op cit). The breadfruit is now well established in the West Indies.

The African Bemba give central place to millet, which forms the bulk of their diet. Meals consist of heavy lumpy millet porridge, known as nbwali, served with a relish of vegetables and, rarely, scraps of meat or fish. Nbwali is akin to ´bread´, in that it represents life and health: the word recurs in proverbs, folktales, puns, jokes, songs and riddles (Williams 1973, p75). The word is used extensively in ritual - in marriage ceremonies, initiation rites, political actions, kinship relations; Nbwali is a central theme in cultural life as well as being the main source of sustenance. It is no accident that the two examples of bread and nbwali both involve a cereal staple.

> No civilisation worthy of the name has ever been founded on any agricultural basis other than the cereals. The ancient cultures of Babylonia and Egypt, of Rome and Greece, and later those of northern and western Europe, were all based on the growing of wheat, barley, rye and oats. Those of India, China and Japan had rice for their basic crop. The pre-Columbian peoples of America - Inca, Maya and Aztec - looked to corn for their daily bread.
>
> (Mangelsdorf 1953, p70)

May (1974) echoes this sentiment, identifying cultures by their staple food products. Thus, he says, there are wheat cultures, millet and sorghum cultures, corn and rice cultures. Wheat is the world´s most cultivated plant. It was probably the earliest cereal cultivated by man, and its domestication, says Mangelsdorf, laid the foundations of Western civilisation. Hanks (1972) describes the Rice Goddess who is central to the lives of Thai villagers; in times past when people were virtuous, rice alone sufficed to nourish them - an idea perpetuated in a fashion by modern Zen macrobiotic practices. For the Indian peoples of much of the American continents, maize was a true

57

cultural superfood.
 Root crops, as well as cereals, can become
cultural superfoods. The potato has a central role
in meals in Western Europe. Originating in Peru as
early as 500 B.C., it only slowly gained acceptance
in other parts of the world. In Peru it became an
important nutritional food for it thrived at
elevations where few other cultivated plants would
grow. It also had an important symbolic value; the
potato motif is common in Peruvian pottery samples,
where it often takes an anthropomorphic design
(Salaman 1952). Moreover, the potato designs are
sometimes mutilated, which, suggests Salaman,
represents an outpouring of blood as in a sacrifice;
blood was often poured over seed potatoes to ensure
fertility of the crop, and bowls of potato meal were
buried with the dead.
Introduced into Europe about 1570, the potato was at
first viewed with some scepticism. It was recognised
as a member of the Nightshade family and so became
identified with its poisonous cousins. The Scots
rejected the potato as an unholy food as it was not
mentioned in the Bible. In Russia, the introduction
of the potato was met with open revolt, and a
linguistic manipulation equated the potato with
something sexually perverse and unclean (Salaman op
cit). It was not until the eighteenth century that
the potato became really popular in Europe - and at
that time it contributed to massive population
increases consequent on raised nutritional
standards. In Ireland though, due to prevailing
climatic conditions and because it fitted into
existing cooking patterns, the potato was quickly
accepted early on. It helped the Irish peasants
survive the hardships inflicted by war and strife,
and soon became the basic food of most of the
population. The potato has been held responsible for
the massive population increase in eighteenth
century Ireland for it provided ´a maximum of
sustenance with a minimum of labour´ (Salaman op
cit, p118). The Irish became so dependant on this
cultural superfood that the failure of the crop
resulted in widespread famines in the middle
nineteenth century. Because they wouldn´t eat fish
unless they could get potato to go with it, and
because they rejected corn maize as being inedible
for humans, the Irish people suffered a famine which
resulted in a halving of the population in a matter
of twenty years. Desperation forced many families to
emigrate to the New World. It is estimated that one

and a half million people died, whilst a further million left the country bound mainly for America. Heisler comments that it is ironic that a New World crop - maize - was rejected as a means of sustenance, when a previously introduced New World crop failed (Heisler 1981).

Because some foods become culturally indispensible, their nutritional value can be over-rated. After all, how can a food which is important to the mind not also be important to the body? Bolivian peasants believe that the potato has insuperable nutritional qualities. The plantain is extensively used in Bantu ritual. Because of this, it has been difficult for health workers to persuade the Bantu people that plantain is not a nutritionally adequate staple, and that supplementary foods are needed.

Meal Patterns

Hunger is a drive which arises periodically, and people of all cultures take at least one meal in a 24 hour period. However, patterns of meal-taking vary widely and are a part of cultural learning. Thus the British typically have four ´food events´ in the day; North American practice favours three daily meals; whilst in continental Europe, five or six ´food events´ are common. There are, of course, considerable variations within the framework of general patterns, and there is some evidence of a general trend away from a small number of large meals to a greater number of small meals as the norm in Northern societies. Changes in family structure and in lifestyles mean that communal meals are less common and that snacks are often fitted into busy schedules as and when time allows. In stark contrast are some African tribes whose members eat only once a day. Children are taught voluntary control of the hunger drive and learn to ´feel hungry´ only at the appropriate time (Williams 1973, p74). In Bemba society, where only one daily meal is taken, children are permitted light snacks throughout the day; but by adolescence they are expected to adopt the adult one meal pattern.

Because many societies suffer sporadic food shortages, they have developed customs of fasting for adult members which make a virtue out of necessity. Fasts of up to three days may be specifically used to delay or displace the hunger drive. Aids to hunger suppression are commonly employed; coca leaves are chewed by Andean Indians

in lieu of food, as cocaine inhibits hunger and
fatigue and also, during long arduous journeys in
mountainous terrain, relieves travellers of the need
to add the weight of food supplies to already large
burdens. Peyote has a similar effect, as does the
betel nut; hunger and thirst are inhibited and
energy-requiring activity is decreased. Tobacco,
coffee and tea may likewise be used to blunt
appetite.

Faced with chronic hunger and long-term food
shortages, some human groups have developed cultural
patterns which reduce their caloric level well below
that normally thought to be necessary for survival.
Because of environmental conditions, the Bemba of
Africa are rarely able to produce enough of their
staple millet crop to last an entire year. They call
the last three months of the year the 'hunger
months'. When millet becomes scarce the whole
community slows down. Adults reduce their food
intake and stop brewing millet beer; children eat
only one small meal per day. Everyone curtails
activity, staying in their huts and drinking large
quantities of water and taking snuff to reduce their
hunger (Williams 1973, p75). This author reports an
average 1706kcal/day for adult male intakes -
demonstrating that the Bemba live consistently at
energy intake levels below those normally thought to
be capable of sustaining life.

Meal patterns, including number of meals and
frequency of eating, differ not only between, but
also within cultural groups. The traditional English
breakfast of fried bacon, sausage and eggs, followed
by toast and marmalade with gallons of tea may no
longer be the norm in middle-class households, but
it is still offered with pride to guests at hotels
and bed-and-breakfast places and on British Rail's
Intercity morning trains. Elsewhere, the continental
breakfast of rolls and coffee has become a firmly
established alternative, partly as a result of
cultural exchange, foreign travel and time
consciousness and partly, perhaps, because of
anxiety over dietary calories and cholesterol.
Within Britain there are many regional variations in
meal patterns and in preferred foods. Yorkshiremen
traditionally enjoy fatty bacon, which distresses
the stomachs of their more sensitive neighbours. An
episode in James Herriot's memoirs of life as a vet
in rural Yorkshire, recalls the time when, after an
early morning's job, Herriot was offered a real farm
breakfast. When the bacon arrived, there was

scarcely any red meat on it - a cause for admiration on behalf of the farmer, but a sore trial for Herriot, who had to somehow force himself to swallow this ´delicacy´.

Even the names given to food events may vary. The Southerners ´dinner´ is often known as ´tea´ in the Midlands and North of England, though both terms refer to the same evening meal. ´Dinner´ is the Northerners midday meal - elsewhere known as ´lunch´; whilst his hearty ´tea´ commonly becomes a light afternoon snack in other parts of the country. There are social class variations in meal term usage which may be more pronounced than regional differences. Whatever the meal is called, though, its structure remains remarkable consistent.

Meal Structure
Meals exhibit underlying structures which change little over time. Although experiments and innovations may be introduced along with new food products, the meal has to remain recognisably the same. In other words, most people have an idea of what would be acceptable as ´breakfast´ or ´dinner´ or ´supper´, and are able to differentiate these meals from ´snacks´. Douglas & Nicod (1974) conducted research into meal structures in Britain as a way of determining the likely acceptability of culinary innovations. They hypothesised that whilst only small reinforcing changes might be possible in the highly structured parts of food patterns, new foods and techniques could be introduced into less structured elements of the traditional diet. Nicod actually lodged with a number of families in order to discreetly observe normal food habits. The researchers divided eating occasions into four types:
(a) food event - any eating occasion;
(b) structured event - social occasion with time, place and sequence rules;
(c) meal - food eaten as part of structured event;
(d) snack - food eaten as part of unstructured event, where there are no formal rules and each food item is self-contained.
Three kinds of meals were identified; a major hot meal at about 6 P.M. on weekdays and early afternoon on weekends; a minor meal at about 9 P.M. weekdays and 5 P.M weekends; and a tertiary meal - often a biscuit and hot drink - available at different times. Breakfast was defined as a snack rather than as a meal as it did not have a consistent structure

61

Figure 2.1 Structure of main meal in British working class household

	Course 1	Course 2	Course 3
	SAVOURY	SWEET	SWEET
	potato staple	cereal staple	cereal staple
	no discretion to omit elements	some discretion	solid optional
	liquid dressing runny	liquid dressing thick	dressing solid thicker
	other sensory qualities of food dominate over visual pattern	visual pattern dominates until serving	visual pattern dominates until eating
	solids not segregated from liquids		solids and liquid segregated

Source: Douglas & Nicod. 'Taking the Biscuit.' New Society, 19th Dec., 1974

or composition. The three meal system focused on potato and cereal; the most important meal featuring potatoes, whilst the minor meal included bread and possibly cakes and biscuits; the tertiary meal included biscuits.

The researchers show that the Sunday meal sequence - main, minor, tertiary - is either fitted into weekday patterns starting with the main meal at 6 P.M. or is adopted in its entirety [eg. with the midday provision of cooked major meals at works canteens]. They analyse the structure of the major meal, illustrating various rules of combination and order (See Figure 2.1). Rules of combination for course 1 are repeated in course 2. The authors comment that the rules for structuring the first course of a major meal are absolutely strict. No deviation is allowed if the food event is to be recognised a a major meal. The three courses of the major meal are structured similarly to the three meals of Sunday; that is, there is a direct structural correspondence between Course 1 and the major ´potato´ meal; course 2 and the minor ´cereal´ meal; course 3 and the tertiary ´biscuit´ meal. The role of the biscuit as a unique expression of the conclusion of a meal or meal sequence in British cuisine is emphasised.

Such a detailed analysis of meal structure (and the authors provide more insights than are recounted here) may at first seem to be mere exotica, and to be without practical implications. However, if rules for meal structures are indeed firmly adhered to then the scope for introducing new foods or for altering food behaviours is formally delimited. Nutrition educators should perhaps be aware of this when they attempt to ´improve´ or modify diets. As an example, Douglas and Nicod point out that there is no place for plain fresh fruit within the meal system described and so suggestions that fresh fruit replace puddings as an economy or nutritional measure are almost inevitably doomed to failure.

Methods of preparation
Methods of food preparation are diverse and many; they are related to types of food available, the state of the material culture and the cultural needs and preferences of the society. A wealth of information on methods and techniques can be found in modern cookbooks and in anthropology texts, and the topic is dwelt on but briefly here to highlight a few examples of cultural influences on, and

consequences of, food preparation.

The greatest revolution in food preparation must have been the discovery of fire. Meats could be eaten raw, but cooking improved their flavour and palatability, whilst many vegetable foods are only edible if cooked. Early cooking methods would have included direct heat roasting, boiling in water heated by hot stones, and the use of animal stomachs as cooking vessels. The invention of pottery would have considerably extended options for mixing and heating foods. Topography may have placed limitations on the use of particular methods and therefore of certain foods; for example, cereals and beans are not usually popular in mountainous regions because of the inordinate amount of time required to prepare them. To bring a pan of water to the boil, of course, takes much longer in the high mountains than at sea-level, and is doubly inefficient where fuel resources are often scarce. Fuel conservation may also be achieved by cutting food into small pieces which can be cooked quickly. On the other hand, the dung fuel used in many Southern countries provides a low heat ideal for prolonged slow cooking of dishes which can be left all day whilst other domestic and agricultural tasks are attended to. These examples suffice to indicate that available energy has a direct impact on the types of foods which can be readily prepared and thus on cuisine. Cultural lifestyles and occupations impose their own requirements for dishes which are ´instant´ or ´slow cooking´, ´oven-to-table´ or easily carried. As an example of the latter, the Cornish Pasty was invented as a convenient ´packaging´ for meat and potatoes so that they could be eaten by miners at the pitface.

Preparation methods can add to or detract from the nutritional value of a food. It is fairly well known that prolonged boiling of vegetables leaches water-soluble vitamins into the cooking water, which is often discarded with a consequent loss of valuable nutrients. The addition of baking soda to green vegetables to keep them brightly coloured also reduces nutritional value. Dripping from roasted meats contain nutrients, lost unless the drippings form the basis of a gravy. On the other hand some methods of preparation actually enhance nutritional value. Pellagra is a disease endemic to many maize-eating societies. For many years, before the elucidation of vitamin deficiency theories, it was held to be an infectious disease so widespread was

its occurrence. Even with discovery of a link
between niacin deficiency and the symptoms of
pellagra, some puzzling anomalies remained. Pellagra
was observed in some groups who had higher average
intakes of niacin than other groups who were
pellagra free. Even after the quantity of tryptophan
in the diet had been taken into account (tryptophan
is an amino acid which can under certain conditions
be converted to niacin) the differences in disease
prevalence persisted. The solution to the puzzle lay
in the discovery that niacin occurs in a bound form
in maize and thus its actual biological availability
is low. The technique of soaking maize in lime water
to soften it before using it in baking has the
effect of freeing niacin from its bound form and
making it available. This cultural practice helps
then to explain why some maize-eaters do not suffer
from pellagra. A further example of nutritional
enhancement is found amongst the Pima Indians of
Arizona, where three methods of preparation all have
the effect of increasing calcium levels in food.
They are, roasting of food in contact with coals or
ashes; grinding of food with stone grinding
implements; and cooking of corn in a Mesquite ash
solution. In the first two instances iron levels are
also raised. When assessing the nutritional adequacy
of a diet it is important to consider the potential
effects of nutrient losses or additions during food
preparation in order to arrive at accurate
conclusions.

The Culinary Triangle. Not only have foods
themselves been categorised in a variety of ways
which reflect how we think about them (see Chapter
1), but methods of food preparation too have been
analysed with a view to understanding both social
structure and human thought processes. Food
preparation as a cultural phenomenon has been
explored in immense detail by Claude Levi-Strauss, a
leading exponent of structuralism. According to
Levi-Strauss the way in which we perceive
relationships in nature leads us to generate
cultural products which incorporate the same kind of
relationships. He claims that cultural elements have
a common inner structure that reflects the common
structure of human thought, and that by seaching for
underlying universals of human culture we can learn
something about the nature of man. Just as every
human society has a language there is no society
which does not process at least some of its food by

cooking. Cooking is a universal means by which
nature is transformed into culture, and categories
of cooking are therefore eminently appropriate as
symbols of social organisation and differentiation
(Leach 1970).

Although the kinds of foods available to
different human sub-groups varies considerably every
society breaks up those foods which are available
into a number of categories, each of which is
treated in a different way. Levi-Strauss claims that
cross-culturally these categories are remarkably
alike, and he identifies them as raw, cooked and
rotted. Cooked food is raw food which has been
transformed by cultural means, whereas rotted food
is fresh raw food which has been transformed by
natural means. The principal modes of cooking food -
roasting, boiling and smoking - also form a
structured set, but one which is in opposition to
the first. Levi-Strauss constructed a culinary
triangle in which ´natural´ vs ´cultural´ and
´prepared´ vs ´unprepared´ properties of food are
linked (Fig.2.2).

Figure 2.2   The culinary triangle

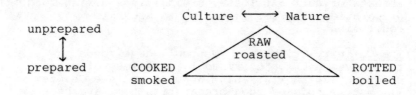

Roasted food is directly exposed to fire without the
intervention of cultural apparatus and therefore
belongs to nature and also to the unprepared
category; boiled food must be cooked in vessels made
by humans and is therefore in the cultural and the
prepared category; smoked foods are prepared with
the mediation of air but without cultural apparatus
and thus belong to the natural and prepared
categories. Roasted food has an affinity with raw as
it is never uniformly cooked; boiled food may be
linked with rotted, as both processes - natural and
cultural - reduce food to a decomposed state;

['potpourri' means rotted pot]; and smoked can be associated with cooked food. Levi-Strauss elaborates on this simple triangle, incorporating other methods of food preparation such as grilling and frying in a more complex diagram. He believes that the system which emerges can be applied to other aspects of society and thus that food preparation is a kind of language which tells us something about societal structure. Indeed, the categories of food as indicated in the culinary triangle are widely accorded very different levels of social prestige. Roasted food is special; it is of high status; it is for men. Boiled food is everyday; it is suitable for children and invalids. It is significant that people in different cultures sort out their foodstuffs in very similar ways and apply similar status distinctions. Levi-Strauss has even claimed that the high status attached to roasted food is a universal cultural characteristic. If this is true, then by studying the use of roasted food in a society - who prepares it, who eats it, when and where it is eaten - we will not only learn a lot about the social structure of that particular human group, but also about the way in which man thinks.

Levi-Strauss's theories have been heavily criticised because of his use of personally selected and often exotic examples with which to prove his point, which arouses suspicions that he has simply chosen those particular examples which will fit into his prearranged matrix whilst ignoring those that are problematical (Leach 1970). He has also been accused of making sweeping generalisations which are not always supported by empirical evidence. Despite such criticisms, it is true that Levi-Strauss has accumulated much evidence for the existence of universal structural principles underlying the way in which foods and food preparation methods are categorised.

Techniques of eating

Before the introduction of the fork as a utensil foods were commonly scooped up in breads or by fingers alone. Breads such as pitas in Europe, chapattis and pooris in India and tortilla in Mexico are still used almost as utensils. In the U.S., finger foods are associated with informal occasions and are not a normal part of regular meals; in other societies, the use of hands is essential. Farley Mowat (1965) describes his first meal with Canadian Inuit:

The tray was magnificent, but its contents were
even more impressive. Half a dozen parboiled
legs of deer were spread out in a thick gravy
which seemed to be composed of equal parts of
fat and deer hairs. Bobbing about in the debris
were a dozen tongues and, like a cage holding
the lesser cuts of meat, there was an entire
boiled rib basket of a deer...The etiquette of
the situation eluded me. I took my sheath knife
and cautiously sawed off a good sized chunk of
leg meat, scraped the encrustation of hairs
from it, and cuddled it in my lap since there
was nothing else that could serve as a plate.
  Now Franz and the three Ihalmiut men
tusked in - I use that word advisedly - and
Ohot seized an entire leg. Sucking the gravy
from it with appreciative lips, he sank his
teeth into the tough muscle while with his left
hand he held the joint away from his face, and
with his right hand made a quick slash at the
meat with his knife...Hekwaw seemed to prefer
the soup. He dipped his cupped hands in it and
then sucked up the greasy fluid with gusty
relish, taking time out now and again to chew
at a deer´s tongue which he dropped back into
the soup to keep warm between bites.
(Mowat 1975, pp100-101)

This description might well have been applied to
mealtimes in Medieval Europe. Before the
introduction of eating utensils table manners were,
what would today be considered to be, disgusting.
Food was eaten from common dishes, plucked out of
sauces by unwashed hands, and discarded on the floor
or even back into the pot. Soups would be slurped
from the bowl, and drinks swigged from communal cups
passed freely around. Elias (1978) presents some
instructive quotations from thirteenth century
treatises on table manners. The following examples
are illustrative of common rules at Upper Class
tables in Europe.

  * A man of refinement should not slurp with his
    spoon when in company.
  * It is not polite to drink from the dish,
    although some who approve of this rude habit
    insolently pick up the dish and pour it down
    as though they were mad.
  * Those who stand up and snort disgustingly
    over the dishes like swine belong with other

farmyard beasts.
* To snort like a salmon, gobble like a badger, and complain while eating - these three things are quite improper.
* Those who like mustard and salt should take care to avoid the filthy habit of putting their fingers into them.

Elias provides many other examples which show early attempts to enforce what we would regard as minimally polite table manners. From the nature of the injunctions it was obviously common practice to spit out food, put it back in the dish, and to offer to others foods which had already been bitten into. At first, such rules of etiquette as those mentioned above were directed at courtly practice; as the bourgeoisie attempted to imitate or prepare for entry into the court they too adopted the new rules of behaviour, in turn influencing provincial practices. Thus the new customs were disseminated from the Upper Class downwards, and were subsequently adopted by ´civilised´ society as a whole. By the nineteenth century, the whole movement which had generated ´manners´ had been forgotten, and proper behaviour at table was taken for granted; what had so recently gone before was now labelled ´barbaric´ (Elias op cit. p 194). Since then there have been few substantial changes in etiquette, and techniques of eating remain basically unchanged.

The manner in which meals are served has changed considerably from the Middle Ages to modern times, and this itself has affected eating techniques. For example, it was common in Medieval Upper Class households to have the whole dead animal - or substantial parts of it - brought to the table for carving. The privilege of carving and distributing the meat was a particular honour, and the ability to carve was thus an indispensible accomplishment of a man of breeding. During the seventeenth century this practice started to go out of fashion - perhaps in deference to female sensibility - and it became relegated to the status of a behind-the-scenes practice to be done by servants and menials. Today, we usually try to avoid any reminders that the meat dish on our plate has anything to do with the killing of an animal - though carving the joint remains as an English tradition to be carried out on high status occasions and celebratory feasts. In this gradual removal of meat from pride of place at the table there may be

69

implications for the future of meat-eating and vegetarianism - a theme which is taken up in Chapter 4.

The presentation of large amounts of meat at table demanded the extensive use of knives - both for carving, and as the most important eating utensil. There were few restrictions on the use of knives and it was taken for granted that they were lifted to the mouth for purposes of eating. Knives were at first pointed, but were later ground down both as a safety measure and for reasons of etiquette. 'In 1669 a royal edict of Louis XIV, probably issued with a view to discourage assassination at meal-times, made it illegal for anyone to carry pointed knives, for cutlers to make them, or for inn-keepers to put them on their tables; it also commanded that any existing knives with pointed blades should have their points rounded off.' (Bailey 1927, p8). Although one might cut oneself when eating from a knife the element of danger in using knives has been overplayed. According to Elias it is the generalised symbolic meaning of danger which underlies the later restrictions and taboos placed on the knife (Elias 1978, p 123). Knives are passed handle first because of the implicit and emotive threat of offering the point; we do not put knives to our mouths because that represents potential danger and would discomfort others. Consequently, the use of the knife has been gradually restricted and there is a continuing trend to use it less and less. Knives are only necessary when large pieces of food are presented on the plate. Even then, North Americans favour the use of fork only, and after cutting food as necessary, frequently lay the knife aside. Chinese food, which is pre-cut into bite-size pieces does not require the use of a knife; instead, chopsticks are an efficient technique of handling food, acting basically, as an extension of finger and thumb. Elias speculates that eventually the knife may follow the pattern set by the joint of meat, and be banished from the table altogether.

Elias comments that the correct use of utensils is limited and defined by a multiplicity of very precise rules, the reasons for which are not self-evident. They only appear apparent to us because they have been culturally learnt and internalised. Why, for example, did civilised eating require the use of forks? It was not for hygienic reasons, as we might now suppose, but rather to

spare the user the shame of being seen with soiled
hands; use of the fingers in eating led to a number
of other unavoidable piggish manners which were
deemed to be disagreeable and offensive. About 1600
A.D. forks appeared in Italy, though they were not
generally used in England till the mid-eighteenth
century. From then on, table utensils continued to
become more elaborate and differentiated; and
instead of communal implements everyone had his or
her own set of utensils each with its specific use.
    Customs form and evolve gradually in response
to the structure of society and to changes in human
relationships. Thus Medieval advice on etiquette was
aimed at the upper class so that they would know how
to behave at court - not because of any intrinsic
value attached to the new behaviours themselves.
Adopting the new manners was a mark of ´civilite´;
as the practices spread throughout society they no
longer served as distinguishing marks of the elite
and so further refinements had to be made in order
to maintain a social separation. As the concept of
civilite pervaded society as a whole, it was
absorbed into normal practice and ceased to be
commented on. We tend to assume that manners were
refined and utensils introduced for reasons of
hygiene, whereas the real motivation stemmed from
the idea that ´civilised´ people behaved in certain
ways. ´Rational understanding is not the motor of
the civilisation of eating´ (Elias p116). We will
see other examples later of how there is a tendency
for members of modern societies to ascribe their own
rationalistic motivations to traditional practices
when trying to interpret cultural patterns.

SUMMARY

The food ideology subscribed to by a given cultural
group represents a collection of learned attitudes
and behaviours which dictate not only what is
acceptable as food, but also when and how that food
is to be prepared, served and eaten. Each culture
tends to think of its own rules and practices as
being ´normal´, and so deviation from common
practice is usually ridiculed or dismissed as being
´heathen´ or ´foreign´ - both terms of
disapprobation. The traveller in a foreign land has
many hazards to negotiate in adjusting to new eating
behaviours, as does the immigrant in his newly
adopted country. The foods on offer may be
substantially different from normal fare, whilst the

etiquette of eating may prove to be elusive and
challenging - as in Mowat´s experience with the
Inuit. Shared food habits provide a sense of
belonging; they are an affirmation of cultural
identity and as such are not easily given up. The
fact that it is hard to retain a commitment to
cultural relativism: hard to accept that one´s own
practices are simply the product of one codified
system amongst many, indicates the great importance
we attach to our food habits. Our unwillingness to
accept just anything as food betrays the notion that
food is consumed for nourishment of the body alone.
Food also nourishes the heart, mind and soul.

REFERENCES

Back, K.W. ´Food, Sex and Theory.´ In T.K.
    Fitzgerald (ed.), Nutrition and Anthropology
    in Action. van Gorcum, Amsterdam 1977
Bailey, C.T.P. Knives and Forks. Medici Society,
    London 1927
Balfet, H. ´Bread in Some Regions of the
    Mediterranean Area: A Contribution to the
    Studies on Eating Habits.´ In M. Arnott (ed.),
    Gastronomy: the Anthropology of Food and Food
    Habits. Mouton Publ., The Hague 1976
Barer-Stein, T. You Eat What You Are. McClelland
    & Stewart, Toronto 1979
Bass, M.A., L.M. Wakefield, and K.M. Kolasa.
    Community Nutrition and Individual Food
    Behaviour. Burgess Publ., Minn. 1979
Bornstein-Johanssen, A. ´Sorghum and Millet in
    Yemen.´ In M. Arnott (ed.), Gastronomy: the
    Anthropology of Food and Food Habits. Mouton
    Publ., The Hague 1976
de Esquef, L. ´Dietary Habits of the Peasant of the
    Bolivian Highlands.´ FAO Nutrition Newsletter ,
    10 (2):16-20, 1972
de Garine, I.L. ´Food, Tradition and Prestige.´ In
    D. Walcher, N. Kretchmer and H.L. Barnett
    (eds.), Food, Man and Society. Plenum Pr.,
    New York 1976
de la Reyniere, G. Almanach des Gourmands P.
    Waeffe, 1968
Douglas, M. and M. Nicod. ´Taking the Biscuit: the
    Structure of British Meals.´ New Society ,
    19th Dec., 1974
Eckstein, E.F. Food, People and Nutrition. AVI
    Publ. Co. Inc., Westport 1980.

Elias, N. The Civilising Process. Urizon Books,
    New York 1978
Farb, P. and G. Armelagos. Consuming Passions: the
    Anthropology of Eating. Houghton Mifflin Co.,
    Boston 1980
Gifft, H.H., M.B. Washbon. and G.G. Harrison.
    Nutrition, Behaviour and Change. Prentice
    Hall, New Jersey 1972
Hanks, L.M. Rice and Man: Agricultural Ecology in
    Southeast Asia. Aldine-Atherton, Chicago 1972
Harwood, A. ´The Hot-Cold Theory of Disease.
    Implications for Treatment of Puerto Rican
    Patients.´ J.Am.Med.Assn. , 216:1153-58, 1971
Hasan, K.A. ´The Hindu Dietary Practices and
    Culinary Rituals in a North Indian Village.´
    Ethnomedizin , 1:43-70, 1971
Heisler, C.B.Jr. Seed to Civilisation. (2cnd ed.)
    W.H.Freeman & Co., San Francisco 1981
Howard, R.A. ´Captain Bligh and the Breadfruit.´ In
    N. Kretchmer and W. van B. Robertson (eds.),
    Human Nutrition: Readings from Scientific
    American. W.H.Freeman, San Francisco, 1978
    (Original paper 1953)
Ingham, J.M. ´On Mexican Folk Medicine.´ Am.
    Anthrop. , 72:76-87, 1970
Jelliffe, D.B. ´Parallel Food Classification in
    Developing and Industrialised Countries.´ Am.
    J. Clin. Nutr. , 20:279-281, 1967
Jelliffe, D.B. and F.J. Bennett. ´Cultural and
    Anthropological Factors in Infant Nutrition.´
    Fed. Proc. , 20 (No.1 part 3): Supplement 7,
    185-187, 1961
Jerome, N.W. ´American Culture and Food Habits.´ In
    Dimensions of Nutrition. Proc. Colo. Diet.
    Assn. Conference, Colorado Assoc. Uni. Pr.,
    Boulder, Colorado 1969
Katona-Apte, J. ´The Socio-cultural Aspects of Food
    Avoidance in a Low Income Population in
    Tamilnad, South India.´ J. Trop. Pediatr.
    Environ. Child Health , 23:83-90, 1977
Leach, Sir E. Levi-Strauss. Fontana, Glasgow 1970
Levi-Strauss, C. The Raw and the Cooked. Harper &
    Row, New York 1969
Lindenbaum, S. ´The Last Course: Nutrition and
    Anthropology in Asia.´ In T.K. Fitzgerald
    (ed.), Nutrition and Anthropology in Action.
    van Gorcum, Amsterdam 1977
Logan, M. ´Humoral Folk Medicine: A potential Aid in
    Controlling Pellagra in Mexico.´ Ethnomedizin
    1:397-410, 1972

Mangelsdorf, P.C. ´Wheat.´ In N. Kretchmer and W.
    van B. Robertson (eds.), Human Nutrition:
    Readings from Scientific American.
    W.H.Freeman, San Francisco, 1978 (Original
    paper 1953)
Martin-Ibanez, F. Cited in Lowenberg, M.E., E.N.
    Todhunter, E.D. Wilson, J.R. Savage, and J.L.
    Lubawski. Food and People. J. Wiley & Sons,
    New York 1979
May, J.M. ´The Geography of Nutrition.´ In J.M.
    Hunter (ed.), The Geography of Health and
    Disease. Studies in Geography No.6.,
    University of N. Carolina Pr., Chapel Hill 1974
McCracken, R.D. ´Lactase Deficiency: An Example of
    Dietary Evolution.´ Current Anthropology ,
    12:479-517, 1971
Molony, C.H. ´Systematic Valence Coding of Mexican
    "hot"-"cold" Food.´ Ecol. Food. Nutr. ,
    4:67-74, 1975
Mowat, F. People of the Deer. McClelland and
    Stewart Ltd., Toronto 1965
Nash, O. There´s Always Another Windmill Little,
    Brown & Co., Boston 1962
Passim, H. and J.W. Bennett. Social Process and
    Dietary Change. Nat. Res. Council Bull. 108,
    Washingon D.C. 1943
Ramanamurthy, P.S.V. ´Physiological Effects of ´Hot´
    and ´Cold´ Foods in Human Subjects.´ J. Nutr.
    Diet. , 6:187-191, 1969
Salaman, R.N. ´The Social Influence of the Potato.´
    In N. Kretchmer and W. van B. Robertson (eds.),
    Human Nutrition: Readings from Scientific
    American. W.H.Freeman, San Francisco 1978
Sanjur, D. ´Food Ideology Systems as Conditioners of
    Nutritional Practices.´ Archivos
    Latinoamericanos de Nutricion , 24 (1), 1974
Sanjur, D. Social and Cultural Perspectives in
    Nutrition. Prentice Hall, New Jersey 1982
Schultz, H.G., M.H. Rucker, and G.F. Russell. ´Food
    and Food Use Classification Systems.´ Food
    Tech. , 29 (3):50-56; 60-64, 1975
Williams, B.J. Evolution and Human Origins: an
    Introduction to Physical Anthropology. Harper,
    New York 1973
Yeung, D.L., W.Y. Cheung, and J.H. Sabry. ´The
    Hot-Cold Food Concept in Chinese Culture and
    its Application in a Canadian-Chinese
    Community.´ J. Can. Diet. Assn. , 34:1-8, 1973

Chapter 3

SOCIAL FUNCTIONS OF FOOD

Whilst it is true that food and the act of eating
have innumerable non-biological associations and
meanings, nowhere is this more evident than in the
common everyday experiences of social interaction.
For food is a vehicle for expressing friendship - or
at least acceptance, for smoothing social
intercourse, for showing concern. It is also ridden
with status symbolism and is manipulated to
demonstrate subtly or blatantly differences in
social standing. There might almost be a dictum
which says: 'where two or more people gather
together then let there be food and drink.' Rituals
and celebrations are usually centred around food,
and sometimes the type of food served can define the
event, as with the Thanksgiving turkey or the
Christmas pudding. The major transitional crises of
the life cycle, the rites of passage, are marked in
almost all societies by ritual or ceremonial
distribution and consumption of food (Cohen 1968).
Cohen hypothesises that these important life events
signify changes in socioeconomic relationships and
responsibilities; as food usages commonly symbolise
social relationships changes in the latter are noted
symbolically by displays, exchanges and consumption
of foods. If food symbolises social relationships,
then food-sharing attitudes and practices are
indicative of social structure. The following
discussion is derived largely from the work of Cohen
(op cit), who identifies four patterns of food
distribution and consumption.
        'Recurrent exchange and sharing' is a feature
of societies where community solidarity is maximal.
Kin groups are highly integrated, families live in
close physical proximity, and there is little change
in community membership. Under these conditions
there is an almost constant flow of food between

groups. ´Mutual assistance and sharing in times of
need´ is characteristic of a second type of social
structure. Although kinship ties are still strong
there is greater physical mobility and change in
community membership. Communal sharing of a hunter´s
kill, and willingness to help in times of economic
difficulties would be typical of this type of
structure. ´Narrowed and reluctant sharing´ -
Cohen´s third type, is characterised by reluctant
and grudging rendering of assistance between social
units. It is associated with a fragmented social
system in which the isolated nuclear family is the
predominant social form. Food is served to the
immediate family only, and this serves to define the
boundaries of the family and to symbolise its
separateness from other nuclear families. Physical
and social distance is great, and there are rarely
any functioning kin groups outside the immediate
family. Although ideals of generosity and mutual
assistance in times of need are articulated, in
practice they are severely restricted in quality and
quantity and to a limited group - usually based on
kinship. Finally, ´non-sharing´ is characteristic of
societies in which there are no stable social
groupings and where the accumulation of individual
wealth and power is paramount. Cohen comments that
this is an uncommon social form, citing the Alorese
and the highland peasants of Jamaica as rare
examples.

Food behaviour is thus a guide to both social
relationships and to social structure. A rich
tapestry of social meaning is woven around every
food event in complex strands; assimilation of these
meanings begins in childhood and may be so
internalised as to become an implicit part of adult
behaviour and routine, understood and carried out
without conscious thought or effort. At the same
time it is true that an act involving food may have
more than one meaning, depending on the actors and
the circumstances of the play; thus some overlap
will be apparent in the categories created below for
purposes of discussion.

PRESTIGE AND STATUS

The table is the centre around which all
reputations are formed.
(de La Reyniere 1968)

Historically, food has always been linked to social

prestige and status. Some foods confer high status
on the eaters, others assume high status because of
the groups who habitually eat them. The discrepancy
between the nobility and peasantry of medieval
England was exemplified by the contrast in their
food intakes. Whilst the poor sustained themselves
with bread, cheese and other simple fare, nobles and
landowners might sit down to suppers consisting of
twenty or thirty different dishes, many of them
containing meat of one kind or another. These grand
feasts had a socio-political purpose in that they
symbolised the power which nobles held over the
common people and also over food supplies (See
Tannahill 1973). Meat was greatly desired by the
general populace and in order to curb the common
appetite and to maintain social distinctions several
attempts were made to introduce sumptuary laws
limiting the quality and quantity of foods which
could be served. 'Meatless days' were proclaimed by
law, but such legislation was largely unenforceable
and other measures had to be adopted to preserve
status differences. For example, the hunting of
venison was forbidden to all but the nobility. In
nineteenth century France, social position and food
consumption were intimately connected. A 'gentleman'
was judged not by his wealth but by his knowledge
and appreciation of the arts of the table.

In the modern world food continues to be a
major way in which to assert social status. Prestige
may be attached to foods themselves or to the
circumstances and manner in which they are served.
Nice social distinctions can be subtly underlined
through food behaviour or can be overtly stated by,
for example, social rules which dictate who can eat
with whom. High-caste Hindu Brahmins do not eat with
untouchables; high-status medical consultants do not
share the same dining room with low-status interns,
or with nurses or dietitians. In many parts of the
developing world it is traditional for the person
with the highest prestige to eat first. Some of the
strictest rules governing who may eat with whom are
enshrined in the Hindu caste system. These rules are
linked with concepts of purity and pollution. What
foods may be eaten by each caste and food exchanges
between castes are also subject to control. Such
practices were largely derived from tribal customs
which set peoples apart by the foods they accepted
or rejected as food; inevitably, some food practices
came to be regarded as superior, as did the people
who practised them. Eating habits thus became a mark

of social rank which persists today, intrinsically
bound to the economic and social systems of village
India. (See, Hasan 1971, Dumont 1972, Mayer 1960 and
Marriott 1968 for detailed discussions). Another
example of non-food sharing as a symbol of social
differentiation was seen in America in the 1950s and
1960s resulting in the barring of Blacks from eating
in certain restaurants. The implication was that
only equals eat together, and it is not surprising
that race riots have been triggered by such
insensitive behaviour (Lowenberg et al 1979, p126).

Status and Food Behaviour
Impressing others through the vehicle of food events
is a widespread method of asserting status. Eckstein
(1980) says that status is conferred by:
* freedom to choose rare and costly items to
  impress others
* freedom to select expensive restaurants for
  personal gratification
* freedom to prepare difficult and time-consuming
  dishes

In Western society, freedom of choice is greatly
prized, and to be denied a choice is nearly always
viewed in a negative fashion. If one has a large
array of choices then one has high status. The
ability to choose freely is linked closely to
economic factors; financial position has always been
a measure of status and this is reflected in the
goods and services which are purchased. Thus new
cars, expensive paintings, and exotic holidays have
traditionally been symbols of wealth and status;
they function by emphasising the differences between
those who have and those who have not. Lack of
freedom to choose decreases self-esteem. Whenever
food choice is restricted, most people will feel
cheated and ill-at-ease. In institutions such as
hospitals and schools food complaints are common,
and are at least partly attributable to the lack of
freedom to choose; with therapeutic diets which
severely limit food choice and yet are not
life-threatening, there is a high rate of
non-compliance - perhaps for very similar reasons.
People living in impoverished circumstances, on
social assistance or welfare, sometimes seem to make
irrational choices by buying expensive luxury items,
and are frequently criticised for extravagant
behaviour. However, such behaviours provide an
escape mechanism from the day-to-day reality of
poverty, and have the effect of increasing

self-esteem by creating the illusion of freedom of choice.

Status is also earned by the nature of the foods served. High status is attached to exotic foods, complex dishes and, usually, to expensive items. The source of status-points may be the wealth which the food signifies - in which case the fact that the foods come largely from cans (caviar) or are prepared by someone else (servants) hardly matters; indeed, prestige may be enhanced by this distancing of actual food preparation. On the other hand, status may derive from time and talent brought to bear on creating elaborate dishes. Perhaps here we can distinguish the ´good cook´ from the ´good host´, both of whom attract social kudos and thus acquire high status. As well as reflecting on the host´s own status, the foods served at dinner parties can also be a comment on the status accorded to the guests. Thus for high-status guests more trouble is taken to prepare elaborate fare. The very question of who invites whom to dinner may be fraught with status implications. When the boss invites subordinates to dinner the social messages are quite different than when the subordinate invites the boss. At one time, before the era of raised consciousness toward sexism, it was almost impossible to open a popular magazine without seeing either an article or a cartoon which depicted a nervous and harrassed wife caught in indecision over what to serve to her husband´s boss in order to create just the right impression.

Food and Fashion

Foods may assume a high status within a society simply because they are consumed by high status groups. Historical examples of this are provided by the stories of white bread and white sugar. When white sugar first became available in Elizabethan England it was an expensive commodity which could only be afforded by the rich. It thus became a symbol of affluence and status to which others, lower in the social hierarchy, aspired in an attempt to elevate their own social standing. Once white sugar became widely used throughout all strata of society it lost its status value; now, brown sugar has assumed the mantle of prestige. A similar pattern may be seen with white bread. As milling procedures became perfected, white flour replaced the coarse dark flours which continued to characterise peasant status; everyone wanted white flour, despite its inferior nutritional value and taste. Cussler and Degive (1952) comment that; 'changing the appearance of food usually involves complex techniques proportionate to the degree of civilisation, so that highly milled and refined foods hold an approved position'. Even though it often looks like plaster-board and tastes like sponge, sliced, pre-packaged white bread has become widely desired. With this symbol of status undermined, social leaders are now heading the movement back to wholemeal flours and breads. As a final historical example consider dairy produce, which was known in Medieval and Tudor England as 'white meat' and which was eaten by people of all social classes; but which, with the increasing prosperity of the sixteenth century came to be regarded as inferior food, fit only for the use of the common people (Drummond & Wilbraham 1957). Ultimately it regained its general popularity, and came back into favour; throughout these vicissitudes of fashion the nutritional value of dairy produce remained exactly the same.

A modern example of circular food practices, motivated at least partly by status considerations, is that of breast versus bottle feeding. When artificial milk formulae first became widely available commercially in the 1930s and 1940s they were eagerly seized on as an alternative to the near universal practice of breast-feeding, which as a natural function became degraded and 'low-class'. By the 1970s the social elite were spearheading the return to breast-feeding, claiming untold virtues for a practice which they once affected to despise. Bottle feeding persists among less educated women from lower socio-economic groups, who will no doubt in time also rediscover their biological capabilities. Meanwhile, in many parts of the developing world, an earlier phase of the cycle is still in evidence. Bottle-feeding is perceived as being 'Northern' and 'modern' and therefore greatly to be desired. An extensive literature attests to the unsuitability of bottle feeding in conditions prevalent in rural areas of Africa, Asia and Latin America; yet families will expend large proportions of their total income to buy artificial formula milk. The often tragic consequences of this status-seeking are seen in the awful toll of malnutrition and infant mortality. For a fuller discussion of the 'bottle-babies' syndrome, see: Raphael (1973), Wade (1974), Jelliffe & Jelliffe

(1978). Readers may also wish to consider the
ubiquitous spread of cola drinks in the light of
status-seeking.

Preferences may develop for high status foods
without regard to actual taste or nutritional value.
De Garine (1976) examines food prestige amongst the
Moussey, Massa and Toupouri tribes of central
Africa. He comments that only humans deliberately
eschew the use of nutritionally valuable foods
because they are considered to be of low status, and
eat organoleptically mediocre or nutritionally poor
foods in order to display economic prosperity
(p150). De Garines' fascinating account supports the
view that: 'The more societies are able to free
themselves from subsistence and have at their
disposal surpluses, the more food is used in a
prestigious way.' (Herkovits 1950). In our affluent
societies we fret over what foods are 'in' and
'out'; quiche has been popularised; fondue is passe;
kiwi has replaced grapefruit and brioche are one up
on croissants; Sushi and steak tartare take over
from grilled trout and t-bones. The importance of
prestige food lies in how much social recognition it
confers, and the wrong choice could spell social
disaster!

Status and Food Ownership
The above examples show how food consumption acts as
a mark of status, or as a symbol of the desire to
rise in status. In some parts of the world, food
ownership has similar functions. In large parts of
East, South and Southwest Africa, cattle have an
overriding social and economic importance reflected
in the fact that ownership of cattle is necessary if
a man is to fully participate in social life.
Without cattle he may be barred from certain rites
of passage and be condemned to low social status.
For example, amongst the Massa, bridewealth of ten
cows must be paid to the father-in-law in order to
obtain a wife. Cattle are kept as a symbol of wealth
and status - a sort of bank account. They are also
used to buy other goods and to pay fines. Although
there is no actual prejudice against beef-eating,
the animals are not commonly killed for food.
Simoons (1961) describes the cattle-keeping complex
extant in Sub-Saharan Africa. The Fulani of Nigeria
regard cattle as symbols of wealth; ownership of
many cattle adds to a man's prestige; consequently,
cattle are rarely slaughtered except on special
festive occasions. Elsewhere too, cattle have

represented wealth; the word ´pecuniary´ is derived
from a Latin root meaning ´wealth in cattle´ (Farb &
Armelagos 1980, p61). For the ancient Irish,
Germans, Homeric Greeks and earliest Latins, cattle
were the most important measure of wealth. The
modern-day Western rancher who keeps large herds of
steers is just as clearly demonstrating his wealth
and status, though in this case it is not ownership
per se, but the money represented by the cattle,
which is important.

FOOD, FRIENDSHIP AND COMMUNICATION
As noted above, food is a universal medium for
expressing sociability and hospitality. The
closeness of social relationships between people
might almost be gauged by the types of foods and
meals they share together. For example; a new
neighbour may be invited for tea and biscuits;
casual acquaintances attend a cheese and wine
soiree; business associates are offered a buffet;
close friends are invited to sit down and share a
full meal. Douglas (1972) comments that a cocktail
party which offers food is a bridge between the
intimacy of meals and the distance of drinks. Food
and drink is a part of most social functions, and
even of more formal meetings - albeit only coffee
and biscuits. The act of eating together indicates
some degree of compatability or acceptance; food is
offered as a gesture of friendship - the more
elaborate the fare, the greater the implied intimacy
or degree of esteem. Offering to share food is to
offer to share a bit of oneself; to refuse food when
offered is easily seen as a rejection of friendship.
To accept an invitation to a social function and
then to refuse the food is viewed as being
unacceptable behaviour.
    It is common, especially in European homes, to
always have a food item - usually something rich and
sweet - to offer to casual callers. To not provide
food is to fail socially and thus lose status.
Exceptionally, the Bemba people of Africa show their
respect for a person not by inviting them to a meal,
but instead sending food to be eaten in private.

Peer Acceptance
As indicated by Maslow´s needs hierarchy, the social
need to belong is an important motivator of human
action. Food readily becomes an expression of the
search for belongingess.

As a lad he had grown up in a poor family of
Italian origin. He was raised on blood sausage,
pizza, spaghetti and red wine. After completing
high school, he went to Minnesota and began
working in logging camps where - anxious to be
accepted - he soon learnt to prefer beef,
beans, and beer, and he shunned all Italian
food. Later, he went to a Detroit industrial
plant and eventually became a promising young
executive... In his executive role he found
himself cultivating the favourite foods and
beverages of other young executives; steak,
whiskey and sea-food. Ultimately he gained
acceptance in the city´s upper classes. Now he
began winning admiration from people in his
elite social set by going back to his knowledge
of Italian food and serving them, with the aid
of a manservant, authentic Italian treats such
as blood-sausage, pizza, spaghetti and red
wine.
(Packard 1959)

This quotation from Packard nicely illustrates the
changing patterns of food uses and preferences in
the attempt to ´fit in´ as social circumstances
alter. The wish to eat what everyone else eats may
result in very specific patterns, which sometimes
raise issues of nutritional concern. A paramount
example is that of teenagers and so-called ´junk
foods´. For many teenagers and adolescents it is
very important that whilst they dress and behave in
ways which stress their non-identity with the adult
world, they do at the same time conform carefully to
the expectations of their peer groups. This is
equally true of food behaviour; if everyone else is
drinking cola and eating burgers then it is a
strong-minded teenager who chooses milk and salad.
Food is often associated with meeting places; the
coffee bar, the pub, the fish shop, the fast-food
outlet. In each of these circumstances the
appropriate food or drink is consumed. Schuchat
(1973) aptly comments that eating is a social
experience whilst nutrition is a health phenomenon.
´Junk food´ is eaten in the context of a social
experience which includes music, noise and company;
whilst in the structured meal, where these elements
are missing the teenager feels that the social
experience has been denied. In North America,
nutritionists are often alarmed at a diet which
seems to be based on burgers, pizzas, french fries

and soft drinks. However, these food are often
consumed in addition to regular meals and provide
the extra calories needed by growing adolescents.
Such a diet does in any case provide a reasonable
selection of nutrients - albeit, one heavily laced
with sugars and fats. Only when salad bars become
the ´in-places´ to forgather can we expect to see a
drastic change in adolescent eating habits!

Peer pressure is often associated with children
and adolescents, though, as the first quotation
illustrates, it can operate within the context of
any social grouping. In addition, food choice in
specific instances is governed by social niceties
which may limit individual freedom to choose (though
it is doubtful whether we often think of it in terms
of peer pressure). For example, in a restaurant
setting, once one person has chosen a soup and salad
combination it is highly unlikely that others in the
party will choose full three-course meals (Eckstein
1980). It is unacceptable or, at least, embarrassing
to be still eating long after everyone else has
finished.

Food as Reward and Punishment

The role of socialisation in the acquisition of food
habits has been discussed earlier; at that time we
saw that attitudes to food could also be passed on
in the socialising process. One of the specific ways
in which children learn what is approved of and
acceptable as food is through a system of reward and
punishment. Rewards and punishments may be explicit
or implicit and are often accompanied with other
reinforcing messages. The child who has been ´good´
is rewarded with a chocolate bar; the ill-behaved
child is sent to his room and deprived of supper.
Concepts of good and bad which are quickly attached
to foods through early social experiences with them
may give rise to feeding problems which can and
often do persist into adulthood. Margaret Mead has
summed up these feelings and it is worth quoting her
at some length. In contemporary America, she says:

> Resistances and acceptances of food are thought
> of in terms of morality. People feel that they
> ought to eat correctly, or, more concretely
> -´It´s wrong to eat too much sweet stuff´.
> Foods that are good for you are not good to
> eat, and foods that are good to eat are not
> good for you. So ingrained is this attitude
> that it may come as a surprise to learn that in

many cultures there is no such contrast, that
the foods which are thought to make people
strong and well are   also exclusively the
foods which they like to eat, which they boast
of eating, and without which they would be most
unhappy.
(Mead 1980)

Having made the point that it is indeed possible to
choose ´wrong´ foods, Mead continues:

Each generation of children is taught that bad
food habits are a possibility against which
they must continually be on guard. That is,
traditionally, we have tried to make the
correct consumption of foods an act of
repetitive personal choice, instead of a
semiautomatic behaviour. In many homes the
´right´ food and the ´wrong´ food are both
placed on the table; the child is rewarded for
eating the ´right´ food and so taught that the
right food is undesirable because, from the
child´s point of view, rewards are never given
for doing things which in themselves are
pleasurable or enjoyable. At the same time,
children are punished by having the ´wrong´
food taken away from them. Here again, the
lesson is taught to the child that that which
is delicious is an indulgence for which one is
punished or with which one is rewarded. A
dichotomy is set up in the child´s mind between
those foods which are approved and regarded by
adults as undelicious and those foods which are
disapproved but recognised as delightful. A
permanent conflict situation is established
which will remain with that child throughout
life; each nutritionally desirable choice is
made with a sigh, or rejected with a sense of
guilt; each choice made in terms of sheer
pleasure is either accepted with guilt or
rejected with a sense of puritanical
self-righteousness. Every meal, every food
contact becomes an experience in which one must
decide between doing right and enjoying
oneself.
(op cit p3)

Probably, most parents have experienced the ´table
as battleground´ syndrome at one time or another. It
might be well to remind them that (a) there is no

special merit in consuming a particular vegetable or harm in omitting one which is disliked; (b) children do have genuine dislikes; and (c) that making the availability of one food contingent on the consumption of another is simply asking for trouble. Foods should be served in a positive family environment, and removed, if not eaten, with the least fuss possible. There is little sense in chastising a child for leaving on his or her plate those very same foods refused by Dad. Nutritionally acceptable desserts, incorporating fresh fruit and minimal sugar for example, can help avoid any necessity for the ´no pudding if you don´t eat your dinner´ gambit. As Mead indicates above, by insisting that a child remain at the table until the plate is clean, parents help to inculcate unhealthy attitudes and negative feelings about eating and mealtimes. Before parents protest too much about a conflict of theory and practice, it should be made very clear that eating and manners are quite separate affairs and that acceptable table behaviour, which is often what is desired of children, is not predicated on actual food consumption. Many food wars, I think, are due to confusion of the two.

FOOD GIFTS AND SHARING

Food is commonly viewed as an item to be shared - as a symbol of social relationships quite apart from any monetary value it may represent. Observation of food-sharing behaviour amongst children at a summer camp revealed that items shared tended to be ´extras´ rather than basic foods, and that they were used to establish friendships and cliques (Dyson-Hudson and van Dusen 1972). Food-sharing has been studied as a psychological phenomenon too. Where children are reared in an environment of food abundance and their food needs are readily gratified, then a psychological predisposition to sharing is created (Cohen 1961). The opposite is true in situations where food resources are scarce and where children are reared in an atmosphere of anxiety and deprivation.

Food is a universally acceptable gift by means of which the donor can express a variety of emotions such as concern, sympathy, or gratitude; food is frequently used to say ´you are loved...you are important´. Chocolate and other sweets are commonly used in this latter context. Mom gets a box of

chocolates for her birthday; a sweetheart is
presented with chocolates on Valentine´s day; a
hostess receives chocolates as a thank you token for
hospitality. Sometimes gifts have value in that they
are homemade; a loaf of fresh bread, or a pot of
country jam are personal tokens. At other times it
is the cost or exotic value of foods which carries
the social message; food hampers are popular gifts
at Christmas, and usually contain delicacies and
exotica rather than everyday foods. A gift is
something given freely; a good or service for which
no payment is required. It is true though that
gift-giving is usually based on an unstated, but
nevertheless expected, repricocity. Three types of
repricocity may be identified each of which has
different rules for exchanges.

1. Generalised reciprocity is characterised by
exchanges which involve: (a) no immediate
expectation of return; (b) no attempt to assess the
value of gifts; (c) no attempt to make gift-giving
´balance out´. That is records, mental or otherwise,
are not kept (Harris 1971, p238). Generalised
reciprocity occurs between family members and close
friends in most societies.

2. Balanced reciprocity, which occurs between
people who are social equals and have some kind of
personal relationship, does involve expectation of
return - perhaps delayed - and takes account of the
value of the gift. Thus in some commercial concerns
smoked hams, bottles of whiskey, or wine may be
given to valued customers at Christmas time in the
expectation that the gift will be reciprocated
through continued business orders. Similarly,
salesmen entertain clients to dinner, offering a
meal in exchange for a contract. An invitation to
supper is issued with the general expectation that
the hospitality will be returned at a later date; if
it is not, then social relations may be damaged or
even terminated. A well-understood social code such
as this is open to deliberate manipulation. For
example; a middle-manager invites the director to
supper where he has the chance to impress and
flatter his boss by serving an elaborate meal. Under
the rules of reciprocity, the manager later attends
a supper at the director´s house, thereby increasing
his own status in the eyes of others.

3. Negative reciprocity involves immediate
exchange and strict accounting of value; the
exchange is impersonal (Hardisty 1977, p83).
Commercial transactions typify this kind of

exchange.
Food exchanges can also be ways of expressing
friendship whilst maintaining economic parity;
exchanges diffuse the status meanings of a food
event. Thus, wine may be given in exchange for a
meal, an arrangement which allows guests to
contribute and to establish a feeling of mutual
friendship, whilst relieving some of the economic
burden placed on the hosts. Another view of this
exchange process might see it as lessening
obligations on the part of the meal-recipients.
Having been wined and dined at the expense of
another, a guest may feel to have been placed under
an obligation to the hosts. Offerings of wine, for
example, repay this obligation on the spot. The
potluck dinner is another example of mutual exchange
which allows sociability without status or
obligation considerations intruding; each guest
contributes to the overall ´meal´ and also shares in
the gifts bought by others.
Food exchanges based on some form of
reciprocity principle are common in situations where
environmental resources are limited and where it
would be disastrous to encourage intensive
productive effort. This is the case with forager
cultures, where a low and irregular work effort is
best suited to ecological conditions. Generalised
repricocity helps to maintain this low-level
activity and to prevent excessive exploitation of
the environment in attempts to gain social status.
It ensures that no-one boasts about their generosity
in gift-giving, which would create a social
atmosphere conducive to status competition and which
in turn would stimulate extra work and intensive
resource exploitation. In instances where
reciprocity has not been adopted, the use of food as
a means of establishing social status has in several
societies given rise to the practice of competitive
food giving. Amongst the Massim of New Guinea food
giving is a form of social control. Wrongdoers are
given more food than they are able to return - which
draws attention to the transgression and restores
honour to the victim (Young 1971). Perhaps though,
the ultimate example of ´fighting with food´ is to
be found in the North American Indian ceremony known
as ´potlatch´. Display feasts, such as potlatches,
are elegant examples of food exchanges based on
principles of redistribution rather than
reciprocity, and in which status is a central issue.

Potlatch

Potlatch was the name given to great feast of the
North-West Coast Indians in which the giving away of
material wealth was a central occurrence. The name
´potlatch´ was derived from the Nootka verb
´Pa-chitle´ - to give, and the noun ´Pa-chuck´ -
article to be given, and thus described the specific
type of festival in which public gift-giving
occurred. The potlatch has been regarded by some as
being merely an extravagant and wasteful display of
wealth in which prestige is gained at the cost of
material impoverishment (Hou 1973). In contrast to
this view, Bozak (1973) says that potlatch feasts
symbolised religious, ethical and legal concepts and
were an important functional part of Indian society.
Also, by accepting food and gifts at these feasts,
guests acknowledged the host´s status.

Potlatches commonly celebrated major
life-events such as birth, puberty, marriage and
death; elaborate festivals signified the death of a
great chief. Other potlatches were termed
´face-saving´; by giving a feast, an Indian who had
suffered embarrassment or misfortune or who had
offended against social law, could redeem himself
and maintain his position in society (Rohner &
Rohner 1970). Then there were penalty potlatches,
imposed on those who breached ceremonial taboos; for
example, laughing, stumbling or coughing at winter
dances (Rohner & Rohner op cit). Whatever the
motivation for the potlatch, it was always a public
rather than private affair. The host, with the
support of his family, clan or tribe invited members
of other tribes to witness his actions and claims.
The guests legitimised the use of any songs, dances
or other privileges claimed by the host. Dancing,
feasting, speech-making and gift-giving occupied the
time. During the potlatch, gifts were distributed
according to the rank of the guests. Food, money,
property - all could be and were given. Originally,
gifts were handmade or home produced, but these were
eventually superseded by manufactured wares obtained
through trading with White men. Guests were shamed
by the large amounts of wealth given to them and
immediately started to plan their own potlatches in
which the wealth could be returned - with interest.
Though it might take many years to accumulate
sufficient wealth to be able to give a potlatch,
this wealth was sometimes conspicuously destroyed
simply to add to the grandeur of the occasion;
canoes were burnt, and blankets and precious sheets

of copper destroyed, all in the pursuit of gaining status.

The collection, storage and preparation of food prior to the festival was of great importance; many delicacies would be painstakingly gathered and prepared. In addition to the food needed for gifts, meals had to be served every day of the ceremony, which commonly lasted for one full phase of the moon. Food was served generously and excess was taken home by visitors to eat later or to share with those who did not attend the feast. It was important to ensure that no-one was left out, and it would have been a source of great shame if guests had been able to eat everything provided. The potlatch was a means of sharing: ´your good fortune, wealth, affluence with fellow men...be it your worldy belongings, your food or your goodwill...´ (Clutesi 1969, p21).

The government of the White settlers held a different view. They could not understand the ceremonial functions of potlatching and saw only the poverty and destitution which descended on those who had given away all their possessions. In fact, potlatches were usually reciprocated by the guests, and they acted as a means of redistribution of wealth amongst the tribes - similar to that seen in some African societies (See for example, Gerlach 1964). Different tribes lived in different environments - river, coast, woods; in any given year the food harvest in one area might be prolific whilst in another region food could be scarce. By holding a potlatch, a rich tribe could share its bounty with others not so well off, at the same time accumulating much prestige and status (Suttles 1960). For example; the Kwakiutl West Coast Indians were organised into local kinship groups, known as numaym, which owned fishing locations, hunting territories, houses and goods. They were led by a chief who was custodian of the resources and who performed rituals; each numaym was self-sufficient and not tied to other groups. When the microenvironment changed so that resource availability declined - for example, when ocean currents moved salmon runs to other coastal areas, self-sufficiency was endangered and warfare sometimes resulted. More often though, surplus food from other numaym could be obtained in exchange for material wealth - blankets, canoes, etc. Competitive feasting, by stimulating resource production, was a way of ensuring that one group would have a food surplus so that this exchange could take place. If a famine was prolonged and a numaym exhausted its material wealth, it could still obtain food - in exchange for social status (Hardisty 1977, p85).

Farb & Armelagos (1980) see the potlatch as an adaptive behaviour which provided the setting and reason for exchange of resources, as well as encouraging high food productivity in readiness for the next feast (p150). Rivalry and prestige were not the moving principles, but rather excuses for keeping the potlatch going. However, in 1884, a law was enacted which forbade direct or indirect involvement with potlatching on pain of imprisonment (La Violette 1973). It proved impossible to consistently enforce this law, and in time the positive values of the potlatch became to be more appreciated. It was recognised as being an important event for expressing respect and honour, for entertainment and for sharing resources. In 1951 the potlatch law was abolished, but by this time there had been considerable changes in Indian culture and the potlatch never regained its former prominence and glory.

Because the Indian potlatch is carried out within the context of an unfamiliar culture and is strikingly overt in its competitive aims it may be classified as an ´irrational´ and ´alien´ practice. However, de Garine (1970) comments that most meals on social occasions are held in a spirit of competition, with each group attempting to outdo the others, though in post-industrial societies quality is usually more important than quantity; European wedding feasts are cited as an example. Conspicuous consumption and prestige economies are still very important in many developing countries, as illustrated in examples already cited in earlier sections of this chapter. Harris (1974) adds that among peoples who do not have a defined ruling class, competitive feasting is a near universal mechanism for assuring production and distribution of wealth within the society (p 116).

FEASTS AND FESTIVALS

Of course, feasting is not always overtly competitive in its intent. The word ´feast´ denotes a special occasion, commonly public, on which food is consumed of a different quality and quantity to that of everyday meals. Feasts are held for many and varied reasons:

* Celebrate a particular religious event
* Celebrate a harvest
* Offer appeasement to a God at the winter
  solstice when in early times people feared that
  the sun would desert them
* Bless the sowing and celebrate the coming of
  Spring
* Honor the dead and pay homage to ancestors.
  (Lowenberg et al, 1979, p134)

They are also used to mark national events such as
Independence, and personal celebrations such as
birthdays and anniversaries. The Wedding Feast of
Henry IV and Joan of Navarre, in 1403, provides an
example of conspicuous consumption on a grand scale
(Table 3.1), and Cosman (1981) gives a colourful
account of a typical medieval banquet, describing
not only the foods, but also common entertainments
and general etiquette.

In general, the foods used for feasting are:
(a) scarce, (b) high quality, (c) often expensive,
(d) difficult and time-consuming to prepare; i.e.
they have high status. (Lowenberg et al 1979, p136).
Sometimes, as with potlatches, public feasts may be
a way of spreading food to all sections of the
population - for everyone joins in. They may also
lead to overeating or even to exhaustion of food
supplies, which results in a glut and famine pattern
of eating.

Festivals are complex and colourful events,
being forms of ritual found in practically every
society in one guise or another. They are public
events which may be of a religious or secular
nature, and which usually include feasting as part
of more general celebrations. Often they occur at
vital points in the human and cosmic lifecycle and
themselves incorporate a cycle of events which
represent or reflect the society's philosophy of
history (Abingdon 1981); thus themes of birth and
death, decay and renewal, sowing and reaping, summer
and winter, are common. Four major types of festival
can be distinguished. Ecofests celebrate
astronomical or seasonal events and are frequently
associated with preliterate or pagan rituals which
were designed to ensure control of the food supply.
Theofests celebrate religious events and are often
wedded to ecofest predecessors; for example,
Christmas celebrates the birth of Christ and also
the winter solstice.

TABLE 3.1   WEDDING FEAST OF HENRY IV

First Course

Braun en peuerade	slices of meat cooked in spiced sweet sauce
Viaund Ryal	puree of rice and mulberries sweetened with honey, flavoured with wine and spices
Test de senglere enarmez	boar's head and tusks
Graunde chare	large piece of roasted meat
Syngettys	cygnets
Capoun de haute grece	capon a la foie gras geese
Fesaunte	pheasants
Heroun	heron
Crustarde Lumbarde	pie of cream, eggs, dates, prunes and sugar
Storieoun graunt luces	sturgeon and great pike
Subtlety	

Second Course

Venyson en furmenty	venison served with a spiced grues of cream, wheat and eggs
Gely	calves foot jelly with white wine and vinegar
Porcelle farce enforce	stuffed suckling pigs
Pokokkys	peacocks served in their plumage
Cranys	cranes
Venyson roste	roast venison
Conyng	rabbits over a year old
Byttore	bitterns
Pulle endore	glazed chicken
Graunt tartez	great pies of meat, game and poultry
Braun fryez	fritters of meat
Leche Lumbard	spiced date cakes
Subtlety	

93

TABLE 3.1 ctd   WEDDING FEAST OF HENRY IV

Third Course

Blaundesorye	almond and chicken mousse
Quyneys in comfyte	quinces preserved in syrup
Egretes	a kind of heron
Curlewys	curlews
Pertrych	partridges
Pyionys	pigeons
Quaylys	quails
Snytys	snipe
Rabettys	young rabbits
Smal Byrdys	small birds
Pome Dorreng	rissoles of pork roasted on a spit, basted with spices and herbs
Braun blanke leche	meat in white sauce
Eyroun engele	eggs in jelly
Frytourys	fritters
Doucettys	custard tarts
Pety perneux	small spiced tarts of eggs, cream and raisins
Subtlety	

Source: Warner, R. (1791) Antiquitates Culinariae . Cited in Drummond & Wilbraham, The Englishman's Food J. Cape, London 1957 (revised ed.)

Many festivals had an agrarian origin, but as they became associated with particular events or deities they ceased to be seasonal as such. As well, new festivals were instituted which had none of the agrarian rationale of earlier celebrations; instead, they celebrated national, local and political occasions. These may be labelled, as a third group, secular festivals. A fourth category of festival embraces personal rituals; into this grouping can be placed birthdays and anniversaries, together with rites of passage such as weddings and funerals.

Brief accounts of some different types of festivals are given below, together with a table of festivals around the world. For a delightful account of medieval celebrations the reader is referred to Cosman (1981). Thelma Barer-Stein gives extensive details of festivals and traditional foods in her 1979 book, ´You Eat What You Are´, which is also recommended reading on this topic.

May Day, celebrated in many parts of the world, is a good example of an ecofest. It originally represented pagan attempts to force Spring to return to the world, and was focused on themes of freshness and renewal. Cosman describes the medieval uses of green foods at this time; green parsley bread slices, green salads, green fruit and green apple cider: green peppermint rice and minted green whipped cream - all representative of the victory of Spring after the barren Winter months. Halloween marks the end of the ancient Celtic year - the division between the end of summer and the beginning of winter. It also precedes the church holiday of All Saint´s Day and the following All Soul´s Day. On this latter day, prayers were offered up for the souls waiting in Purgatory, a practice introduced by Odilo, Abbot of Cluny in 998 A.D., but abolished in England during the Reformation, though it survived amongst Continental Protestants. It is essentially an adaptation of an almost world-wide custom of setting aside part of the year for the dead. Historically, children would beg for ´soul cakes´ - shortbread biscuits with currants, cinnamon and nutmeg - for the wandering spirits. If no cakes were offered then the souls would play pranks. This custom is of course continued in the ´trick or treat´ visits of North American children to neighbour´s houses on Halloween. The householder gives sweets, candies or other food treats to placate these modern day spirits - or else risks becoming the victim of (usually) harmless pranks.

Table 3.2   Festivals around the world

DATE		NAME	COUNTRY	TYPE *
Jan.	6	Epiphany	Various	T
	25	Robbie Burns Night	Scotland	N
Feb.	14	St. Valentine´s Day	Various	TP
Mar.		Easter	Various	ET
	19	Feast of St. Joseph	Italy	T
	21	New Year	Persia	E
Apr.	1	All fools´ day	Various	T
May	1	May Day	Various	ET
	5	Children´s day	Japan	P
	14	Independence Day	Israel	N
Jun.	24	Midsummer Day	Various	E
	24	St. John´s da	Brazil	ET
Jul.	25	Feast of St James	Spain	N
Aug.	15	Assumption of Mary	Various	T
Sep.	29	Michaelmas	Various	T
Oct.		October fest	Germany	N
	14	Thanksgiving	Canada	ET
	31	Halloween	N.America	E
Nov.	1	All Saints Day	Various	T
	2	All Souls Day	Various	ET
	5	Guy Fawkes Night	Britain	N
	20	Anniversary of the Revolution	Mexico	N
Dec.	5	Sinterklaas	Holland	P
	13	St. Lucia Day	Sweden	T
	25	Christmas	Various	ET
	31	Hogmannay	Scotland	N

* E = Ecofest, T = Theofest, ET = eco+theo fest,
  N = National, P = Personal
NB. This classification is not rigid. Many festivals
have multiple origins.

Christmas is celebrated in varying ways and on varying days in many places throughout the world. Although it is predominantly a religious festival it is blended with older pagan and agrarian customs. (In a similar way, many churches were built on the sites of earlier pagan worshippers.) Indeed, the extent to which religions can adopt and adapt existing practices may account largely for their survival and spread. For example, when Sweden became a Christian country in 1537, the Church immediately assimilated certain pagan traditions. Lussi, the Queen of Light, was linked to the Italian St. Lucia - and celebration of St Lucia´s Day now marks the beginning of Christmas festivities in Sweden. The pagan custom of feeding birds and animals to ensure fertility in the coming year is continued, for example, in Baltic and Slavic countries where, on Christmas Eve, bread and barley is fed to farm animals before the family eats its own evening meal. Christmas is an example of a festival which has spread around the world even though it has not always retained its original meaning. The Bushmen of Africa hold a special feast and dance for Christmas; their knowledge of Christmas originated from the London Missionary Society´s work in Africa and, according to Lee (1969) they view it as being a celebration to ´praise the birth of white man´s god-chief´. At this time a great ox is slaughtered by the Tswana headman and distributed amongst the Bushmen. Lee describes the difficulties he encountered when, having lived with the Bushmen for some time, he tried to donate the festive ox (Lee 1969). In other parts of the world, the religious meaning of Christmas is being deliberately eroded. In Russia, Christmas is symbolised by the confrontation between Grandfather Frost and the villainous Baba Yaga; nationalist plays, songs and dances are performed in which Grandfather Frost, aided by the Young Pioneers, defeats his evil adversary (Barer-Stein, p475).

Easter is widely celebrated as a religious festival, often spreading over several weeks, though Easter Sunday and the week preceding have become the focus of modern Easter celebrations. It was named for the pagan Godess, Eostre, the Goddess of dawn and Spring, and occurred at the time of the Spring Equinox in March. The cycle of celebration heralded the triumph of light over dark: of summer over winter. Echoes of the pagan ecofest are seen in the traditional Hot Cross Buns served at Easter. The

cross represents the four seasons, whilst the round
bun itself is the sun.

Religious festivals abound in the Hindu
calendar. In Southern India certain foods are
offered to specific deities and are specific to
particular festivals. Pure deities may only accept
vegetarian food. In the eighteen major Hindu
festivals, special foods are featured; rice and
bananas symbolise fertility; ghee (clarified butter)
symbolises purity, and coconut and mango symbolise
sacredness and auspiciousness (Katona-Apte 1976).
Other examples of religious festivals are given in
Chapter Four.

National holidays mark events in the history of
a people or in the lives of notable figures. The
well-known German Oktoberfest originated as a
holiday to celebrate the wedding of Crown Prince
Ludwig in 1810. Scots the world over pay homage to
the poet Robbie Burns on the anniversary of his
birth, January 25th, with a feast featuring the
ethnic delicacy known as haggis. Many countries
include feasting in their Independence Day
celebrations.

Personal celebrations usually revolve around
major life events. The Greek writer, Herodotus, says
the custom of birthdays was well-established amongst
ancient Persians of rank. Modern birthday parties
call forth special birthday foods, often in the form
of sweet treats, jellies and cakes. In Japan,
birthday celebrations include the serving of
lobster; the hump of the lobster represents the bent
back of old age and by partaking of it the celebrant
is desired of living to an old age. In Korea, a
child´s first birthday is an occasion for special
celebration. The infant is dressed in bright clothes
and given rice cakes, fruit and cookies; he or she
is placed in the midst of symbols which represent
possible future careers and onlookers try to guess
which one the child will grasp first (Barer-Stein,
p357). Wedding feasts, although perhaps not always
as elaborate as the royal meal described above, are
prepared with particular care. Wedding cake is
traditionally shared out amongst guests so that
blessings and happiness can be shared. Sometimes,
the top tier of the wedding cake is kept to be used
at the christening of the first child. On the day
before a Lebanese wedding, guests are served sweet
pastries, nuts and candy-coated almonds as a symbol
of a sweet and prosperous life.

Feasts are commonly held to honour the dead.

Homer's Iliad describes how King Priam ends the
funeral for his slain son, Hector, with a banquet -
an early example of a wake. In many Western
countries, it is traditional after a burial service
to invite guests back to a funeral meal prepared by
relatives and friends of the deceased. In Italy, All
Soul's Day is celebrated with feasting in
rememberance of loved ones.

These example illustrate the variety and
extensiveness of festivals in marking the events
held to be important in a society. In the next
section, we examine a different type of ritual event
- the sacrifice.

RITUALS AND SACRIFICE

When we speak of something having been ritualised we
envisage a repetitive act carried out in a codified
manner. Thus we can point to the morning ritual of
shower, newspaper and breakfast; or to the cinematic
ritual of popcorn, icecream and soft-drinks. Farb
and Armelagos (1980) amusingly describe the ritual
of the modern fast-food outlet, predominant in North
America, but spreading quickly in other parts of the
world. In this ritual, the same words are exchanged
and the same actions performed a thousand times a
day with little if any variation.

More often, we think of rituals as connoting
religious or supernatural activities. They permit
the expression of sentiments which can not always be
put into words and can thus act as a unifying social
force. Many rituals, both pagan and religious,
involve food in some way. Indeed, the need for
particular foods for use in rituals may have
contributed to their spread throughout different
parts of the world. Thus Hindus needed tumeric,
Christians needed wine and Jews needed citron; when
these peoples migrated they took their ritual foods
with them (Farb & Armelagos 1980, p132; Isaac 1959).
Rituals often involved some kind of offering. Food
offerings, which in modern civilisations may be of a
plant nature, were previously almost always animal
in nature. For example, the Brahman sacrifices of
rice cakes were actually substitutes for human
beings. Abraham's substitution of a ram for his son
Isaac (Genesis 22:1), indicates that Hebrews were
aware of the custom of human sacrifice and of its
substitution by animal. 'Human sacrifice was a
religious practice rife among the Semitic peoples as
well as their Egyptian and Aryan neighbours.' (Hertz

1965). Animal sacrifice was a well-established mode of religious worship, though as life became more urbanised even this was discontinued by the Israelites, and instead they were able to purchase redemption with silver (Leviticus 27: 1-8; Tannahill 1976, p26). Eventually it was declared that fasting and prayer would be sufficient; loss of bulk through fasting could be seen as being equivalent to sacrificial offerings in that it represented a ´giving up´, whilst ´He who prays is considered as pious as if he had built an altar and offered sacrifices upon it.´ (Harris 1923). This evolutionary pattern of sacrificial offering: human - animal/plant - money - prayer: is repeated in the history of many societies. Candles, incense and money offerings in modern churches echo primitive offerings of flesh and blood (Tannahill 1976, p19).

An offering is a species of gift and as such it must have certain characteristics. It should be personal, that is something owned rather than a gift of nature; it should have value for the giver and it should be given voluntarily. Sacrifice implies an asymetrical status relationship. Whilst a gift puts the recipient in an inferior social position, an offering emphasises that it is the giver who is of inferior status (Firth 1965). Sacrifices may be offered for a number of different reasons of which the following are perhaps the most common.

1. As food for the Gods. (Man was created to serve the Gods.)
2. To propitiate an affronted deity. ·
3 To effect communication with a deity by eating of victim. (Omophagy.)
4. For maintenance or renewal of life.
5. For divination purposes.
6. To confirm a covenant.
7. To ward off evil.
8. In exchange for favours.

1. The custom of offering something to a deity is ancient and widespread; it is an instinctive part of human nature. Food, as a gift of the Gods, is sacred, and most cultures have particular rituals or procedures to desanctify the first crop in order to make it suitable for ordinary man. Offering food shows devotion to a supernatural force, and in all rural societies, offering of first fruits is practised (de Garine 1970). Tannahill suggests that this is an evolved version of the offering of the

first-born which is commonly mentioned in ancient
literature. She refers to the Rig Veda creation myth
in which the Universe was created from the body, not
of a God, but of a man. Re-enactment of this myth
thus required sacrifice of the first-born (Tannahill
1976, p22).
    2. ´Shall I give my first-born for my
transgression´ (Micah 6:7). Sir Edward Tylor
regarded sacrifice as being essentially a gift to
the supernatural being to minimise its hostility
(Tylor 1871). Homeric Greeks occasionally killed
prisoners to placate an angry God, and Romans made
sacrifices of Greeks and Christians. More often,
animal sacrifices were used, until with time such
gifts developed into homage then abnegation, as
described above.
    3. The anthropologist W. Robertson-Smith viewed
sacrifice as a communion between members of a group,
and between them and their God. Sacrifice acted as a
buffer between the sacred deity and the profane
human thus avoiding any dangerous direct contact.
Cannibalistic elements arose because by eating a
portion of the sacrifice man identified himself with
what was being offered to the Gods. Sometimes the
sacrifice symbolised the God himself so the eaters
could in this way absorb the Divine. When the urban
Aztecs of Tenochtitlan dedicated their great temple
in 1487 A.D. they sacrificed - according to
different sources - between ten and eighty thousand
people. Ritual killings proceeded without pause from
sunup to sundown for four days. Priests prayed that
the victims would ´savour the fragrance, the
sweetness of death by the obsidian blade´ (McDowell
1980). Afterwards, the priests each cooked a bowl of
stewed maize in which was a piece of the flesh of
the captive; this feast was a sacrament - a means of
participating in the divine grace of the victim.
    4. Frazer saw these rituals as a kind of magic
in which the sacrifice was a way of rejuvenating a
God. Kill the God to save him from decay and to aid
his rebirth; kill a victim to feed and strengthen
the God; kill the rivals of the God to facilitate
his resurrection (Frazer 1963). The Creation myth
and Resurrection myth were dominant in primitive
religions and these original dramas had to be
re-enacted each year by the Gods with the help of
man. To aid the return of the fertility deity to the
soil the farmer contributed strength and power in
the form of human sacrifice (Tannahill 1976, p20).
Such sacrifices persist; the Aymaras of Bolivia

ritually kill llamas and sprinkle their blood on
newly planted potatoes (Heisler 1981, p23).
    5. Animals have often been used for divination
arts. The entrails of a sacrifice would be examined
and from this great prophecies made. Andean Indians
sacrificed llamas and examined their lungs and
entrails for omens. Shakespeare gave an example of
this type of functional sacrifice in Julius Caesar;
in reply to Caesar´s demand to know what the
augurers have said, his servant pronounces:

> They would not have you stir forth today.
> Plucking the entrails of an offering forth
> They could not find a heart within the beast.
> (Julius Caesar, Act II scene ii)

    6. Cattle and sheep were sacrificed at the
Temple of Solomon as an act of repentance and in
fulfillment of vows.
    7. A well-known Biblical example of sacrifice
designed to ward off ill is the Iraelite sacrifice
of the Paschal Lamb, whose blood was smeared on
doors so that the Israelites would be spared when
the Egyptians were smitten by the death of their
firstborn.
    8. Normally when sacrifices are made no
material counter-gifts are expected. However,
subsequent fertility of crops or personal health may
be ascribed to such sacrifice. Bantu offer
domesticated animals (not wild ones, for they are a
free gift of nature and have lower status) in return
for demands for the spirit´s blessing. The Nuer of
S.Sudan make offerings which then ´obligate´ the
Gods to return the favour. Many primitive tribes
make blood sacrifices, including human sacrifices,
to ensure a good crop. Examples are found in various
Indian cultures; eg. the Aztec custom of offering
hearts of human victims. The modern Harvest Festival
custom of placing an old grain amongst the new,
parallels the blood and ashes added to corn by
primitive peoples (Firth 1965).
    There is little waste in sacrifice. Once the
Gods have eaten their fill the food becomes a feast
for humans (Farb & Armalagos 1980, p128). Priests,
responsible for officiating at sacrifices, often
lived off what was offered to the Gods. Frequency
and quality of sacrifice are affected by economics
in that there is a relation between what is offered
and resource availability. If animals are scarce
then excuses can be found for not having a

sacrifice. In the case of the Nuer of Sudan, if
prize cattle cannot be spared then older infirm
cattle, sheep, goats or even cucumbers are
substituted. When cattle sacrifices are made, then
meat is shared in the village. Economic calculations
have been ever present in human affairs, and when
the offerer can substitute something less valuable
for the sacrifice, he does so, using a variety of
rationales for his action.

The traditional view that sacrifice should
entail a material loss has been replaced in modern
societies by the idea of a ´moral´ sacrifice.
Abstract piety has replaced concrete food offerings
(Farb & Armelagos 1980, p130). Firth (1965) sums up
by saying that the value of the thing offered is
attributed to it only conventionally by virtue of
its being selected for offering. A more jaundiced
view is offered by Marvin Harris who interprets the
end of animal sacrifice as signifying the end of
ecclesiastical redistributive feasting, and the move
to Heavenly worship as being a means of slipping out
of responsibilities to provide for people on earth.
Thus the open-handed generosity of barbaric chiefs
who held great feasts and fed their followers was
eschewed by Christianity, Buddhism, and Islam whose
leaders were transformed from great providers to
great believers - and who served nothing to eat in
their temples (Harris 1977, p119).

Sacraments

Many cultures, particularly ancient ones, have had
their sacred foods. Frazer points out that a sacred
animal is often an embodiment of the God himself.
Attis of Phrygia was, according to legend, killed by
a wild boar. The pig was identified with Attis and
was thereafter not eaten by his followers. However,
ritual sacrifices could be made of the pig so that
the believers could consume their God sacramentally.
The sacramental killing and eating of an animal
implies that the animal is sacred and is as a rule
spared. The Greek writer Herodotus said that the
ancient Egyptians looked upon the pig with loathing.
No one would touch a pig, drink of its milk or have
social intercourse with swineherds and their
families. However, once a year, pigs were sacrificed
to the moon and Osiris, and the flesh was eaten.
Frazer supposes that this was a sacramental meal and
that the pig was a sacred animal (Frazer 1963, Para
373). He supports this by alluding to the fact that
in many belief systems it is not permitted to touch

103

sacred objects in the normal course of everyday
life. The pig was regarded with both reverence and
abhorrence. Eventually, the feelings of revulsion
took the upper hand and the pig became a despised
animal. (Other foods, initially regarded
ambivalently, are elevated to God-like status).
     There are parallels, noted by early
anthropologists, between the Christian Eucharist and
primitive sacrifices. At the Last Supper Jesus had
said 'Take; this is my body' and 'This is my blood
of the covenant..' (Mark 14:22-24). In the original
Eucharist, or Thanksgiving, the community gave
thanks as they ate bread from the same loaf and
drank wine from the same cup, thus commemorating the
death of Jesus. St Paul, anxious for potential
converts amongst Jews, Romans, Greeks and Pagans,
presented the Last Supper as a sacrifice in which
Jesus was the Paschal lamb who was offered up.
Because of the calendrical proximity of the two
events Paul was easily able to transfer the
symbolism of Passover to the Crucifixion. St Paul
seems to have been responsible for instituting the
custom of re-enactment of the sacrifice by
emphasising the words 'do this in remembrance of me'
as Jesus' instructions at the Last Supper. Only the
gospel of Luke includes these words...and they were
written at a time after Paul's correspondence with
the Greeks in which he had urged the ritual
re-enactment. Also, Luke was a close friend of Paul
(Tannahill 1976, p58). Out of these 'adjustments'
was born the ritual of the Mass. From an early time
some men, like St John Chrystostom, Archbishop of
Constantinople, believed in transubstantiation,
whilst most continued to view the mass as a symbolic
act. A conflict, or at least an inconsistency, arose
which threatened to weaken the concept of Papal
supremacy. The medieval Church wanted to wield
temporal as well as spiritual power and there was no
room in it for dissent; all had to submit absolutely
to the will of God. Hence Pope Innocent III
determined to resolve the dispute. In 1215 A.D.
Innocent held the assembly of the Fourth Lateran
Council where the Catholic church decreed that when
a priest pronounced 'This is my body' at Mass, then
the bread and wine were truly changed to the body
and blood of Christ. The Host was no longer a symbol
but an actuality, and to deny this was heresy. The
Communion was thus transformed from being a symbolic
act to an equivalent of the pagan rituals of
omophagy - or eating of the God. In this way,

Christianity adopted an act of pure cannibalism
(Tannahill 1976, p60). The Communion loaf was later
replaced by unleavened wafers when it was realised
that, as a Jew, Jesus would not have eaten leavened
bread during Passover. Tannahill gives an account of
how the red bacillus which sometimes grew on stale
food was misinterpreted as being bleeding of the
Host. Because the Host was so closely identified by
Christians as the body of Christ, ("Host" is derived
from Latin "Hostia", meaning sacrificial victim.)
the conclusion was reached that it was being
tortured by Jews who had, after all, crucified Jesus
through their hate of him. This resulted in massive
persecutions of Jews in the thirteenth and
fourteenth centuries.

SUMMARY

Truly, food usages are signposts to understanding
different cultures. Patterns of food preparation,
distribution and consumption reflect the dominant
type of social relationships in a society. They are
an expression of status and social distance, of
political power and of family bonds. Food is
extensively used in social intercourse as a means of
expressing friendship and respect. The quality and
quantity of food offered or shared reflects a common
understanding of the closeness of various types of
social relationships. Food is also used as a
manipulative tool to purchase favours or to bring
about desired behaviours, and as a weapon with which
to humiliate rivals. It confers status through
ownership or usage, and is commonly a part of ritual
proceedings. Food is an indispensable element in
festivals and celebrations where it may be again
symbolic of social relationships or where it may
assume supernatural powers. The discussion of the
role of food in sacrificial and sacramental rituals
leads naturally to the main subject of the next
chapter - that of religion.

REFERENCES

Barer-Stein, T. You Eat What You Are. McClelland
     & Stewart, Toronto 1979
Bozak, G. ´Potlatch: Revival of a Lost Culture.´
     Performing Arts in Canada , 10:14-16, 1973
Clutesi, G. Potlatch. Morris Printing Co.,
     Victoria 1969

Cohen, Y.A. ´Food and its Vicissitudes: A
    Cross-cultural Study of Sharing and
    Non-sharing.´ In Y.A. Cohen (ed.), Social
    Structure and Personality. Holt, Rinehart &
    Winston, New York 1961
Cohen, Y.A. ´Food Consumption Patterns.´ In D.L.
    Sills (ed.), International Encyclopedia of the
    Social Sciences. Vol. 5. pp508-13. MacMillan
    Co. & The Free Press, 1968
Cosman, M.P. Medieval Holidays and Festivals.
    Scribner, 1977
Crin K.R., R.A. Bullard and L.D. Shinn (eds.),
    Abingdon Dictionary of Living Religions
    Abingdon, Nashville 1981
Cussler, M. and M.L. DeGive. ´Twixt the Cup and the
    Lip: Psychological and Socio-cultural Factors
    Affecting Food Habits. Twayne Publ., New York
    1952
de Garine, I.L. ´The Social and Cultural Background
    of Food Habits in Developing Countries
    (Traditional Societies).´ In G. Blix (ed.),
    Food Cultism and Nutritional Quackery
    Symposium of the Swedish Nutr. Found., Almqvist
    & Wiksells, Uppsala 1970
de Garine, I.L. ´Food, Tradition & Prestige.´ In
    D.N. Walcher, N. Kretchmer and H.L. Barnett.
    (eds.), Food, Man and Society. Plenum Pr.,
    New York 1976
de La Reyniere, G. Almanach des Gourmands. P.
    Waeffe 1968
Douglas, M. ´Deciphering a meal.´ Daedelus ,
    101:61-81, 1972
Drummond, J.C. and A. Wilbraham. The Englishman´s
    Food. Rev. Ed., J. Cape, London 1957
Dumont, L. Homo Hierarchus: The Caste System and
    its Implications. Paladin, London 1972
Dyson-Hudson, R. and R. Van Dusen. ´Food Sharing
    Among Young Children.´ Ecol. Food & Nutr. ,
    1:319-24, 1972
Eckstein, E.F. Food, People and Nutrition AVI
    Publ.Co.Inc., Westport 1980.
Farb, P. and G. Armelagos. Consuming Passions: the
    Anthropology of Eating. Houghton Mifflin Co.,
    Boston 1980
Firth, R. ´Offering and Sacrifice: Problems of
    Organisation.´ In W.A. Lessa and E.Z. Vogt.
    (eds.), Reader in Comparative Religion: an
    Anthropological Approach. Harper & Row, New
    York 1965

Frazer, J.G. The Golden Bough. Abridged. Macmillan
    Publ. Co., New York 1963
Gerlach, L.P. 'Socio-cultural Factors Affecting the
    Diet of the Northeast Coastal Bantu.' J. Am.
    Diet. Ass. , 45:420-24, 1964
Hardisty, D.L. Ecological Anthropology. J. Wiley &
    Son, New York 1977
Harris, M. Cows, Pigs, Wars and Witches. Random
    House, New York 1974
Harris, M. Cannibals and Kings. Random House, New
    York 1977
Harris, M.H. A Thousand Years of Jewish History.
    Bloch, New York 1923
Hasan, K.A. 'The Hindu Dietary Practices and
    Culinary Rituals in a North Indian Village.'
    Ethnomedizin. 1:43-70, 1971
Heisler, C.B.Jr. Seed to Civilisation. 2nd ed.
    W.H.Freeman & Co., San Francisco 1981
Hercovits, M.J. Man and his Works Knopf, New York
    1950
Hou, C. To Potlatch or not to Potlatch. B.C.
    Teachers' Federation 1973
Isaac, E. 'Influence of Religion on the Spread of
    Citrus.' Science 129:179-186, 1959.
Jelliffe, D.B. and E.F.P. Jelliffe. Human Milk in
    the Modern World. Oxford University Pr.,
    Oxford 1978
Katon-Apte, J. 'Dietary Aspects of Acculturation:
    Meals, Feasts and Fasts in a Minority Community
    in South Asia.' In M. Arnott (ed.),
    Gastronomy: The Anthropology of Foods and Food
    Habits. Mouton Publ., The Hague 1976
LaViolette, F.E. The Struggle for Survival.
    University of Toronto Pr., Toronto 1973
Lee, R.B. 'Eating Christmas in the Kalahari.'
    Natural History , 78 (10), 1969
Lowenberg, M.E., E.N. Todhunter, E.D. Wilson, J.R.
    Savage and J.L. Lubawski. Food and People. J
    .Wiley & Sons, New York 1979
Marriott, M. 'Caste Ranking and Food Transactions: a
    Matrix Analysis.' In M. Singer and B.S.Cohn
    (eds.), Structure and Change in Indian
    Society. Aldine Publ., Chicago 1968
Mayer, A.D. Caste and Kinship in Central India: A
    Village and its Region. University of
    Calif.Pr., Berkeley 1960
McDowell, B. 'The Aztecs.' Nat. Geog. , 158 (6),
    1980

107

Mead, M. ´A Perspective on Food Patterns´ in L.A.
    Tobias and P.J. Thompson. (eds.), Issues in
    Nutrition for the 1980s. Wadsworth Inc.,
    Monterey 1980
Packard, V. The Status Seekers. McKay, New York
    1959
Raphael, D. ´The Role of Breast Feeding in a Bottle
    Oriented World.´ Ecol. Food & Nutr. ,
    2:121-126, 1973
Robertson-Smith, W. Lectures on the Religion of the
    Semites. 3rd Ed. Macmillan, New York 1927
Rohner, R.P. and E.C. Rohner. The Kwakiutl Indians
    of British Columbia. Holt, Rinehart & Winston
    1970
Schuchat, M.G. ´The School Lunch and its Cultural
    Environment.´ J. Nutr. Ed. , 5:116-118, 1973
Simoons, F.J. Eat Not This Flesh. University of
    Wisconsin Pr., Madison 1961
Suttles, W. ´Affinal Ties, Subsistence and Prestige
    Among the Coast Salish.´ Am. Anthrop. ,
    62:296-305 1960
Tannahill, R. Food in History. Stein & Day, New
    York 1973
Tannahill, R. Flesh and Blood. Sphere Books,
    London 1976
Tylor, E.B. Primitive Culture: Researches into the
    Development of Mythology, Religion, Language,
    Art and Custom. J. Murray, London 1871
Wade, N. ´Bottle Feeding: Adverse Effects of a
    Western technology.´ Science 184:45, 1974
Young, M.W. Fighting with Food: Leadership, Values
    and Social Control in a Massim Society.
    Cambridge University Pr., Cambridge 1971

Chapter 4

RELIGION, CULTISM AND MORALS

Religion is fundamentally a belief system which
includes the myths that explain the social and
religious order and the rituals through which the
members of the religious community carry out their
beliefs and act out the myths to explain the unknown
(Freidl & Pfeiffer 1977). Its purpose is to express
beliefs about the universe and to fulfil a basic
need by helping people to cope with the unknown and
uncontrollable. World religions may be divided
broadly into two types; prophetic and mystical.
Prophetic religions are derived from ancient Jewish
lore and include also Christianity and Islam. The
mystical religions originate in Indian philosophies;
they are sometimes classed as 'Eastern'. Under this
division Islam is properly classed as a 'Western'
religion. Each religion has its own rituals and
ceremonies; its own special beliefs; its own
interpretation of morality. The practices of
religious adherents are an attempt by them to relate
to the 'supreme being' they worship... to explain
those things which they themselves cannot fully
understand or control (Brown 1963), and adherence to
religious laws is important in reaffirming the
beliefs of that religion.
     Many of the factors which shape food habits are
derived from religious laws. These may be actual
restrictions or prohibitions embedded in religious
doctrine or they may simply be strongly held beliefs
common to the members of a particular religious sect
and without any real doctrinal origin. A religious
group may use food laws as a way of drawing
attention to the fact that they are indeed different
from other groups; prohibitions may be arbitrarily
created - or unnecessarily maintained for this very
purpose. When a food law is enshrined in religious
dogma it is given additional force. Obeying the law

is a way of displaying devoutness and of expressing
belief and respect for the religion´s supreme being,
and as such, gives the practitioner a sense of
security and community with co-religionists. The
orthodoxy of religious practitioners determines how
closely they adhere to food restrictions. In many
cases food restrictions are relaxed or even ignored,
this being most likely to happen during a period of
acculturation, and involving especially the young.
At the same time it is true that new converts to a
religion are often the most zealous practitioners of
its various rules and regulations.

Some dietary restrictions can claim direct
origins in Holy books. ´I will set My face against
the soul that eateth blood´. ´For the life of the
flesh is in the blood´ (Leviticus 17:10). ´Thou
shalt not seethe a kid in his mother´s milk´ (Exodus
23:19). ´Ye shall not eat the swine because it parts
the hoof but does not chew the cud´ (Leviticus
11:4). On the other hand, without necessarily
claiming any religious motivation it is possible to
invoke reasons of morality to support particular
eating habits. A good example of this is the whole
business of non meat-eating. Although non
meat-eating is a characteristic of several religions
it is a practice also enthusiastically embraced by
many who would not consider themselves religious in
the nominal sense of the word. Moral attitudes
influence other aspects of food behaviour such as
types of food eaten and amount of money spent on
food, and are expressed in the contrasting
philosphies of ´eating to live´ versus ´living to
eat´.

Cultism is a term used to describe patterns of
eating which are, in terms of conventional
nutritional wisdom, bizarre. Cultism may be centred
around the supposed efficacy of one particular
dietary substance or may involve quite complex
patterns of food behaviour. A cult often assumes a
pseudo-religious mantle amongst its followers, and
indeed has some common ground with orthodox
religions in that faith is usually a strong
characteristic of its adherents. The tendency of
some nutritionists to merely dismiss food cultists
as ignorant and dangerous fanatics is a misguided
one. Cultist food practices undoubtedly answer
social and psychological needs in their
practitioners - in much the same way as do ´normal´
food practices for non-cultists. That the foods
chosen are unusual or nutritionally undesirable does

110

not make the reasons for their use any less important to understand. Unfortunately though, whilst a questionable nutritional practice may be tolerated because it is religiously inspired, the same practice is often derided if it is perceived to be a consequence of cultism.

RELIGION

The various religions of the world dictate patterns of eating for millions of people. According to Eckstein (1980) food can serve three purposes in a religion; to communicate with God, eg. through the saying of a Grace; to demonstrate faith through acceptance of divine directives concerning diet; to develop discipline through fasting. Dietary strictures may include: (a) What foods can and cannot be eaten; (b) What to eat on certain days of the year; (c) Time of day to take food; (d) How to prepare food; (e) When and how long to fast (Lowenberg et al 1979).

Some religious groups hold that it is for the individual to determine what is healthy to eat and that there is no merit in the consumption or avoidance of particular foods. Roman Catholics and most Protestant groups, for example, believe that individual choice is the correct approach to eating, and therefore they do not have far-reaching food laws. Neither would they risk giving offence by refusing certain foods when eating in company; whereas orthodox Jews, Hindus and Muslims will insist on obeying their dietary proscriptions even when it means refusing food offered in friendship. Mormonism is an exception within Christian sects in that dietary laws are observed as a matter of conscience (Eckstein 1980). Examples of various religious dietary proscriptions are listed below under each of Lowenberg's five categories.

Food Restrictions

Judaism.
* May eat only animals with cloven hooves and which chew the cud. ie. cattle, sheep, goats, deer.
* Eat only forequarters of animal.
* Eat only fish with scales and fins.
* Must not mix meat and dairy foods in the same meal.
* No blood.

Islam.
* No blood.
* No pork
* No intoxicating liquor.
Sikhism.
* No beef.
Hinduism.
* Must not kill or eat any animal.

Days of the Year
* Until recently Roman Catholics abstained from
  eating meat on Fridays in remembrance of the
  sacrificial death of Christ. In 1966 this law was
  changed to apply only to Fridays during Lent.
* In the Greek Orthodox church every Wednesday and
  Friday (with the exception of two weeks) are
  considered to be fast days. This recalls the
  betrayal of Christ and His death.
* Judaism does not permit the preparation of food
  on the Sabbath. Similarly, Seventh Day Adventists
  and Mormons must prepare food in advance for
  consumption on the Sabbath.

Time of Day
* Time strictures are often applied during periods
  of fasting. Foods may not be eaten, for example,
  between sunrise and sunset - but may be consumed
  during hours of darkness.
* Seventh Day Adventists do not eat between meals
* Buddhist monks do not eat after midday.

Preparation of Food
* Judaism requires the ritual slaughtering of
  poultry and animals in a way which permits the
  maximum draining of blood - for blood may not be
  used as a food. Meat, before cooking, must be
  Koshered by a complex process of soaking in
  water, salting and draining.
* Moslems also have ritual slaughter proceedings.
* Separate utensils must be used for meat and dairy
  products in orthodox Jewish homes.
* Devout Hindu Brahmins purify themselves by ritual
  bathing and donning of clean clothes before
  eating.

Fasts
* The World Council of Churches, in response to the
  World Food Conference of 1974, recommended that
  one day a month should be a fast day, to save
  food for those in need.

112

* Greek Orthodox followers fast every Wednesday and
  Friday (except 2). Also they have a 40-day ´Great
  Lent´ fast before Easter and a 40-day ´Advent´
  fast beginning on November 15, as well as two
  shorter fasts in June and August. No meat or
  animal products may be consumed during fast
  periods; the devout consume no olive oil.
* Muslims fast during the month of Ramadhan.

The five major religions, which between them account
for about 60% of the world´s population, are in
order of size - Christianity, Islam, Hinduism,
Buddhism, Judaism (Lowenberg et al 1979). Each of
these groups embraces several sub-groups; Eckstein
comments that there are over five hundred religious
sects in the U.S. alone (Eckstein 1980). Modern
reinterpretations of religious teachings give rise
to new splinter groups - each with their own
particular beliefs and patterns of living. The five
major religions are discussed in more detail below.

CHRISTIANITY

Christianity is the most widely spread of all
religions. It embraces the Roman Catholic,
Protestant and Eastern Orthodox churches. Dietary
laws and restrictions differ between and within
sects, being almost non-existent in the case of
Catholicism and quite strict in the case of Eastern
Orthodoxy. Until 1966 Roman Catholics were required
to abstain from eating meat on Fridays - in symbolic
remembrance of the death of Christ. In 1966, by
order of the U.S. Catholic Conference this directive
was amended so that meat was permitted except on
Fridays during Lent. In some areas of the world,
non-Catholics will not eat fish on Fridays for fear
of being mistaken for Catholics - fish being the
traditional replacement for meat.
      The saying of a short prayer before and/or
after a meal is common in Christian groups. Parallel
practices are seen in Judaism and in Islam. The
Blessing and the Grace establish a direct connection
between God and the provision of good food, and
encourage an attitude of reverence whilst eating.
Biblical directive for this action is found in Acts
27:35: ´And when he had thus spoken he took bread
and gave thanks to God in presence of them all, and
when he had broken it he began to eat´.

Seventh Day Adventists

Certain Protestant denominations have fairly strict
dietary rules. The Seventh Day Adventists are a
religious sect whose main tenet of Faith is that the
Second Coming of Christ on earth is imminent.
Although the original prediction by William Miller
that the Second Coming would occur on October 23
1843 proved to be mistaken, the early Adventist
movement continued to gather strength and was
officially organised in 1863. (It may seem
paradoxical that in many cases of unfulfilled
prophecies belief in the truth of the proposition
grows stronger rather than weaker. Social
psychologists have offered explanations for such
behaviour which centre around an individual´s need
to reduce cognitive dissonance. Proselytising can be
at least partly attributed to similar psychological
processes. The apposite discussion in Philip
Zimbardo´s book makes fascinating reading (Zimbardo,
Ebbesen & Maslach 1977).)

Mrs Ellen White, one of the early converts to
Adventism, through her visions and dreams greatly
influenced the thinking of the Adventist Church. One
such vision reminded Mrs White of the Fourth
Commandment, and this led to the celebration of the
Sabbath instead of Sunday as the holy day - hence
the name, Seventh Day Adventists. As in Judaism, the
Sabbath is a day of rest, and no food may be
prepared on that day. Instead, food may be readied
on Friday and the dishes washed on Sunday.

Seventh Day Adventists reject meat for several
reasons. Biblical references indicate that the
swine, for example, is unclean; whilst the writings
of Mrs White reveal a sort of magical thinking in
her declarations that meat consumption makes people
more animalistic and less sympathetic to the needs
of others. Stimulants such as tea and coffee,
alcohol and tobacco are avoided, as are many spices;
eating between meals is discouraged on the grounds
that the body needs sufficient time to digest and
assimilate what is taken at meal times. Taking their
belief from a biblical reference in Corinthians, the
Adventists place much emphasis on the concept of
healthful living. ´Know ye not that ye are the
temple of God and that the Spirit of God dwelleth
within you. If any man defile the temple of God, him
shall God destroy; for the temple of God is holy,
which temple ye are.´ (Corinthians 3:16-17). This is
achieved by eating the right foods and taking
exercise and rest appropriately. Adventists believe

in a simple diet and are basically vegetarian -
though most do consume milk and eggs. As in nearly
all the religious groups there are less orthodox
members who do not follow strictly the admonitions
of the Faith; thus some Adventists will in fact eat
meat.

It is interesting to note in passing, that Dr
John Harvey Kellogg was for many years responsible
for the Sanatarium at Battle Creek, where the
Adventists settled. His attention to the rich and
wealthy eventually brought him into implacable
opposition to the White´s and he left - but not
before he had established a successful ´health food´
trade. One of his products, cornflakes, was
originally seen to be a technologically pure food,
which was therefore pure for the body and the spirit
too.

Mormonism
The Mormons, or Latterday Saints, claim to be the
fastest growing religious organisation in the world;
in 1981 the Mormon church had over four and a half
million members.. Mormons assert the importance of
eating a well-balanced diet in order to nourish the
body as the temple in which the soul resides.
Vegetables and ´herbs´ are emphasised, whilst meat
should be sparingly used. Mormons are expected to
lead physically healthy lives and thus they refrain
from tobacco and alcohol use, as well as avoiding
caffeine-containing beverages. This emphasis on
healthful living is shared by Adventists and by
Muslims. Like the Jews and the Adventists, Mormons
recognise the Sabbath as a time for rest. Basic
foods must be prepared the day before - though
simple finishing touches may be done on the Sabbath
itself. Organised fasting for those in sound health
occurs once a month; a 24-hour fast lasts from
Saturday through to Sunday evening, and money or
food saved is contributed to the welfare of the
poor. This fast is a religious discipline and is not
undertaken for dietary purposes.

Eastern Orthodox Church
There were already, by the fourth century, important
differences in understanding of Christian doctrine
between the Eastern churches, who often used Greek
and were more philosophical in their
interpretations, and the Western churches of Rome,
Cathay, Milan and Lyons. The Eastern Orthodox
movement grew up around several influential bishops

in the centres of Alexandria, Jerusalem, Antioch,
Constantinople, and later, Moscow. Though
Constantinople subsequently retained more importance
than did the other centres the relationship between
them remained more one of collegiality than of
central dominance or control. Eastern Orthodox
beliefs came to differ from those of the Church of
Rome in several ways. ´The Eastern Orthodox Church
believed that the Holy Spirit originated completely
from God the Father, that leavened bread should be
used in Communion services and that priests should
be allowed to marry prior to ordination.´ (Lowenberg
et al 1979, p172). Mutual excommunication of the
Patriarch of Constantinople and the Bishop of Rome
occurred in 1054 partly as a result of the Pope´s
efforts to reform and centralise the Church and his
claim to authority over all of Christendom. (The
fellowship was formally restored in the time of Pope
John XXIII.)

Fasting is a major part of the practice of
Eastern Orthodoxy - though the term fasting is used
differently here to its more usual connotation of
complete abstinence from food. There are two major
fasts: one, the Great Lent, lasts for 40 days
preceding Easter, and another 40-day fast begins in
November at Advent. In addition there are two
shorter fast periods in the summer months and, as
well, every Wednesday and Friday in the year -
excepting two (before Ascension Day) - are
considered to be fast days. Rather than forbidding
foods completely, these fasts require that certain
foods are forgone whilst others continue to be
acceptable. For example, no animal products can be
eaten, and only shellfish are allowed in the way of
fish. Because olive oil is an important food
commodity its avoidance during fast periods is a
sign of true sacrifice and a symbol of devoutness.
Historically, olive oil was stored in casks lined
with stomach of calf, which would ´contaminate´ it
through contact with an animal product. Olive oil
was also associated with aphrodisiac properties;
since fast days are also days of sexual abstinence,
this may provide another explanation for the
avoidance of olive oil.

The Great Lent fast is held in memory of
Christ´s 40-day fast in the desert. In preparation
for the fast there is a two to three week period of
pre-Lenten activity during which all meat and dairy
products in the house are eaten or otherwise
disposed of. Thereafter no animal foods are taken

until Easter Sunday; however, fish is allowed on
Palm Sunday and on the Annunciation day of the
Virgin Mary. On Maundy Thursday lambs are killed and
hung in preparation for the Resurrection feast. Hard
boiled eggs are cooked and dyed red to symbolise
Christ's blood. In the Mani region of Greece, eggs
dyed on ´Great´ Thursday are considered to be
superior to those prepared on other days; they are
dyed early in the morning - at the time the Great
Thursday liturgy is being sung in the church - and
are therefore believed to have the church's special
blessing (Arnott 1975, p301). The red colour is a
sign of mourning, the egg itself symbolising the
tomb of Christ; the eggs are broken open on Easter
morning, symbolising the opening of the tomb. These
eggs are considered to be tokens of good luck; some
are baked on top of the Easter bread which is
prepared on Good Friday. Also, on Good Friday,
lentil soup is eaten to symbolise the tears of the
Virgin Mary; often it is flavoured with vinegar as a
reminder of Christ's ordeal on the cross - another
example of symbolism, common in religious food
practices.The Easter fast is broken after a midnight
service on Easter Saturday when a lamb-based soup is
served, followed by olives, bread and fruit. The
meal is followed immediately, or on Easter morning
by the egg-cracking game. On Easter Sunday, the
austerity of Lent is ended with the spit-roasting of
lambs.

Food symbolism is manifest during these special
Easter celebrations, but ritual food is also
important in other ceremonies. Special altar bread
called Prosphoron - the bread of offering - is
prepared by laywomen for use at Sunday Communion.
This bread is free from milk, sugar, eggs and
shortening, and is stamped with a Prosphoron
seal.The centre portion of the loaf represents a
lamb, and during the Communion becomes transformed
into the body of Christ. Other parts of the loaf
represent the Virgín Mary and the Angelic Host and
Saints. The Prosphoron offering is bought to the
altar with two lists of names. One, of living
friends and relatives, who are wished good health;
and another of the dead, who are wished a peaceful
repose. Kolyva - which is boiled whole grain wheat
is used as a symbol of everlasting life. It is mixed
with pomegranate seeds, nuts and spices and is
offered at the altar three, nine, and forty days
after the death of a family member, and also on the
first and third anniversaries. The mixture is

117

sprinkled with sugar and offered on a silver tray; the sugar represents the wish that the dead will have a sweet and blissful life in heaven. A cross is made in the Kolyva with either brown sugar or Jordan almonds and the name or initials of the deceased is similarly inscribed beneath the cross. The Kolyva is blessed by a priest at morning service and later distributed to friends of the deceased (Lowenberg et al 1979, Barer-Stein 1979). According to Barer-Stein, modern-day Greeks rarely return directly home after a funeral, but stop to eat and drink in a symbolic act which represents purification and the driving away of the spirit of death (Op cit, p248).

JUDAISM

The sacred writings of the Jewish faith, contained in the Torah, include what are perhaps the most detailed directions for dietary practices of any of the major religions. The Torah, which consists of the books of Genesis, Exodus, Leviticus, Numbers and Deuteronomy, is the authoritative guide to human conduct and is followed faithfully by orthodox Jews. Although animal foods are eaten, only certain ones are acceptable; others are considered to be unclean and are therefore forbidden. Animals which have cloven hooves and which also chew the cud are considered clean; those which meet neither or only one of these criteria are forbidden. Thus the cow, sheep, ox and goat are clean - whilst the pig, and indeed, the camel, are unclean. In addition, birds of prey, creeping animals, most winged insects and reptiles are forbidden. Only fish with fins and scales can be used, thus excluding shellfish. Meat must be obtained from animals which have been ritually slaughtered; if the animal dies of disease or of natural causes it becomes unclean. There is a taboo against the consumption of blood, which is considered to be the vital life of an animal. Leviticus 17:14 declares : ´Ye shall eat the blood of no manner of flesh for the life of all flesh is the blood thereof: whosoever eateth it shall be cut off´.

Orthodox Jews will not eat meat and dairy products at the same meal and even preparation of these foodstuffs must be kept separate. Therefore, two sets of utensils are commonly used for preparation and serving of meat and dairy products. Strictly, six hours must elapse after eating meat

before dairy products can be taken; after
consumption of milk or dairy products a half-hour to
one hour wait is necessary before meat can be eaten.
The advent of margarine and artificial creamers has
eased the inconvenience caused by this prohibition
by providing acceptable substitutes for butter and
cream. Fish is stored and served in utensils
separate again to those used for meat or dairy
products.

The term ´Kosher´ is used to refer to those
foods which are permitted and which have been
prepared in the prescribed manner. Foods which are
unclean or which have not been prepared in the
ritual manner are referred to as ´trayf´. To be
kosher meat must be ritually slaughtered in a
procedure supervised by a Rabbi. A person known as a
shochet slashes the animal´s throat with one deep
cut in order to completely drain the blood from the
body. It is then stamped with the shochet´s seal of
approval. Further treatment of the meat ensures the
complete removal of blood from the animal. Meat is
soaked for thirty minutes then allowed to drain on a
slotted board after which it is sprinkled with salt;
after another hour it is washed again and is then
ready for cooking. This preparation was
traditionally a domestic task, but it is now
possible to buy meats which have been thus prepared
commercially. The shochet is the modern equivalent
of the priests who controlled slaughter of animal
sacrifices in the Temple of Jerusalem. Berman
provides a detailed list of the characteristics
required in a shochet as well as the duties the
position entails (Berman 1982, p32). Eating of the
sciatic nerve of the animal is forbidden, as is
abdominal and intestinal fat. As it is difficult to
remove the sciatic nerve from the animal, only the
forequarters of an animal are used.

Processed foods may contain ingredients which
are not acceptable under the kosher laws.
Identification symbols are placed on many products
to signify that they are kosher. The letters K. or
M.K.U., U, and COR are commonly used. Critics such
as Berman have called kosher food processing a
billion dollar business. Large food corporations
hire Rabbis as advisers or consultants and
supervisors, and the kosher symbol is placed on
foods which don´t need it - just to provide a
competitive edge in the supermarket (Berman, p39).
This author draws parallels between the big-business
orientation of modern kashrut practices and the

ancient excesses of Temple sacrifice, and declares
that because of the often cruel methods of animal
rearing employed, approved meats are kosher in name
only.

Jewish Holidays and Festivals

The Jewish history of persecution is reflected in
many of the particular food usages and heavy
symbolism of feasts and fasts. There are no secular
holidays in the Judaic calendar; all are religious
in nature, and most festivals have seasonal and
historical significance. The Jewish faith holds the
Sabbath sacred as a day of rest; food preparation is
done on Friday. A traditional item for the Sabbath
is Challah - a type of bread; an ancient practice of
placing twelve challah loaves on the altar of the
Temple in Jerusalem to represent the twelve tribes
of Israel is here copied and adapted. Two loaves are
used, which symbolise the double portion of manna
which God provided to the Israelites on Fridays for
the following Sabbath during the 40 years they spent
wandering in the wilderness (Lowenberg et al 1979).
       At the beginning of the New Year, on Rosh
Hashanah, the Day of Judgement, the Challah is
decorated with birds or ladders to carry the prayers
of the family to heaven. Bread and slices of apple
are dipped in honey as a symbolic wish for a sweet
year. Pomegranates are eaten as a resolve that all
merits become as numerous as those of the seeds of
the fruit, whilst nuts and almonds are to be avoided
as they are thought to stimulate the flow of saliva
and thus interfere with the recital of prayers. Ten
days later, Yom Kippur, the Day of Atonement, is a
complete fast for all over the age of thirteen
years. It is a religious duty to eat a full meal on
the eve of Yom Kippur so that the pain of the fast
will be felt more acutely. Traditionally,
meat-filled pancakes - Kreplach - are eaten, which
symbolise stern judgement wrapped in mercy.
       Extensive food symbolism is seen during the
major feast of the Passover, or Pesach, which
commemorates the flight of the Israelites from Egypt
- and also the beginning of the Spring barley
harvest. (This is an example of a common process by
which new teachings are incorporated into older
traditions. New meanings are attributed to old
practices by endowing them with revealed status.)
Special foods must be used during this feast and
everyday supplies from the kitchen must be avoided.
An unleavened bread called matzah is prepared ahead

of time and lasts for the duration of the Passover.
In place of flour a preparation of matzah meal is
used. Some Orthodox Jews sell all the leavened
products they own to non-Jews for the duration of
Passover, on the understanding that the goods will
be returned after the festival. Otherwise, any
leavened products in the house must either be eaten
or discarded before Passover begins. Pieces of
leavened bread may deliberately be placed in each
room of the house so that they can be found and
removed, representing the removal of 'leaven' or
evil impulse from the soul. In Orthodox Jewish homes
a special set of utensils are used during the
Passover.

On the eve of Passover it is customary for the
first-born to fast, symbolising the slaying of the
first-born when the Israelites were spared. On the
first and second nights of Passover a seder plate is
used; seder is the Hebrew word for order. This plate
contains various foods which are symbolic of events
in Jewish history. A roasted egg symbolises the
burnt offerings made in the Temple at Jerusalem, and
also exemplifies the beginning of life in Spring –
an imported pagan custom; a roast shank bone
symbolises the ancient sacrifice of the Paschal
lamb. Horseradish represents the bitterness of
slavery in Egypt, and celery or parsley stands for
the poor diets of the years of slavery. Parsley is
dipped in a dish of salt water before eating.
Haroseth, a mixture of chopped apple, nuts, cinnamon
and wine has the consistency of clay as used by the
Jews to make bricks in Egypt. Three pieces of matzah
bread represent the three estates of Israel; –
priests, Levites and laymen. They also recall the
three measures of meal which Abrahaham bade Sarah
prepare for the three angels who visited him on the
night of Passover. The middle matzah is broken by
the celebrant to symbolise the parting of the Red
Sea. A minimum of four cups of wine must be drunk
during the course of the meal: recalling the four
biblical promises of deliverance given to the
Israelites (Gaster 1968).

Fast days are observed by girls over the age of
12 yr and one day and by boys over 13yr and one day.
The purpose is less to do with the physical event of
going without food than to prepare for repentance.
Jewish law emphasises discipline and self-mastery;
dietary restrictions teach adherents not to consider
the pleasure of eating and drinking as the ends of
man's existence. Fasting can be used as a response

to any one of a number of exigencies (Eckstein 1980). Jews may fast to show sorrow and repentence; when in need of Divine guidance or when facing great temptations or tests; when studying or meditating; and when faced with dangers they may fast as a means of avoiding or terminating a calamity. Jewish fasts may be divided into three categories: (a) those decreed by God or referred to in the Scriptures, eg. Day of Atonement; (b) those decreed by the Rabbis, eg. Eve of Passover; (c) private fasts, eg. anniversaries of parents´ deaths (Eckstein op cit p253). Fasting is laid down as a precept, to be carried out on days which commemorate sad days in the history of the Jews. A series of fasts to express sorrow are associated with events concerning the siege and fall of Jerusalem under Nebuchadnezzar (Table 4.1). Gaster (1968) suggests that these fasts were probably adopted from popular pagan observances and made to fit Jewish history.

Table 4.1   Jewish Fast Days Commemorating Siege and Fall of Jerusalem

Fast of the tenth month	(10th of Tebeth) commencement of siege
Fast of the fourth month	(17th of Tammuz) first breach of the walls
Fast of the 5th month	(9th of Ab) destruction of temple
Fast of the 7th month	(3rd of Tishri) assassination of Gedahiah governor of Judah.

As the Jewish culture spread around the world and integrated with different societies so the practice of traditional customs became less rigid. Three divisions of Judaism formed, each reflecting a different attitude to traditional practices and to the outside world. Orthodox Jews are devout in their continued practice of the strict rules of the ancient faith; this tends to set them apart from social intercourse with non-Jews, although Berman (1982) estimates that a sizeable percentage of American Orthodox Jews have also forsaken dietary regulations. This has given rise to a classification of ´Non-observant Orthodox´. Reform Jews have

abandoned many of the dietary restrictions as well
as other ritual practices. Conservative Jews are a
blend of the first two; they still eat kosher foods
but have forsaken some of the strict ways of
Orthodoxy. Generally, transgressions of dietary laws
are sanctioned, and even encouraged if critical
questions of health arise.

ISLAM

Islam, which means submission, or resignation to the
Will of God, is the youngest as well as the second
largest major religion in the world. The number of
adherents - around 800 million, living mainly in the
Arab world and in North Africa and Asia, rival that
of Christianity. There are also large Moslem
populations in the Americas and in Europe. Mohammed,
the founder of Islam, was a merchant by trade. He
was born in Mecca and spent much time in solitary
meditation in the surounding hills. One night he was
visited by the Archangel Gabriel who told him he was
to be a prophet. When Mohammed began to teach
submission to one God, he was chased out of Mecca
and, in 622A.D. fled to Medina. Later he was to
return in triumph to the city which is now the
centre of the Islamic world.
     Adherents of the Islamic faith are known as
Moslems (sometimes spelled Muslim). Moslems believe
that Mohammed (The Praised One) was the last of
God´s prophets. They accept the divinity of the
Bible, but believe that this is superseded by the
Holy writings contained in the Qur´an, as given to
Mohammed by Allah. One of the suras, or chapters of
the Qur´an, known as ´The Cow´ contains directions
concerning dietary regulations.
     Mohammed would have been familiar with
Israelite history and customs, and this, together
with the geographical proximity of the two religious
worlds and the presence in the deserts of Arabia of
heretic Christians driven out of Rome, has resulted
in certain similarities between Jewish and Islamic
practices. The religious practices of Moslems are
guided by the Five Pillars of Islam. These are
faith, prayer, alms giving, fasting and pilgrimmage
to Mecca. All Moslems repeat once a day: ´I bear
witness that there is no other God but Allah and
that Mohammed is the prophet of Allah´. Prayers are
said regularly throughout the day. If no mosque is
nearby, a devout Moslem will kneel on his personal
prayer-rug, facing Mecca, and pray. Moslems are

expected to give a proportion of their wealth, in
money or livestock, as ´Zakat´. Originally intended
to support the poor, Zakat is often used to support
mosques and schools, especially in non-Moslem
countries. The pilgrimmage to Mecca is the often
once-in-a-lifetime trip made by devout Moslems from
all over the world. The great Mosque there holds
over 35,000 people, and a 100 square mile area
around Mecca is closed to all who are not Moslems.

Fasting is a way of reaping spiritual rewards.
The major fast is that of Ramadhan which occurs in
the ninth lunar month of the year and which
commemorates the first Quranic revelations to
Mohammed. Those who keep the fast will be pardoned
all their past sins. Ramadhan is derived from the
word ´ramz´, which means ´to burn´; its origin may
be found in the fact that the fast was first
observed during the hot season or may arise from the
belief that the fast burns away sins. The fast,
which includes abstinence from water as well as food
lasts from sunrise to sunset each day for the whole
month. When the fast occurs during summer months
abstention from water during the long hot days is a
major hardship. (Moslem schoolchildren in England
have been known to faint in the classroom during the
period of Ramadhan, due to a prolonged period
without food). With a few exceptions, this fast is
prescribed for all Moslems who have reached ´the Age
of Responsibility´. (12yr in girls, 15yr in boys).
Groups which are exempted are:

* elderly persons in poor health
* pregnant and nursing women
* menstruating women
* the sick
* travellers on a journey of more than three
  days
* individuals engaged in hard labour

The first two groups have to fast for an equivalent
number of days later in the year, or ´substitute
fast´ by feeding the poor. People in the latter four
categories cannot substitute fast but must make up
the lost days when they are able. Young children are
expected to undergo one or two days fasting to
prepare for when they reach the Age of
Responsibility. The fast is one of the most strictly
observed of Islamic practices though in some modern
Islamic countries it is losing ground. After sunset,
light meals may be taken, and a meal is usually

eaten just before sunrise. Wealthy classes often give large feasts and dinner parties in the evenings. Other fast days are observed throughout the year, and there are two holy festival days on which fasting is forbidden (Sakr 1975). The 10th day of Muharram is a voluntary fast but one which is generally observed. Fasting on every Monday and Thursday of the week and on the 13th, 14th and 15th of each month is practised only by strict Moslems. Mohammed said: 'Every good act that a man does shall receive from ten to seven hundred rewards, but the rewards of fasting are beyond bounds for fasting is for God alone and He will give its rewards'.

As in the Jewish faith, so too in Islam, certain foods are considered to be unclean and not fit to be eaten. The Qur´an forbids the eating of pork, and blood too is avoided. Any animal that dies of disease or by strangulation or beating is not fit to eat. To be acceptable, an animal must be ritually slaughtered with a blow to the head; the words 'Bismi 'llahi. Allah akbar' (I begin with God´s name. God is most great) are spoken. Carrion, blood, swine flesh and anything over which the name of another God has been invoked is forbidden, though if one eats of such foods under constraint, one is free of sin. Carnivorous animals and birds which seize their prey with talons are forbidden as is the flesh of the domestic ass. Alcohol is forbidden, there being strict penalties for its illegal use. The left hand is unclean, and the right should be used for eating, though now, in many places, Western-style cutlery is used. Unlike Hinduism, Islam does not recognise separate classes or distinctions between people; all worship and eat together before the One True God.

Farb and Armelagos (1979) suggest that the Islamic taboo against pork was adopted because it provided them with a clear distinction from the Christians, who ate pork. Also it encouraged the support of Jewish neighbours and facilitated the possible conversion of the latter to Islam. Moreover, the pig was not a suitable animal to raise in the prevailing ecological conditions. Farb notes that if the swine had been a useful domestic animal then the prohibition would never have arisen. However, Diener & Robkin (1978) revive the view that, historically, Middle East rulers saw the raising of pigs as being too profitable for the villages, making them dangerously autonomous. Rulers prohibited pig-rearing to curtail this profit. A

political motive is thus postulated. The extent of
pork avoidance varies considerably in modern Islamic
populations. Whilst it is abhorred in Iran, pork is
eaten by Chinese Moslems...especially if it is
called ´mutton´ or some other name (Simoons p28).

EASTERN RELIGIONS

Although Jewish and Islamic law specifically outlaw
certain foodstuffs, Christians were warned by the
Holy Spirit that such proscriptions were the
doctrine of the Devil (Eckstein 1980). For many
Christians, prohibition of meat-eating is a sign
that a religion is degenerate and ungodly. The
reverance for life which is expressed in Western
religions through the avoidance of blood as a food
is frequently shown in Eastern religions by
abstinence from meat-eating. In the cases of
Hinduism and Buddhism, this is related directly to
concepts of reincarnation and eternal spirit.

Hinduism
Originating in India over four millenia ago,
Hinduism is usually considered to be the oldest
living religion. The word is a corruption of
´Sindhu´ and means ´the people and culture of the
Indus river region´ - indicating its geographic
origin. In the early religion sacrifice was very
important but it was the Aryan invasion of North
West India which gave Hinduism its modern cultural
and mythic form, largely through the hymns or
sciptures known as the Veda. Hindus worship a
multitude of deities, but all of them are part of
the one supreme Universal Spirit - Brahman - who
pervades and upholds the structure of the universe.
Brahman originally created the universe as the God,
Brahma; as Vishnu he sustained the Universe, then as
Shiva he destroyed it. The Universe is thus
cyclical. The present Universe was created by Brahma
and will in time be destroyed again by Shiva. The
Hindu belief in renewal can be likened to the second
law of thermodynamics...energy is not created or
destroyed, it merely changes form. On an individual
level too, the Hindu views life as a process of
renewal, firmly believing that past and future
reincarnations reflect on one´s spiritual progress.
    Pervading Hindu life is the social structure
known as the caste system. Unlike class, caste is
something one is born into and which one has no

opportunity to move out of in one´s present
lifetime. It is determined by actions in previous
lives and is thus accepted with a surprising degree
of fatalism and docility. Social injustice, poverty
and discrimination can thus be reconciled, even by
those who suffer most. The caste system arose from
the four Vedic estates or varnas; according to a
creation myth, Purusa - who was an original Divine
whose body filled the universe, was sacrificed by
the Gods. Parts of his body formed the various
elements of Creation. The highest caste - the
Brahmin - sprang from Purusa´s mouth. Originally,
Brahmin were priests and teachers and were not
permitted to take up any other type of work. They
were supported in food and money by members of other
castes - who attracted merit to themselves by the
act of giving. Modern-day Brahmins often hold
powerful professional and business positions. From
Purusa´s arms came the Ksatriyas, the rulers and the
warriors. They were expected to take the role of
protecting the community - and particularly the
Brahmins - with their lives if necessary. They were
allowed to kill animals and were meat eaters. The
Vaisyas - farmers and traders - were formed from
Purusa´s thighs; their duty was to support the
community economically. The Sudras came from the
God´s feet; they were the menial labourers whose
duty was to serve the other three castes. There was
some degree of social mobility and social
intercourse between the divisions. The system of
Varna was codified in the Law of Manu during the
second century A.D. It coincided with a hardening of
social divisions in society, and the rights and
duties of the four estates became markedly
differentiated. Numerous castes developed within the
varna framework - including the Untouchables, who
were often denied even menial work, and who were
banned from the villages and towns. Most castes are
subdivided and are closed social groups who practice
endogamy, and thus reinforce the caste divisions.
Although they maintain a social independence,
because of a strict demarcation of jobs the various
castes are in fact extremely interdependent and are
indispensable to each other. This system resembles
to a degree, the feudal relationships extant in
Medieval Europe. Although Mahatma Gandhi struggled
to end the concept of untouchability and although it
was officially declared illegal in 1949, the concept
of impenetrable social barriers remains strong. Only
by leading a high moral existence in one life can

one be reborn at a higher level in the next; one´s
future is the direct consequence of one´s current
actions.

The caste system is reflected in eating
practices. There are many rules governing who may
eat with whom or give food to whom, and these rules
are so embodied in the social system that it is
often possible to work out the status of a person by
observing his or her food behaviour. Carstairs
(1957) studied a Hindustani population and found
that eating together was a very important social
event; members of different castes must not eat
together and any family member who renounces caste
differences is not allowed to eat with his kin lest
he pollute them with his heresy. Preparation of food
is a matter for reverence in a Brahmin household.
Those who prepare and those who partake of the meal
must cleanse themselves with ritual bathing, and
perhaps by putting on clean clothes. Ritual purity
attaches to each caste so that eating with members
of a lower caste or accepting food or water from
them, defiles members of higher castes. For example,
a Brahmin will not accept cooked food from a member
of a lower caste, although he will accept ghee
(clarified butter) and milk, which cannot be
contaminated by touch as they are products of the
sacred cow. Coconut is also considered to be sacred,
its three ´eyes´ representing the eyes of Shiva. If
a Brahmin touches food cooked by a person of a lower
caste he loses his ritual purity and his own caste
status.

Other dietary regulations are outlined in the
Code of Manu which enshrines the sacred laws of
Hinduism.

* Wound not others, do not injury by thought or
  deed, utter no word to pain thy fellow creatures.
* One should cease from eating all flesh. There is
  no fault in eating flesh, nor in drinking
  intoxicating liquor, nor in copulation, for that
  is the occupation of beings, but cessation from
  them produces great fruit.
* Meat can never be obtained without injury to
  living creatures, and injury to sentient beings is
  detrimental to the attainment of heavenly bliss.
* There is no greater sinner than that man who,
  though not worshipping the Gods or the manes,
  seeks to increase the bulk of his own flesh by the
  flesh of other beings.

Devout Hindus - especially Brahmins- are vegetarians
because of their belief in the sanctity of life.
Many reject eggs, for these are also potential
lives. Part of the reason for the rejection of flesh
as food is the belief that the soul of one's
ancestors may be reincarnated in the animal. The
strict prohibition against beef is examined in more
detail under the heading 'Sacred Cow'. Members of
lower castes may eat meats other than beef, and even
beef-eating may be tacitly condoned. In early
Hinduism, fish swimming in the seas represented
stars swimming in heaven - and the stars were
equated with deities; this is a possible origin for
the notion of sacred fish in modern India, though
fish may be used, especially in the Bengal region,
and in the tribal subcontinent. Simoons (1974)
suggests that this represents the situation before
fish-avoiding Aryans arrived in about 1500 B.C.
People living along these routes of migration, still
largely avoid fish. Other foods forbidden under the
Code of Manu are domestic fowl, salted pork, onions,
garlic, turnips and mushrooms. Such avoidances are
most strictly practiced by the higher castes, but
their impact seems to be slowly dying amongst other
castes. Simoons (op cit) also points out that there
are wide-spread evasions of dietary restrictions
through the imperatives of nutritional need. Hindus
may fast for various reasons associated with family,
calendar, religion, caste, age or sex. Abstention
can be partial or total. There are eighteen
festivals at which special foods are eaten and in
which food is spread to a wider population
(Katona-Apte 1976).

Hinduism began by absorbing other, older forms
of worship and making these other Gods subservient
to Brahman. Throughout its history it has tended to
absorb what is good in other religions. From
Jainism, orthodox Hinduism took over the ideas of
monasticism, non-injury and vegetarianism. From
Buddhism it adopted monasticism and the idea that
the meaning of existence is not to be found in this
world, but outside it. From Islam, Hinduism adopted
the notions that the caste system should be
abolished, that idol worship should be abolished and
that religion should be defended by the sword. Of
course, not all Hindu sects accepted these new
tenets; those that did, formed new sects - such as
the Sikhs.

Sikhism

Sikh means disciple. Originally part of a movement
to seek unity between Hindu and Muslim, Sikhism was
founded by Guru Nanak, who was born in 1469 A.D.
Although Hinduism remained the predominant
influence, Sikhs rejected both idol worship and the
caste system. They worshipped one God. Nanak
propounded a coherent theme for living, and also
started up institutions to carry out his ideal.
Dhamsalas or kitchens were established where people
could share communal meals without distinction of
religion or caste. But it was Gobind, the tenth and
last of the Sikh Gurus, who welded them into a
distinctive community. As well as the outward signs
of turban and beard-wearing for men, dietary laws
were laid down. Alcohol was forbidden, as was the
eating of meat killed according to the Muslim
manner. Sikhs have a reverence for cattle similar to
that of Hindus and so do not eat beef - but they may
eat pork; some are vegetarians. Usually they are
less rigid about their food practices than are
Hindus and Muslims, and adapt more easily when they
encounter new cultural conditions.

Jainism

At one time an early rival to Buddhism, Jainism
rejected the notion of sacrifice and the Gods
central to Brahminism. Jainas do not accept God or
the Supreme Spirit as the creator and controller of
the world; every soul can be a supreme spirit and
there can be an infinite number of Supreme Spirits.
Self-discipline and self-control replaced sacrifice
as the path to self-realisation. Jainas make vows,
the foremost of which is non-injury to living beings
- a concept known as ahimsa. Jainas will sweep the
floor in front of where they walk in order to avoid
crushing insects; monks strain their drinking water
so that the animalcules therein will not be
destroyed. Orthodox Jainas believe that it is better
not to eat at night for then they may inadvertently
eat some living thing. The laity strive to imitate
these ideals of asceticism. Strict observance of the
principle of non-killing meant that agricultural
occupations were denied to Jainas; instead they took
up business and professional activites, increasing
their general power and influence in the world out
of proportion to their actual numbers. Jainism has
survived in a few regions of Western India, though
it has made some compromises with orthodox Hinduism.
Some Jainas intermarry with the Vaisya Hindu castes.

Buddhism

Buddhism, like Jainism, was originally a sect of
Hinduism - a branch of the Aryan Way of Life
(Arya-Dharma); some of its teachings are still found
in orthodox Hinduism. Buddhism arose in the sixth
century B.C. as a result of the teachings of
Siddartha Gautama. The story of Gautama is
well-known. Leaving home at the age of 29yr, he
wandered for six years before attaining
enlightenment and becoming the Buddha. He spent the
next forty-five years teaching about the path of
righteousness. In 250 B.C., through the efforts of
King Asoka, Buddhism became India's state religion;
though now it is predominant in Sri Lanka, Burma,
Thailand, Laos, Cambodia and Japan, it remains only
as a small force in India itself (Lowenberg et al
1979).

Buddha taught the Four Noble Truths:

* Existence is suffering
* This suffering is due to selfish desires
* The cure of suffering is to destroy these
  selfish desires
* This cure can be effected by following the
  Eight-fold path; *right action * right speech *
  right livelihood * right effort * right
  mindfulness * right concentration * right views
  * right intentions.

Following the Eight-fold path is the way toward
attaining Nirvana, absolutism or perfection - the
extinction of individual desires. Like Hindus,
Buddhists believe in reincarnation and the idea that
what a person is today is the sum total of their
actions in previous existences. This is sufficient
to explain current injustices in the world; by Right
action it is possible to improve one's lot in the
next world.

Buddhists vow to abstain from killing or doing
any injury to living creatures, though in many
Buddhist areas meat is eaten. The spread of Western
influence in South East Asia has encouraged the use
of beef, and it is likely that the taboo will become
progressively weaker (Simoons 1961, p53). The
non-eating of meat is most strictly observed by the
monks and by devout laymen, who also renounce
alcohol which 'clouds the mind'. Such Right action
attracts merit which helps progress toward higher

levels of existence. Buddhist monks are embodiments
of the ideal. Traditionally they are dependent on
voluntary contributions of food and clothing; they
do not eat after midday, taking only tea and coconut
milk. In Thailand and Burma each morning they go to
the villages to beg, though they are not allowed to
announce their arrival or to give thanks for what
they receive. In some regions food is taken to the
monasteries by families on a kind of rota basis.
Even if a family does not eat at noon it will still
send food to the monks - and the very best food at
that. DeYoung estimated that the cost of maintaining
the large population of Buddhist monks in Thailand
was equivalent to each household feeding an extra
family member for a year (DeYoung 1955). By
supporting the monks, lay people show their devotion
to Buddha and also attract great merit to
themselves, aiding their own progress toward
Nirvana. Food is always offered to visitors in a
Buddhist home; not to do so would be a source of
demerit.

Thirty years ago, fully one quarter of the male
Tibetan population were monks. Now the number is
around one thousand. These monks are not allowed to
live off the labours of others and are expected to
work in the fields and orchards around the
monasteries. The Chinese influence has resulted in a
secularisation process including destruction of
monasteries (Abingdon 1981). Crop production takes
precedence over animal rearing because of the
emphasis on the non-taking of life. Animals may
occasionally be eaten by lay Buddhists, or raised
and sold to Chinese merchants. Simoons comments that
in modern China and Japan economic considerations
rather than cultural prejudices are mainly
responsible for the low consumption of flesh foods
(Simoons 1961, p11). In Thailand fish is commonly
eaten, the rationale being that the fish is not
killed, it is merely removed from the water.
Emphasis is laid on wrongful killing of a sentient
being rather than on wrongful eating; it is the
slayer who attracts demerit rather than the eater.
This is in contrast to Hindu laws, which place
emphasis on the eater as wrongdoer.

Origins of Religious Dietary Laws
Religious dietary laws stem from several possible
origins. For example, foods may symbolise past major
events in the history of the religion and thus serve
as a reminder of past sufferings and thereby

132

reinforce dedication and faith. In this way
religious practices readily assume symbolic values.
In primitive religions food offerings were made to
the Gods in order to placate them and buy their
favours; love and loyalty could thus be shown and
protection sought. In some cases it was thought that
the Gods actually ate these offerings. Berman, a
champion of vegetarianism within the Jewish
tradition, suggests that modern Jewish dietary laws
are a form of atonement replacing the older custom
of sacrifice. By focusing attention on eating
practices the laws remind people of the biblical
references to a vegetarian way of life and of their
own short-comings in persisting to eat meat (Berman
1982).

   Although dietary regulations are obeyed because
they are written down in Holy Books their origin
must be looked for in particular environmental and
cultural conditions. Many of the food prohibitions
of the various religions involve meat. Simoons
(1961) deals with the widespread rejection of the
pig as food noting that the Middle East is a centre
of pork avoidance, where Christians and pagans, as
well as Moslems and Jews, all reject pork as food.
He suggests that amongst the pastoralists of Asia
the pig was not a commonly eaten food but that it
was eaten by those who settled permanently in the
area. The taboo arose as an expression of contempt
by one group for the other and the consequent
ridiculing of each other´s customs. There are many
examples in food lore which show the use of food as
a means to demonstrate differences between groups at
society and at sub-group level. Once the prejudice
against pork-eating was established it could have
been incorporated into religious writings as a means
of accentuating and perpetuating the cultural
division.

   It is also possible that certain prohibitions
developed as a protective device against some
apparent hazard. This latter explanation is commonly
offered in respect to the Jewish prohibition on
eating pork. Pork is readily infected with the
parasitic worm, Trichinella Spirella, and therefore
can be a source of disease and sickness. Its
´unclean´ reputation may thus have derived from its
propensity to cause sickness, though the symptoms
are not specific to Trichinosis and the relationship
would probably have been unclear to pre-scientific
peoples. The spoiling of meat in warm climates would
not have been restricted merely to pork; neither is

the pig a naturally dirty animal. Simoons sees
hygienic explanations as being the result of
rationalising tendencies of a later scientific
generation (Op cit p39).
    Grivetti & Pangborn (1974) also challenge the
contention that Semitic avoidance of pork is based
on health and sanitation and propose instead that it
involved ecological factors and the retention of
ethnic identity. The Jews may have prohibited it to
set themselves apart; however this does not explain
why a prohibition was placed particularly on pork.
Other types of meat were eaten in common by the
different cultural groups in the area and other
cultural practices were also similar. Additionally,
the Jewish prohibition against pork is not recorded
in the Bible until after the Exodus from Egypt.
Until then, every living thing was considered to be
suitable food for consumption: ´Every moving thing
that liveth shall be meat for you´ (Genesis 9:3).
Farb & Armelagos (1980) are of the opinion that the
taboo can be solely explained by the Prophetic
admonitions to avoid imperfection. The book of
Leviticus is concerned with themes of wholeness and
perfection; only that which is blessed as being
perfect is acceptable to God. Such animals were
those that were already domesticated when the
Israelites first inhabited the Holy Lands (Douglas
1970). The pig was thus excluded, together with
other ´imperfect´ creatures such as shellfish,
rodents and lizards, insects and flightless birds.
These were considered to be abominations which did
not conform to what was expected of their class of
living beings. Farb points out that the biblical
prohibition against the pig is no more prominent
than that against other imperfect animals and asks
why then the pig taboo has come to be almost
symbolic of Jewish diets. In the second century B.C.
Antiochus IV desecrated the Temple of Solomon and
ordered that swine were to be sacrificed there and
that Jews were to eat the meat as an act of
submission to the Syrians. This gave prominence to
what had been only one of a number of dietary taboos
(Farb & Armelagos p117). The Hellenistic world was
outraged at the enormity of this act which involved
the deliberate pollution of a place of worship, and
in self-defence Antiochus was forced to spread a
story that Jews were in the habit of fattening up
Greek prisoners, sacrificing them, and eating them
whilst swearing hostility to the Greeks (Tannahill
1976, p93). When the Macabees captured Jerusalem and

re-established the Temple, pork avoidance became an
assertion of opposition to Pagan rule - a
declaration of allegiance to the ancient Law of
Moses.
    Yet another view is provided by Marvin Harris
who advances the cause of ecological imperatives. He
argues that pig raising came to incur costs that
posed a threat to the entire subsistence system in
the Middle East (Harris 1977). When the pig was
first domesticated there were extensive forests
covering the upland zone of the Middle East -
conditions ideal for pig raising. The spread of
mixed farming and herding economies converted the
forest first to grassland then eventually to desert.
The pig is maladapted for these latter environmental
conditions and so the pastoralists found that they
were feeding valuable grain to the pigs and were
having to provide artificial shade and moisture.
Although the short-term benefits of pigs as meat
sources remained, the long-term effects of continued
pig rearing would have been costly and maladaptive.
Harris says:

> Cultures tend to impose supernatural sanctions
> on the consumption of animal flesh when the
> ratio of communal benefits to costs associated
> with the use of a particular species
> deteriorates. Cheap and abundant species whose
> flesh can be eaten without danger to the rest
> of the system by which food is obtained, seldom
> become the target of supernatural
> proscriptions.
> (Harris 1977, p131)

The Leviticus prohibition, he says, helped to remove
any temptation to raise pigs. The other forbidden
species were similarly proscribed because of the
disproportionate amount of time and effort that
would have had to have been expended in hunting.
Thus there is a general rationale of banning
inconvenient and expensive foods. Diener & Robkin's
political explanation has been already mentioned in
the section dealing specifically with Judaism.
    The prohibition on mixing meat and milk,
referred to earlier, is widely identified as a
specific Jewish practice. However, Grivetti (1980)
points out that the meat/milk separation is also
observed in parts of South West Asia, Central
Sahara, East Africa and South West Africa, and that
its origin in Jewish lore is therefore

questionable. In the Old Testament books of
Leviticus and Deuteronomy, where many of the Jewish
dietary laws are set down, there is no prohibition
placed on the mixing of milk and meat products;
indeed such a combination is seen to be of high
status. It is the commandment against ´seething´,
found in Exodus, which is the basis for the
prohibition. Grivetti pursues this discrepancy and
reviews evidence for a number of possible origins
for the practice, of which the biblical commandment
is only one. Hypotheses include notions of health
and of ethnic identity, which we have already
encountered in relation to pork; the idea of
self-denial (undue pleasure is gained from eating
both foods); conservation of staples (protein foods
were too precious to be used unsparingly); and
sympathetic magic. In regard to the latter Grivetti
says that African pastoralists do not boil milk as
they believe that this will prevent further milk
production from that cow; boiling a kid in its
mother´s milk would therefore represent a threat to
the whole herd. Some scholars have suggested that
the problem rests on the mistranslation of ´blood´
as ´milk´ in the Biblical injunction. Grivetti finds
little to commend this idea but instead favours an
explanation based on semantic manipulation. The
biblical text, he says, referred to the preparation
of food rather than to the consumption of it. It did
not forbid the mixing of milk and meat at the same
meal, but only during preparation of the meal;
modern Orthodox practice is thus based on a
misunderstanding. Examples such as this illustrate
the difficulty in determining the origin of food
practices and also the ease with which later
rationalisations become established and are accepted
as true explanations .

A final example illustrates the tendency for
religions to adopt and adapt earlier customs for
their own purposes. The Jewish Passover can be seen
to have origins which predate the writing of the Old
Testament. The Festival of the Shepherds and the
Festival of Matzos were celebrated by nomadic Jews
long before the deliverance from Egypt (James 1961).
Modern Jews have forgotten the origins of the
various customs and have reinterpreted them in their
contemporary festivals. Matzahs are no longer a
propitiatory offering to assure a good harvest but
instead commemorate the fact that the Jews did not
have time to allow the bread to rise on the night
they fled from Egypt.

Even if prohibitions arise for sound ecological or cultural reasons there is still the question of why they persist when conditions change. It may become obvious that the breaking of a particular food law does not have any adverse consequences, in which case prohibitions may indeed be lifted. However, if the consequences - real or imagined - are severe enough then the prohibition will persist. The social sanctions against eating forbidden foods may be strong enough to cause fear and guilt sufficient to deter anyone from even trying them. This fear may cause actual physical symptoms; thus the very thought of eating pork is enough to make an Orthodox Jew feel physically sick. Those who do dare to break the taboo may also suffer symptoms of physical sickness induced, perhaps psychosomatically, by the expectation of a negative reaction to the eating of forbidden foods. This is in the nature of a self-fulfilling prophecy, and those who survive such distressing experiences are unlikely to ever touch the food again (Farb & Armelagos 1980).

MORALS AND ETHICS

Is it wrong to eat certain foods, even if they are culturally acceptable and are not restricted by religious taboos? Some people certainly think so, and the case of non meat-eating is discussed at length below. Other foods or food products may be occasionally singled out by individuals or groups as being morally unacceptable because of the way in which they are produced or marketed. Such was the case with South African food products which were heavily boycotted by anti-apartheid supporters in the 1960s and 1970s. The foods themselves were not of course the source of moral contention, but rather they were chosen as symbols of what was viewed as a morally distasteful political system. In a similar vein, Nestlé food products became the focus of an international boycott by those opposed to the marketing of infant formula milks in developing countries. Although infant formula is a satisfactory alternative to breast milk where clean water and hygienic environmental conditions prevail, it easily becomes a source of infection when polluted water and dirty feeding bottles are used. In addition, it is expensive for low-income rural dwellers to buy and whilst money needed for other things is spent on the prestigious formula nutritionally and

economically valuable breast milk is wasted. Costly
formula is often diluted to make it last longer and
thus becomes nutritionally unsatisfactory as well.
The argument of the boycotters is not that there is
something intrinsically wrong with formula milks,
but they are eminently unsuitable for use in the
countryside and villages of the developing South. To
actively promote them, as Nestlé and other companies
do, is therefore at least unethical - if not
downright immoral.

The Nestlé boycotters coordinated their
protests by forming hundreds of action groups
throughout the Northern world. They collected
evidence, wrote letters and even published their own
newsletters - all with a view to influencing company
and government policy. Other food boycotts are not
so high profile and may indeed operate simply at an
individual level, having no discernable effect apart
from that of answering the conscientious needs of
the boycotter. For example, many large multinational
food companies import raw foodstuffs from poor
countries of the South. Such products as fruit,
coffee and cocoa command far higher prices when they
reach the American and European markets than are
paid to the primary producers. On foreign-owned
plantations, local workers may be paid poverty-line
wages to grow and harvest crops which will make huge
corporate profits abroad. By refusing to buy the
products of particular companies consumers in the
affluent world make their own protest against
exploitation and greed. Although they do not expect
to be able to change the system they can at least
decline to participate in one part of it.

Boycotts do of course have political and
economic as well as moral implications. Many people
would not consider joining a boycott because they
would see it as being politically motivated and
quite ineffective as a tool for change. However,
practicality and efficiency are not generally the
criteria used for making moral or ethical choices;
more to the point is what is considered to be right
or wrong.

Non Meat-Eating
Vegetarianism as a style of eating may be the result
of necessity - either economic or ecological - or of
choice. As a matter of choice it can be freely
practised on an individual basis or collectively
adopted for religious or philosophical reasons. Meat
is an expensive component of the traditional Western

138

diet; the cost of the shopping basket can be
considerably reduced if this class of foods is
restricted or omitted. Normally, no nutritional harm
results if suitable adjustments are made; for
example, if consumption of fish and of dairy
products is increased or if cereals, nuts and pulses
are used as protein sources. It was once common for
nutritionists and dietitians to exhort their clients
- particularly the poor and the elderly - to
substitute less expensive cuts of meat for prime
cuts as a way of saving money. Although seemingly
rational from both an economic and nutritional point
of view, this advice entirely ignores psychological
effects on esteem and status. Meat is usually
considered to be a high-status food and its forced
disappearance from the table - in quantity or
quality - has negative connotations. There is no
doubt though that meat consumption does decline to
some extent when household economics dictates cuts
in food expenditures. In many parts of the world
meat is simply not available, at least in other than
very small quantities; diets consist largely of
cereal or starchy root staples. Under these
circumstances vegetarianism is a condition imposed
by the material environment; were meat to be readily
available then it would be eaten.

For many others though, non meat-eating is a
personal or collective choice which reflects certain
views about the world and the place of animals in
it. Eastern philosophies often emphasise the mutual
dependence of man and his environment; human beings
are part of the world and must live in harmony with
the rest of creation. Hindu and Buddhist beliefs in
metempsychosis, the transmigration of souls,
disallow the taking of a life which, after all, may
contain the soul of an ancestor or of a potential
child. This reverence for life is most fully
expressed by sects such as the Jainas (See earlier).
In sharp contrast is the Judao-Christian view that
Man was given dominance over the Earth and thus has
the right to exploit world resources - including
animals - for his own ends. Berman, who acts
sometimes as a critic sometimes as an apologist for
meat-eating by Jews, maintains that compassion
toward animals is a major theme in the Bible and
that meat-eating was only permitted by God after the
Flood because that was what ordinary men wanted. It
was thus a concession to man´s imperfection; after
two millenia, still we are not morally ready to
forgo the eating of flesh (Berman 1982, p18).

Vegetarianism as a tenet of religious faith has been more fully described in preceding sections. Whilst some religious practitioners are not entirely conscientious in following dictates concerning food avoidance, other individuals without particular religious beliefs deliberately eschew the use of meat for a variety of reasons. (For historical insights into flesh avoidance see Simoons 1961.) Some believe that a vegetarian diet is healthier for the body and they therefore adopt a simple pattern of eating which emphasises the use of fruits, vegetables and whole cereals and pulses. Such a diet tends to be higher in bulk and lower in calories, sugars and fats than a typical meat-centred regime; thus it is not surprising that limited studies have found vegetarians to be lighter on average than non-vegetarians, and to have lower blood cholesterol levels and lower blood pressures.

Another group of vegetarians avoid meat for ecological reasons; meat production is an energy-intensive process, particularly when it is carried out in large-scale feed-lots. Grain which could be used directly for human food is instead fed to cattle; in the process of converting grain to meat large amounts of food energy are wasted. The rising world demand for meat, epitomised by the meat-centred diet of North Americans, encourages the use of energy-intensive methods of food production. In U.S. feed lots grain is fed to cattle with a tenfold loss of energy. Battery hens utilise 5-10 lb grain per hen to produce 1lb of meat or eggs. Barbara Ward presents a sobering picture of the

---

Figure 4.1   Energy efficiency in food production

	Energy output as % energy input
Urban allotment	200 - 400
Chinese intensive farm	4000
British wheat farm	300 - 400
Milk	50
Beef	10
Commercial Fisheries operation	1

Information based on Barbara Ward, ´Progress For A Small Planet´ 1979

impact of energy-intensive food production on present and future food supply. She compares the energy we get from food with the energy required to produce it (Figure 4.1). Statistics such as these prompt some authorities to claim that vegetarianism allows for a more equitable sharing of the world's resources.

Ethical vegetarians believe that it is wrong to kill or harm animals, though they do not necessarily subscribe to particular religious doctrines. This group includes the anti-vivisectionists. Peter Singer in two books, Practical Ethics, and Animal Liberation, explores the moral basis for non-use of animals as food. He argues that animals, as sentient beings, have as much right as humans to existence and that morally there is little difference between the taking of a human life and of an animal life. Singer is concerned with the basic moral principle of equal consideration of interests and argues that such consideration should not be arbitrarily limited to members of our own species. He begins by making a case for not causing suffering to animals, which rules out the use of animals raised in 'factory farm' conditions, a parallel to the human degradation of factory conditions during the industrial revolution. Unfortunately many people who oppose cruelty to animals continue to support cruel practices through their buying and eating habits. Singer quotes Oliver Goldsmith, who said (somewhat hypocritically): 'They pity, and they eat the objects of their compassion' (Goldsmith 1966). He continues: 'People who eat pieces of slaughtered non-humans every day find it hard to believe that they are doing wrong, and they also find it hard to imagine what else they could eat' (Singer 1976, pxii). The practice of dining on animals reflects our fundamental view that they are merely a means to our ends. By boycotting meat and adopting a vegetarian diet we decrease demand and contribute to a decreased slaughter of animals. Although individual action may have little impact on the meat industry, in the short-term at least, it assures us that no animal was slaughtered to meet our personal desires.

> Becoming a vegetarian is the most practical and effective step one can take toward ending both the killing of non-human animals and the infliction of suffering upon them.
> (Singer 1976, p173)

141

There is an ambivalence in our attitude toward animals in that whilst we profess to love them we do not hesitate to kill them when it suits us to do so. Sometimes emotions can over-ride the impulse as in the case of a favourite rabbit saved from the pot through a mixed sense of love and guilt. For the primitive hunter there was a direct connection between the animal and the act of eating; although animals were killed they were also respected and often worshipped or given as offerings to the Gods. In modern societies where a complex food supply chain has replaced the direct hunter-animal relationship, meat has become merely another convenience product to be bought at the retailers. The ultimate result is seen at the modern supermarket, where the precut, plastic-wrapped, aseptic-looking product bears little resemblance to anything that was once an animal./Indeed this sense of animal as commodity is epitomised by modern methods of animal rearing on feed lots and in batteries where the animal is raised in the most cost-efficient manner, often under miserable conditions, expressly for the purpose of being slaughtered. It is difficult to see that there is any respect for life here.

Delicacy and aesthetic considerations may prompt the refusal of meat. The work of Elias was discussed earlier in relation to table manners. This same author interprets vegetarianism as a logical development in the ´civilising´ process in which there is a strong tendency to remove the distasteful from the sight of society (Elias 1978, p120). He suggests that those who from ´more or less rationally disguised disgust´ at eating meat refuse it altogether are in the vanguard of a larger social movement. Though their ´threshold of repugnance´ is lower than that of twentieth century civilised standards as a whole, and they are therefore considered to be deviant by their contemporaries, they are following the same direction that has produced changes in the past. Whereas the carving of a dead animal at table was once entirely acceptable, nowadays any reminders that a meat dish has anything to do with the killing of an animal are avoided to the utmost. The rejection of meat altogether is the next logical step on this typical civilisation curve. Berman too, though he writes from a religious perspective, associates meat-eating with an earlier stage of human history and claims that vegetarianism is a better response to today´s world.

'Vegetarianism is surely a foretaste of life on earth in generations ahead' (Berman 1982, p xiv).

Finally, vegetarianism in one of its many forms may be adopted by specific sub-groups and counter-cultures as part of a rigid belief structure. Sims (1978), in a study of the values, attitudes and beliefs of vegetarians and non-vegetarians, found that vegetarians had stronger food-related orientations of ethics, religion and health. She found that value-orientation, attitudes and beliefs could be used to predict vegetarianism/non-vegetarianism with a ninety percent accuracy. Vegetarians can be characterised as 'loners' or 'joiners', and their dietary restrictions may be 'circumscribed' or 'far-reaching' (eg. Lacto-ovo vegetarians include eggs and dairy products in their diets, whilst vegans reject all animal products.) Further work in this area by Dwyer and co-workers showed that attitudes and lifestyles varied with respect both to membership in vegetarian groups and to extent of dietary restrictions. Though health factors were the most common reason given for the decision to adopt vegetarianism, 'joiners' were more likely to base their diets on quasi-religious convictions, and to regard diets, cooking and eating as being essential to their beliefs. Joiners with far-reaching food avoidances behaved as cultists or quasi-religious groups (Dwyer et al 1974). The example of Zen Macrobiotics is discussed below.

Macrobiotics
Zen Macrobiotics has nothing at all to do with Zen Buddhism. It is the creation of George Oshawa, a Japanese author/scientist/philosopher born in 1893, who has said: 'Macrobiotic medicine is in reality a kind of Aladdin's lamp - a flying carpet with which you can realise all your dreams.' A Macrobiotic diet is said to offer spiritual enlightenment through a combination of pseudo-psychology and ascetic eating habits. Among its precepts is the notion that brown rice contains healing qualities that guarantee freedom from aging, tension and illness (Stare 1970). '(Macrobiotics) cures, decidedly, not only all the diseases of the present and to come but every misfortune too' (Oshawa 1966).

The concept of macrobiotics was resurrected from ancient oriental traditions and philosophies. The principles of yin and yang have been applied to a vegetarian-style diet in which brown rice and miso soup are the main principles. Yin and Yang represent the opposing forces of the universe, which are also present within man himself. Foods are placed on a continuum ranging from extreme Yin foods like sugar and dairy products to extreme Yang products such as meat and eggs (Figure 4.2). Whole grain cereals and vegetables are in the centre of the yin-yang continuum and thus are most appropriate in bringing about a harmonious condition in the body. This concept bears some resemblance to the hot/cold principle found in other food ideologies.

Figure 4.2   The Yin-Yang Continuum

YANG...meat-eggs-fish-grains-vegetables-fruits-dairy products-sugar-alcohol-drugs-chemicals...YIN

The macrobiotic diet consists of a series of numbered regimes which comprise ever-increasing proportions of cereals with gradual elimination of animal foods, of fruits, and finally, of vegetables so that the highest level number 7 diet consists solely of brown rice. Every mouthful is to be chewed fifty times, and at the same time fluid intake is severely restricted. The diet first achieved notoriety when a young woman starved to death on a brown rice diet during her effort to reach a state of enlightenment. According to the American Academy of Pediatrics (1977) the Zen macrobiotic diet is the most dangerous of current cult diets. The lower-level diets, like other vegetarian regimes, can meet nutritional needs but the cereal-based higher levels are too restrictive. Strict adherence to the more rigid diets can result in scurvy, anaemia and hypoproteinemia, hypocalcaemia and ultimately, death. Calorie intake is usually low, and poor growth is the main clinical finding in infancy. A 1974 report of two infants fed on kokah (A Zen macrobiotic food mixture for infants, consisting of a mixture of brown rice, wheat, oats, sesame seeeds and beans) from birth to 7 and 14 months respectively, showed that they were substantially underweight and short in length (Robson 1974).

Why should people be attracted to dietary
doctrines which are nutritionally questionable and
potentially dangerous? An easy answer would be that
they are simply not aware of the dangers and are
duped by the claims of doctrinaire charlatans.
However:

> We might also raise the hypothesis that food
> cults and food fads can be considered as
> compensatory items in our materialistic
> society, as an attempt
> to restore the symbolic and emotional content
> and the affective role of food and nutrition in
> a society where scientific thinking and social
> isolation are the rule.
> (de Garine, 1970)

This theme is taken up again in the next section,
but first a brief overview of cultism and quackery
is presented so that modern practices can be put
into the context of a continuing tradition of
unorthodoxy.

CULTISM AND QUACKERY

According to the Concise Oxford Dictionary, a quack
is an: ´Ignorant pretender to skill esp. in medicine
or surgery; one who offers wonderful remedies or
devices´ (Concise Oxford Dictionary 1976). One of
the foremost crusaders against nutritional quackery
is Dr Victor Herbert of the New York Hematology and
Nutrition laboratory. In his popular writings
Herbert contrasts what the faddist and quacks say
with what actual happens in their own lives and
gives pointers to recognising the quack (Table 4.2).
For example he says Adelle Davis spent much of her
life giving nutritional advice to prevent cancer;
she herself died of cancer. The Shute brothers claim
that megadoses of Vitamin E protects against heart
attacks; one of the brothers had triple coronary
bypass surgery. Using many more examples, and
focusing on the story of Laetrile, the so-called
miracle cancer cure, Herbert ruthlessly exposes the
multi-million dollar industry of quackery, revealing
corruption, deception and brainwashing on a mammoth
scale (Herbert 1980).
Food cultism and the associated quackery of
self-styled nutrition practitioners is however not
new; it has had a long and enduring history.
Medicinal and magic properties were ascribed to

particular foods even in Neolithic cultures and
elaborate divisions of foods according to humoral
properties were devised by the Ancient Greeks. Food
and medicine were inextricably linked, paving the
way forever after for the practitioners of cultism
and quackery. In Medieval times it was astrology
which influenced food selection; Nicholas Culpepper,
the English herbalist, was of the opinion that
´Cucumbers, cold and moist, governed by the moon´,
were good for ´hot stomachs and hot livers´. Barley,
being a ´notable plant of Saturn´ was hence
´unwholesome for melancholy people´. Numerous
herbals were written, extolling the virtues of
plants as medicines. Modern food faddism has revived
the notion of food as medicine as one of its
fundamental appeals. Contemporary food fads usually
fall into one of three categories. (1) Those in
which the virtue of a particular food or food
component are exaggerated and purported to cure
specific diseases; eg. garlic, lecithin. (2) Those
advocating omission of certain foods because of
harmful properties ascribed to them; eg. white
bread, sugar. (3) Those emphasising ´natural foods´,
eg. organic vegetables. Faddist claims raise doubts
about the purity of the ordinary food supply, and
create a market for the ´special products´ pushed by
the health food stores.

Preoccupation with a ´natural diet´ developed
over the last century and has persevered especially
amongst those who are opposed to the ever-increasing
artificiality of life. Graham, in the U.S. in the
1830´s proclaimed vegetarianism as being the natural
diet. ´The simpler, plainer and more natural the
food of man is, the more healthy, vigorous and
long-lived will be the body, the more perfect will
be all the senses, and the more alive and powerful
may the intellectual and moral faculties be rendered
to suitable cultivation´ (Graham 1883, cited in
Young 1970). The Reverend Sylvester W. Graham was a
Presbyterian preacher, born in Connecticut in 1794.
He had many food theories, one of which was that the
right food would save not only man´s life but his
soul. ´Fruits, nuts, farinaceous seeds and roots,
with perhaps some milk and it may be honey, in all
rational probability constituted the food of the
first family and the first generations of mankind.´
(Graham op cit). Meat and fat were bad because they
heated the temper and led to sexual excess. (Note
the resemblance of this to the humoral theory of

Table 4.2   16 tips to recognise the Quack

---

1. He advises that you go out and buy something
   which you would not otherwise have bought.
2. He is a fake specialist with imposing ´front´
   titles. Use of Institute and Society titles which
   mean nothing.
3. He says that most disease is due to a bad or
   faulty diet.
4. He says that most people are poorly nourished.
   (Sub-clinical deficiency gambit.)
5. He tells you that soil depletion and use of
   chemical fertilisers causes malnutrition.
6. He alleges that modern processing methods and
   storage remove all nutritive value from our food.
7. He tells you that you are under stress and that
   in certain diseases your need for nutrients is
   increased.
8. He says you are in danger of being poisoned by
   food additives and preservatives
9. He tells you that if you eat badly, you´ll be ok
   if you take a vitamin or vitamin and mineral
   supplement. (This is the ´nutrition insurance´
   gambit.)
10. He recommends that everyone take vitamins or
    health foods or both.
11. He claims that natural vitamins are different
    from synthetic ones.
12. He promises quick, miraculous and dramatic cures.
13. He uses testimonials and case histories to
    support his claims
14. He´ll offer you a vitamin that isn´t. (Pangamate
    - Vit B15; Laetrile - Vit B17.)
15. He espouses the ´conspiracy theory´ and its twin,
    the controversy claim. He says he is being
    persecuted and his work supressed. Or that there
    is a controversy between himself and orthodoxy.
16. He is legally beligerent. If a nutritionist
    travels with a lawyer and threatens.libel actions
    against those who disagree with him, he is
    probably a quack.

Source: Herbert V. Nutrition Cultism. G.F.Stickley Co.
Phil. 1980

the ancient world). Mustard, catsup and pepper could cause insanity. White bread was bad but bread made from coarse unsifted flour was good, provided it was slightly stale and had bran in it, as bran was good for regularity. Graham´s teachings were quickly taken up; Graham hotels opened, operating on his exposued principles, and Grahamites adhered faithfully to their leader´s dietary strictures. As his fame spread, Graham became more and more outrageous with his claims for the virtues of a vegetarian diet. But although his dietary ideas were somewhat bizarre and often taken to excess, Graham did awaken an interest in and realisation of the health value of foods. During his lifetime he did not profit personally through the sale of his health food products or through his writings; his name is now remembered because it is used widely in the breakfast food industry.

The case of Dr Kellogg has already been mentioned in a previous section. His famous cornflakes were at first known as ´Elijah´s manna´ and were admired for their technological, and hence spiritual, purity. Many entertaining accounts of the emergence of early food faddists as well as more contemporary cases can be found in Deutsch (1977).

Gullability and Food Cults
A number of explanations have been offered for why people experiment with alternative diets or become involved in food faddism and cultism. Kandel and Pelto (1980) present insights into the health food ´sub-culture´ as practised in the Boston area of the United States. They see the movement as arising from a number of factors including growing ecological and environmental awareness, increasing consumer consciousness and as a legacy of hippie lifestyles and contact with Eastern mysticism. Although the various religious and secular subgroups which make up this movement are often derided for holding bizarre and nutritionally unsound beliefs, it is possible to suggest that their vegetarian-oriented eating patterns are well ecologically adapted to future food supplies on this earth. As Kandel and Pelto put it: ´Participation in the health food movement may prove to be one of the most successful preadaptations to life in the coming century´ (Op cit p362).

Whilst this unorthodox view has much to commend it there is no doubt that thousands of people unthinkingly become victims of food faddism through

misconceptions about the nature of food and diet.
Wang (1971) defined a misconception as, ´a belief
commonly held as true but which is not in accord
with scientific evidence´. Misconceptions include
fallacies, fads and half-truths. Social
psychologists as well as nutritionists have studied
the phenomenon of food faddism and have isolated a
number of explanations for its persistence. The
major ones of these are reviewed below.

Cult of Appearance. Desires like good health,
personal beauty, relaxation and extension of youth
are commonplace (Lynch 1970). Society glorifies
youthfulness and exhorts everyone to employ a myriad
of strategies and of products in the effort to
remain young, at least in external appearance. Huge
amounts of money are spent on products which promise
to improve complexion and bring about rejuvenation.
Lynch comments: ´The ritual involved in seeking the
goal of physical attractiveness among the young
sections of the population has probably had more
influence on food patterns in modern Western
society, than any other cults.´ Frederick Stare adds
that:

> Millions of Americans are convinced that the
> road to utopia is paved with fad diets...one
> can...purportedly achieve eternal youth and
> beauty, perfect and enduring health, sexual
> potency, better memory, freedom from nervous
> tension, acute mental powers, peace of mind,
> and attunement with the universe: in short,
> they promise the impossible to the gullible.
> (Stare 1970, p53)

Megadoses of vitamins may be promoted on their
supposed ability to ward off the effects of aging
and to retain youthfulness. Health food stores
number the elderly amongst their best customers.
Eckstein (1980) points out that many old people grew
up at a time when the drinking of tonics and the use
of herb remedies was still common. When all else
fails they revive these practices and invest them
with magical potentials. A subsequent feeling of
well-being occurs as a result of the satisfaction
derived from employing old remedies to deal with
modern ills. Beal (1972) also refers to this
aspiration for a long-life, calling its followers
´super-health seekers´.
    Another aspect of the cult of appearance is the

desire for the correct body image. Slimness is the
current preoccupation, and is reflected in the
number of best-seller books on diet and weight loss
and the innumerable products which supposedly aid in
the slimming process. Teenage girls may be
particularly susceptible to cultural pressures to be
slim, and commonly will view themselves as being
overweight - whether they really are or not.
Slimming behaviour is also explainable in terms of
the second reason for food faddism:-

Tendency to Follow Popular Trends. Beal (1972)
interprets this tendency as an ego defence and
patterning need to establish an identity and gain
approval and acceptance from others. It parallels
the well-known use of food to gain acceptance and
express belongingness, as discussed later in Chapter
6. The only difference is that in this case the food
practices employed are not always considered to be
orthodox. According to Gifft, Washbon and Harrison
(1972) teenagers are in general more psychologically
and socially prone to food fads. Their need to
express independence and to reject adult values may
take the form of dietary experimentation. Such
changes as are made are often based on erroneous
information and misconceptions about diet, leading
to the possibility of increased nutritional
vulnerability.

Uncritical Belief in Bizarre and Unrealistic
Promises. Hilde Bruch draws on an example from
Solzhenitsyn's Cancer Ward to illustrate the potency
of even false hopes. The hospital inmates hear of a
miracle cure - a fungus from birch trees; they all
take extreme steps to procure it, even those who
doubt its claims. Potentially, anyone when desperate
and confronted with danger of death may come to
believe in or hope for miracle drugs, herbs and
foods as long as they offer a ray of hope (Bruch
1970). Hope is the greatest commodity food faddists
have to offer. The benefit of many products and
'cures' may lie solely in a placebo effect of
suggestion. If the products themselves are harmless
then perhaps this placebo effect should not be
dismissed as being without use. All too often though
there are potentially harmful side effects
associated with the use of dietary supplements which
make their use undesirable.

Denial of Illness /Hypochondriasis. ´The new danger
to our wellbeing, if we continue to listen to all
the talk, is in becoming a nation of healthy
hypochondriacs, living gingerly, worrying ourselves
half to death´ (Thomas 1975). The opposite side of
the coin to hope, is fear. For those concerned with
uncertainities of living there is a patterning need
for stability concerning the world. Frederick Stare
says that fear is a basic cause of vulnerability to
quackery. ´Fear of illness, physical or mental
incapacitation, weakness and death returns us to the
childish condition of wanting reassurance and
strength from an uncritical adult who promises
safety and well-being´ (Stare 1976, p180). For some
people, a decrease in physical strength is
associated with a decrease in feeling of well-being.
These people will grasp at anything which holds a
promise of retaining vigour (Eckstein 1980, p299).
Hypochondriasis gives rise to fear and tension which
result in a decrease in coping ability and an
increase in irrational and magical thinking.
Emotional and mental strains are readily translated
into physical discomfort. Bruch adds:

> It is not surprising that the underprivileged
> and poor, the uneducated and the sickly often
> become the victims of quackery; they are more
> prone to be below par in their health, and more
> apt to convert stresses and deprivations in
> their lives into physical symptoms. Decrease in
> strength and efficiency and loneliness and fear
> of being deserted, make many of the elderly
> susceptible to the promises of quackery: the
> dream of the Fountain of Youth has a long and
> respectable history.
> (Bruch 1970, p85)

Mistrust of Medical Profession. Kandel and Pelto
(1980) suggested that the health food movement could
be viewed as a process of social revitalisation and
also as an alternative health maintainance system.
´Frequently, health food users are trying to improve
their health, their lives, and sometimes, the world
as well´. It is also a system which emphasises
preventive rather than curative approaches to
health. The medical model of health care, which
emphasises high-tech. curative medicine, makes
flawed assumptions about its own limitations and
demands ever-increasing financial and material
inputs in order to keep functioning. Also, people do

not share in decisions about their own health and must defer to the superior knowledge of the health care specialists. In the professional concern with being scientific there is often a danger that the patient's emotional needs are disregarded; cultists and quack nutritionists quickly prey on these unmet needs.

One of the criticisms levelled at food faddists is that they have a propensity to attempt to treat their own ailments with folk and quack remedies, thus delaying consultation with qualified medical practitioners. At the same time the public is constantly warned off consulting a doctor for minor illnesses; an atmosphere is built up which leads the patient to believe that he or she is 'wasting the doctor's time' unless the complaint is serious. But how is the ordinary person to know what is serious and what is not? Similarly, nutritionists have been at the forefront of those who have advised the use of vitamin and mineral supplements for therapeutic reasons. Having demonstrated that such supplements can be used to cure ills they then expect the public to refrain from trying to do the same on their own behalf. The ambivalence of this position detracts from the credibility of the authoritative health professional.

Anti-Establishment Attitudes. Food habits arise from a need to express the self in a manner consistent with personal values. These values often contradict those espoused by the Nutrition establishment, the Health-care establishment, and the Food-processing establishment. Wolff (1973) coined the term 'foodists' for those who choose organically grown foods and avoid processed and packaged items. These individuals hold beliefs differing from the culture in which they were raised and which developed during a time of rapid cultural changes when alternate choices of lifestyle were perceived to be available and realisable. Their beliefs, though derided by the establishment as foolish or misguided, are reinforced by a sense of community with those of like mind.

Needs for Emotional Fulfilment. It has been suggested that health food is symbolic of a continuing search by users for peace of mind and that some try health foods as if in constant search for a new solution (New & Priest 1967). They are sometimes referred to as 'truth seekers'.

> The great majority...of faddists...are not
> physically ill at all but are anxious about how
> to face the problem of living and become
> concerned about their bodies and their health.
> Many suffer from discomforts and chronic aches
> and pains which are not well-defined, and for
> which medicine fails to offer clear-cut
> diagnoses or remedies. The more chronic a
> condition, the more susceptible a sufferer to
> the false promises of a quick and easy cure.
> (Bruch 1970, p85)

Schafer and Yetley (1975) suggest that differences
in food behaviour from what is usually considered to
be normal or mainstream are attempts to meet
internal psychological needs. They believe that food
faddism - however seemingly bizarre - does have a
real effect in meeting psychological needs, a view
which contrasts with the traditional orthodox
nutritionist´s explanation that food faddism is
merely the result of ignorance, gullability and
exploitation. Classical theories of cognitive
dissonance tell us that when a person is faced with
non-fitting relationships between ideas internal
conflict or dissonance is created. Most people try
to minimise dissonance and this may be done in a
number of ways. One is to modify existing beliefs so
that new information can be assimilated; another is
to reject the new non-fitting information. Applying
this theory to food behaviour, Schafer and Yetley
propose that individuals interpret external
information in a way which is consistent with their
existing beliefs and which meets their internal
needs. Nutrition information which does not fit in
with existing beliefs is rejected as it tends to
cause anxiety and instability - when what is
required is exactly the opposite - stability. When a
cherished belief is undermined the faddist turns to
support from his own reference group to reestablish
stability. Beal (1972) comments that the comfort
derived from this reassurance that one´s existing
nutrition knowledge is correct meets a
self-realisation need for recognition of
self-competency.
     Schafer and Yetley also emphasise the role of
fad diets in projecting a self-image. Again, this
parallels the normal use of food as a vehicle for
self-actualisation as further discussed in Chapter
6.

Artificiality of Modern Life. Dr Victor Herbert,
who has made a particular study of food cultism and
faddism, comments that nutrition cultism has
cleverly benefited from distorting the decision by
millions of people to become more self-reliant into
a cry to abandon science and prove their
independence, freedom of choice and personal
responsibility by making decisions based on
anecdote, fraud and misrepresentation (Herbert
1980). Food processing and the use of food additives
is portrayed by the faddists as being unnatural and
therefore detrimental to health. Public concern has
also been aroused over the possible relationships
between food allergies and additives used in
processed foods. Back-to-the-earth movements reject
the claim that in a modern complex industrial
society it is essential to turn the food supply
system into an ultra-sophisticated commercial
venture in order to feed people adequately. Indeed
the growing dependence of individuals on this
production and marketing system increases their
vulnerability in times of crisis. They are many
steps removed from primary food production and thus
are at the mercy of whatever changes - political,
economic or environmental - affect the production
chain. There is more security in a return to home
gardens and raising of small animals as food than is
generally admitted. Recognising the appeal of such
reasoning, advertisers who at one time made
technological claims about their products are now
joining the bandwagon and emphasising how close
their product is to ´nature´.
     One strange note which is struck in all this is
the fact that many of the people who criticise the
artificiality of the food supply and who abhor the
use of additives are the same people who willingly
swallow a multitude of dietary supplements in the
form of pills, powders and potions. The evils of
manufactured foods are fought by the virtues of
manufactured tablets. The physiological action of
vitamins and minerals consumed in quantities greater
than dietary requirements dictate are at a
pharmocological rather than nutritional level. A
reclassification of mega-vitamin supplements as
´drugs´ rather than ´foods´ might give pause for
thought to many people who conceive of such pills as
being somehow ´natural´.

Consequences of Food Faddism
Some of the rationales described above have become
part of mainstream consumer wisdom (White 1979).
Lack of laws covering advertising and claims that
may be made for products have contributed to this
situation, together with a willingness on the part
of the public to accept information at face value.
Hamilton and Whitney suggest ways to judge the
credibility of nutrition information (Table 4.3)
though many people are not willing to be convinced
that any claim is false even if there is a unanimity
of expert opinion, and they continue to make health
decisions on the basis that anything is worth a try.
This type of behaviour is identified as ´rampant
empiricism´; in such an approach rational judgement
is ruled out since even a total lack of scientific
evidence does not eliminate the possibility that a
treatment or practice may appear to benefit some
users. Psychosomatic effects and unaided recovery,
which occurs frequently, reinforce faith in the
results obtained from this uncritical trial and
error method.

Table 4.3   List of useful tags to apply when judging
            the credibility of nutritional
            information.

Logic without proof
Bent truth
Incomplete truth
Scare tactics
Misuse of terms
Sales pitch
Personal gain
Amateur diagnosis
Unreliable publication
Authority not cited
Fake credentials

Source: Hamilton E.M & Whitney E.N. Nutrition
Concepts and Controversies. West Publ. St.Paul 1982

Normally, food faddism is regarded with
distaste and even contempt by orthodox
nutritionists. Its practitioners are seen to be
ignorant or misguided victims of unscrupulous, if
charismatic, gurus and merchandisers. Even when it

is admitted that some people do in fact truly believe in the power of the products they promote or consume the response from the nutrition establishment is still likely to be scientifically simplistic. If only - the lament goes - these people had proper nutrition information then they would cease from their faddish practices and eat in ways of which we approve. Such a view ignores the by now well-known truism that information is not enough when it comes to persuading people to change their behaviour patterns. It also dismisses the idea that such food practices do contribute to the emotional well-being of the eater and may meet essential psychological needs. ´In many cases, the judgements we make on food cults and food fads are value judgements which describe this behaviour as deviating from the modern concept of food as reduced to its nutritional,economic and...organoleptic properties ´ (de Garine, 1970).

Orthodox nutritionists too, it seems, have fallen victim to the current emphasis on physical well-being - itself part of the cult of appearance and fitness. Although it is generally acknowledged that the construct of health includes social and mental as well as physical components it is nevertheless often the case that little or no attention is paid to the first two dimensions. The role of food in promoting and maintaining social and emotional well-being may have been forgotten in the fastidious application of physical criteria as measures of nutritional health. This is not to say that we should cease to be critical of the promoters and users of dietary adjuncts; whilst many of the products sold and bought are harmless (except to the wallet) some are potentially dangerous through inappropriate use. As well they encourage a kind of magical thinking which diminishes the chances of reaching the very goals which are so fervently desired - those of fitness and good health. However, nutrition educators must learn that a strategy based on simply asserting the truth of scientific facts and denying any possible benefits in unorthodox practices is self-defeating and is doomed to failure. In echoing the thoughts of Gerlach and Hine (1970), the modern health food movement exhibits all the characteristics of a major social transformation and should be treated seriously as such.

SUMMARY

Food choices are often circumscribed by what is acceptable under the tenets of the consumer´s religion. Whatever their origins, religious dietary restrictions are one way in which adherents to the Faith are reminded that they are indeed different to other groups. Simoons (1961) gives a fascinating account of the origins and the spread of pork avoidance in the Old World, illustrating the effect of successive waves of conquerors on the beliefs and practices of peoples in different areas. Today there seems to be a general decline in the power of traditional religious beliefs. Whilst in some countries taboos remain strong, proscriptions against the eating of particular foods are being generally weakened and in many areas of the world only the ´clergy´ and the devout laity fully observe them.

Religion is not the only force which has faith at its heart; faith is also the lifeblood of the cultists and food quacks. When one goes into a store and sees row upon on row of nutritional supplements, plant extracts, lotions and potions - all masquerading as ´health foods´ - there is a strong temptation to join the ranks of rationalistic nutritionists who dismiss the whole business as commercial quackery. When the elderly lady in the queue counts out her last pennies to buy a jar of honeybee pollen one feels that something somewhere is not quite right. But whilst purveyors may indeed be frauds and crackpots they would not be able to sell their products unless: ´...there were not people with unfulfilled needs, and if their merchandise, worthless as it is from a naturalistic scientific viewpoint, did not give some relief, however temporary or imaginary, namely, by offering hope where there had been despair and nihilism ´ (Bruch 1970, p82). At our own peril do we ignore this human dimension.

REFERENCES

Abingdon Dictionary of Living Religions Crin, Bullard & Shinn (eds.), Abingdon, Nashville 1981

American Academy of Pediatrics. ´Nutritional Aspects of Vegetarianism, Health Foods and Fad Diets.´ Pediatrics , 59:3, 1977

Arnott, M.L. ´The Breads of Mani.´ In M.L. Arnott
     (ed.), Gastronomy: The Anthropology of Food
     Habits. Mouton Publ., The Hague 1975
Barer-Stein, T. You Eat What You Are. McClelland
     & Stewart, Toronto 1979
Beal, V.A. Food faddism and Organic and Natural
     Foods. Paper presented at Nat. Dairy Council
     Food Writers´ conference. Newport, R.I. 1972
Berman, L.A. Vegetarianism and the Jewish
     Tradition. Ktav Publ., New York 1982
Brown, J.C. Understanding Other Cultures. Prentice
     Hall, New Jersey 1963
Bruch, H. ´What Makes People Food Cultists or
     Victims of Nutritional Quackery?´ In G. Blix
     (ed.), Symposium on Food Cultism and
     Nutritional Quackery. Swedish Nutr. Found.,
     Almqvist & Wiksells, Uppsala 1970
Bruch, H. ´The Allure of Food Cults and Nutrition
     Quackery.´ J. Am. Diet. Ass. , 56:316, 1970
Carstairs, G.M. The Twice-born: A Study of a
     Community of High-caste Hindus. Hogarth Pr.,
     London 1957
Concise Oxford Dictionary. 6th Ed. Clarendon Pr.,
     Oxford 1976
de Garine, I.L. ´The Social and Cultural Background
     of Food Habits in Developing Countries
     (Traditional Societies). In G. Blix (ed.),
     Symposium on Food Cultism and Nutritional
     Quackery. Swedish Nutr. Found. Almqvist &
     Wiksells, Uppsala 1970
Deutsch, R. The New Nuts Amongst the Berries. Bull
     Publ. Co., Palo Alto 1977
DeYoung, J.E. Village Life in Modern Thailand.
     University of Calif. Pr., Berkeley 1955. Cited
     in Lowenberg et al. Food and People. J Wiley
     & Sons, New York 1979
Diener, P and E.E. Robkin. ´Ecology, Evolution, and
     the Search for Cultural Origins.´ Curr.
     Anthrop. , 19:493-540, 1978
Douglas, M. Purity and Danger: An Analysis of
     Concepts of Pollution and Taboo. Penguin
     Books, Harmonsworth 1970
Dwyer, J.T., et al. ´The "New" Vegetarians: Group
     Affiliation and Dietary Strictures Related to
     Attitudes and Lifestyle´ J. Am. Diet. Ass. ,
     64:376-82, 1974
Eckstein, E.F. Food, People and Nutrition AVI
     Publ.Co.Inc., Westport 1980
Elias, N. The Civilising Process. Urizon Books,
     New York 1978

Farb, P. and G. Armelagos. Consuming Passions: the
    Anthropology of Eating. Houghton Mifflin Co.,
    Boston 1980

Freidl, J. and J.E. Pfeiffer. Anthropology: The
    Study of People. Harper´s College Pr., New
    York 1977

Gaster, T.H. Customs and Folk-ways of Jewish Life.
    W.Sloane, New York 1955

Gerlach, L.P. and V.H. Hine. People, Power, Change:
    Movements of Social Transformation.
    Bobbs-Merrill Co. Inc., Indianapolis 1970

Gifft, H.H., M.B. Washbon, and G.G. Harrison.
    Nutrition, Behaviour and Change. Prentice
    Hall, New Jersey 1972

Graham, S. Lectures on the Science of Human Life.
    Fowler & Wells, New York 1883

Grivetti, L.E. and R.M. Pangborn. ´Origin of
    Selected Old Testament Dietary Prohibitions.´
    J. Am. Diet. Ass. , 65:634-638, 1974

Grivetti, L.E. ´Dietary Separation of Meat and Milk.
    A Cultural Geographical Inquiry.´ Ecol. Food &
    Nutr. , 9:203-217, 1980

Hamilton, E.M.N. and E.N. Whitney. Nutrition:
    Concepts and Controversies. West Publ.,
    St.Paul 1982

Harris, M. Cannibals and Kings. Random House, New
    York 1977

Herbert, V. Nutrition Cultism. Facts and Fictions.
    George F. Stickley Co., Phil. 1980

James, E.O. Seasonal Feasts and Festivals. Thames
    & Hudson, London 1961

Kandel, R.F. and G.H. Pelto. ´The Health Food
    Movement.´ In N.W. Jerome, R.F. Kandel & G.H.
    Pelto. (eds.), Nutritional Anthropology.
    Redgrave Publ., New York 1980

Katon-Apte, J. ´Dietary Aspects of Acculturation:
    Meals, Feasts and Fasts in a Minority Community
    in South Asia.´ In M. Arnott (ed.),
    Gastronomy: The Anthropology of Foods and Food
    Habits. Mouton Publ., The Hague 1976

Lowenberg, M.E., E.N. Todhunter, E.D. Wilson, J.R.
    Savage and J.L. Lubawski. Food and People. J
    Wiley & Sons, New York 1979

Lynch, G.W. ´Food and Cultism in Modern Western
    Society.´ In G. Blix (ed.), Symposium on Food
    Cultism and Nutritional Quackery. Swedish
    Nutr. Found., Almqvist & Wiksells, Uppsala 1970

New, P.K.M. and R.P. Priest. ´Food and Thought: A
    Sociologic Study of Food Cultism.´ J. Am.
    Diet. Ass. , 51:13, 1967

Ohsawa, G. The Book of Judgement. Ignoramus Pr.,
    1966
Robson, J.R.K. 'Zen Macrobiotic Dietary Problems in
    Infancy.' Pediatrics. 53:3, 1974
Sakr, A.H. 'Fasting in Islam.' J. Am. Diet. Ass. ,
    67:17-21, 1975
Schafer, R. and E.A. Yetley. 'Social Psychology of
    Food Faddism.' J. Am. Diet. Ass. , 66:129,
    1975
Simoons, F.J. Eat Not This Flesh. University of
    Wisconsin Pr., Madison 1961
Simoons, F.J. 'Fish as Forbidden Food: the Case of
    India.' Ecol. Food & Nutr. , 3:184-201, 1974
Singer, P. Practical Ethics. Cambridge U. Pr.,
    London 1979
Singer, P. Animal Liberation. J. Cape, London 1976
Stare, F.J. 'Current Nutrition Nonsense in the
    United States.' In G. Blix (ed.), Symposium on
    Food Cultism and Nutritional Quackery. Swedish
    Nutr. Found., Almqvist & Wiksells, Uppsala 1970
Stare, F.J. 'Food Faddisms.' In D.N. Walcher, N.
    Kretchmer, & H.L. Barnett. (eds.), Food, Man
    and Society. Plenum Pr., New York 1976
Sims, L.S. 'Food-related Value-orientations,
    Attitudes, and Beliefs of Vegetarians and
    Non-vegetarians.' Ecol. Food & Nutr. ,
    7:23-35, 1978
Tannahill, R. Flesh and Blood. Sphere books,
    London 1976
Thomas, L. 'Notes of a Biology Watcher: The Health
    Care System.' New Eng. J. Med. , 293:1245-6,
    1975
Wang, V.L. 'Food Information of Homemakers and 4-H
    Youths.' J. Am. Diet. Ass. , 58:215, 1971
Ward, B. Progress For a Small Planet. Penguin
    Books, Harmonsworth 1979
White, P.L. (Editorial) Contemporary Nutrition. ,
    4:2, 1979
Wolff, R.J. 'Who Eats for Health?' Am. J. Clin.
    Nutr. , 26:438-445, 1973
Young, J.H. 'Historical Aspects of Food Cultism and
    Nutrition Quackery.' In G. Blix (ed.),
    Symposium on Food Cultism and Nutritional
    Quackery. Swedish Nutr. Found., Almqvist &
    Wiksells, Uppsala 1970
Zimbardo, P., E. Ebbesen and C. Maslach.
    Influencing Attitudes and Changing Behaviour.
    Addison Wesley, Reading 1977

Chapter 5

MYTHS, TABOOS and SUPERSTITIONS

According to the Concise Oxford Dictionary, a myth
is a traditional narrative, usually involving
supernatural or fancied persons, and embodying
popular ideas on natural or social phenomena (C.O.D.
1976). Malinowski (1962) saw myths as being in the
nature of charters; that is, stories of the first
doing of an act that are still repeated in ritual or
that validate some claim in social relationships.
They explain why what is done today is the right
thing to do. Sacredness and ritual are
characteristics of myth and may be combined with
elements of legends or fairy-tales. Legends recount
supposed history whilst fairy-tales deal with
miraculous happenings which no-one supposes to be
true and which are pure entertainment. It may be
that myths also serve to explain and impose order on
the incomprehensible universe (Freidl & Pfeiffer
1977 p432).
     Magnus Pyke offers a number of explanations for
the origin of food myths, the foremost of which is
the rationalisation of natural phenomena. Such
rationalisations occur when an observation is made
but not fully understood. Sympathetic medicine,
based on the idea that like influences like, is an
example of this. The ancient Doctrine of Signatures
attributed properties to foods on the basis of their
appearance; eg. red beet juice was a cure for
anaemia, yellow celandine a cure for jaundice.
Mandrake root was used as an aphrodisiac because its
forked shape resembles a man´s crotch; the root does
indeed contain a mild narcotic which could act as a
calmative for a nervous lover and thus enhance
sexual performance. Pyke comments that the
relationship between the shape and the effect may
have developed as a rationalisation for the observed
effects (Pyke 1970). (The sixteenth century

161

physician, Paracelsus, codified the Doctrine of
Signatures. He suggested that the properties of
foods were based on their composition rather than on
their appearance. Although he had the wrong idea of
what these food principles were, identifying them as
salt, sulphur and mercury, he was correct in
divining the importance of food composition in
affecting biological outcomes.)

Myths can also arise simply as a result of
wishful thinking. Wish-fulfilment is the term
applied to the adoption of a belief even though
there is no empirical scientific evidence to support
it. For example, because doctors are expected to
achieve results they may resort to unusual or
unorthodox treatments when baffled by an illness.
Sometimes such treatments appear to work and they
are then enthusiastically endorsed (Pyke, op cit).
Once they become part of the conventional wisdom,
they continue to be used even though there is no
evidence to support their efficacy. Many examples of
this reification process can be found in the world
of therapeutic dietetics; the Sippy milk diet, for
instance, is still faithfully prescribed by some
physicians even though it has no effect on the
symptomology of ulcers. Pumpian-Mindlin brings a
psychological perspective to this particular
example, noting that gastric ulcers may be related
to dependent personality traits;
sufferers have an unconscious fear of being
successful and therefore independent; their organic
illness provides a respectable excuse for bed rest
and prolonged milk feeding. ´How much more like an
infant could one be - on a symbolic level at least?´
(Pumpian-Mindlin 1954).

Economic theories and considerations of
personal gain not infrequently intrude on
nutritional fact. In the early 1930s the myth arose
that aluminium cooking pots were harmful to health;
this notion was originated by manufacturers of iron
pots in a struggle to maintain their own sales and
thus, their economic status (Pyke 1970). When
machinery first replaced human labour in the canning
industry unemployed workers spread rumours that the
acid used in soldering machine-produced cans
poisoned the contents. This helped to build a strong
prejudice against canned goods (Young 1970). In
contemporary society, vitamin pill manufacturers are
fighting the same kind of battle. One of their
commonest plaints is that the processed foods of
today have been poisoned with additives and that

extra vitamins are needed to make up for deficits lost in manufacturing processes.

One of the commonest reasons for assigning properties to foods which results in their non-consumption is the desire to express separateness. Examples of this in a religious context have already been dealt with in Chapter 4. In much of the Western world, horseflesh is not considered to be a food fit for human consumption. The taboo against horsemeat arose in the eighth century when Pope Gregory III ordered Boniface, his apostle to the Germans, to forbid the consumption of horseflesh by Christian converts to show their separateness from the Vandal pagans (Simoons 1961). The current distaste for horsemeat stems not from intrinsic unpalatability but from this historical sign of superiority and separateness. Horseflesh is readily eaten in modern day France as well as in several other cultures. Strodtbeck (1968) cites the example of the Black Muslim movement which declared through its spokesman, Mohammed Ali, that the swine was: ´the nastiest animal in the world´. The Black Muslims made the pig a taboo animal to distinguish themselves from other American negroes and from Whites who ate the reviled pork. Pyke calls this kind of practice, ´the myth of separateness´.

Finally, Pyke describes the myth of the master race as it arose from Judao-Christian ethics. From the teachings of the Old Testament has grown the belief that man can absolutely control his environment and that he has dominance over the rest of nature. Pursuance of this ´myth´ has resulted in malnutrition, pollution, erosion of resources, and the extinction of hundreds of bird and animal species. Heisler adds that things may have been quite different if the religions of the developed Northern nations had been derived from fertility cults, with an emphasis on Mother Earth and reverence for her creatures, instead of on the monotheism of Jahweh (Jehovah) - a non-fertility deity (Heisler 1981).

Modern science is basically a means of embodying ideas about natural phenomena but is based on observable facts rather than on supernatural beliefs; because observations are subjective in nature and thus are often incomplete, if not actually erroneous, it is possible that nutritional doctrine now accepted may contain unseen errors which, being reified, pass into the mythology of dietary dogma. However, at least in principle,

163

science is to be questioned and changed if the facts dictate change; myth is essentially religious or sacred and is thus not questionable.

Food and Magic
Sir George Frazer expressed the early view that magic was a sort of pseudo-science, preceding genuine science. Malinowski pointed out that it is highly unlikely that magical beliefs would have been generally applied as an explanation of natural phenomena, for if people thought that like affected like all the time then they would become hopelessly confused by what actually happened in the real world (Malinowski 1963). Malinowski maintained that science arose from man´s ability to organise knowledge, whilst magic dealt with the organisation of supernatural realities. Rather than being a way of interpreting the world in general magic is directed toward a specific end and involves manipulation of an object, albeit it in a supernatural manner. It is thus essentially pragmatic, seeking to gain control over forces in the universe which cannot be understood in any other way.
      Frazer, in his classic book, The Golden Bough, suggests that fundamentally there are two types of magic, sympathetic or homoeopathic, and contact or contagious. In the first case, similar things can be considered the same, as in the example of blood and beet-juice given above. Magic effects can be achieved by working magic on an object which resembles or has the properties of the target selected. In the second case, actual contact with the object is required; contagious magic relies on touching or possessing part of the object or its belongings. Thus a hunter may perform magic on the spoor of an antelope in order to catch the beast itself. In addition, undesired effects can be avoided by avoiding contact with sympathetic objects - a case of negative magic. This, suggests Frazer, is the origin of taboo; an avoidance of what it is believed could cause harm. Ideas of sympathetic and contagious magic abound in food taboos. Thus snails and jackals are avoided by hunters who don´t want to become cowardly and weak. Lions, and hearts of predators may be eaten to confer strength and courage. In parts of Nigeria it is believed that if children are reared on expensive foods then they will expect them when they are older...and will steal to get them (Ogbeide 1974).

Shifflett (1976) reports that in the Shenendoah region of the south-eastern U.S. red beets are believed to cure low blood pressure. In Britain, lactating women may be given milk stout to stimulate their own milk production. A modern example of sympathetical magical thinking in the world of commerce is to be found in the case of formula milks which strive to imitate breast milk.

Many foods are endowed with magical properties, and beliefs in their efficacy are firmly held. Any rationalisation for such beliefs recedes into the background with the passage of time, and the beliefs themselves become part of the conventional wisdom or folklore of the society.

Folklore and Old Wives´ Tales

Traditional beliefs and superstitions are passed down the generations in the form of folklore or, more pejoratively, old wives´ tales. A wealth of traditional wisdom is bought to bear on weather prediction, birth rites and on food practices. Country cures, often involving the use of tisanes, are eagerly adopted by ´scientific man´ as though their very antiquity confers on them certain power. Whilst it is true that there is a strong empirical basis to support many practices others rely on the kind of non-scientific rationalisations described above. For example, fish is widely touted as being a ´brain food´; in P.G. Wodehouse´s timeless stories, Bertie Wooster is forever advising the inimitable Jeeves to eat fish in order to come up with a brainy scheme or ruse. (See for example, Wodehouse 1957). As it happens, fish is a good source of dietary potassium and potassium is indeed found in significant quantities in brain cells. The imaginative leap which is taken to ascribe a cause and effect relationship between eating fish and mental prowess is entirely fanciful. Does the belief that crusts will make hair curly have similar pseudo-scientific origins? Bringeus (1975) provides an account of Swedish folk beliefs surrounding the boiling of blood sausage. Silence is required during the process for when the lips are sealed the sausage skin will remain sealed also. Traditions which held that the sausage would burst its casing if a stranger came in probably derived rationally from the fact that draughts could blow the fire and cause uneven cooking.

In traditional Appalachian culture non-nutritional uses of food may be classified as

occult or non-occult (Shiffet & Noel 1979).
Non-occult uses mainly take the form of household
remedies in which food is used in a non-nutritional
manner. These remedies are handed down over many
generations - sometimes in writing, but often orally
- and frequently pertain to poultices made of food
and to the use of food in pain relief. The authors
give some examples from their study: ´For fever
"take a grated potato - salt it down heavy and put
it on the forehead". For rheumatism "rub mustard and
beet leaves on the pained part; tie it on with a
cloth".´ Occult uses are usually based on principles
of sympathetic magic: ´To cure yellow jaundice
"break an egg, take the white and put it in a sack
and hang it around the neck. They say the egg white
will turn yellow".´ In a Californian investigation,
Newman (1969) found that the recitation of folk
beliefs to a primiparous woman symbolised her entry
into the new estate of motherhood. Snow and
Johnson´s study in Michigan showed widespread belief
in the efficacy of dietary avoidances during
menstruation. Fruits, vegetables, spices, pickles
and pork were to be avoided as they were ´cold´ or
´too acid´ and could stop the flow and cause
cramping and sterility. Blood is ´hot´, so eating a
cold food whilst blood is flowing might cause it to
clot (Snow and Johnson 1978).

PROHIBITIONS

Table 5.1   Reasons for Food Taboos and Avoidances

Disgust - fear of contamination
Unfamiliarity
Intimate familiarity
Fear of infertility
Condition of flesh - decayed, diseased
Hygiene - health
To restrict slaughter of useful animals
Sympathetic magic
Transmigration of souls
Totemism
Sacredness of animal
Religious sanctions
Cultural identity

Whilst magical thinking leading to the avoidance of
certain items can explain the basis of many food
practices and taboos it is only one of several
factors contributing to varied and elaborate systems
of prohibitions found throughout the world (Table
5.1). A belief basic to all religions, modern or
primitive, is the attribution of a spirit or soul to
living things. This belief is known as animism, and
inherent in it is the worship of some spirit which
is thought to have supernatural power and which may
be either animate or inanimate. The Melanesians
called this power mana, and it could be a source of
both danger and beneficence (Mair 1965). Food is
loaded with power, or mana, which affects its
suitability for consumption by certain individuals
and at particular times of the year. Taboo is a
restriction on human behaviour to avoid contact with
mana. This, according to de Garine (1970), is the
basis of many prohibition systems. The same author
provides us with a schema to classify prohibitions
(Table 5.2).

A taboo is a kind of sacred law which replaces
secular law in maintaining social control (Freidl &
Pfeiffer 1977, p431). It should be carefully
distinguished from avoidance, which is usually based
on empirical common sense. Let us say, for example,
that eating a particular berry always causes
vomiting; after sufficient trials to establish the
cause and effect relation, that berry will be
henceforth avoided; if it is believed that eating
over-ripe bananas during pregnancy causes brown
spots on the skin of the baby, the supposed
relationship is a magic or supernatural one and
leads to the establishment of a taboo. There are
also plenty of examples of ´inverse´ taboos, where
only certain groups of the society are allowed to
consume particular foods. Most permanent taboos and
avoidances have little effect on the nutrition of
the individual practising them. However, temporary
avoidances affect individuals at certain crucial
periods of their life cycles and can have a very
adverse effect. Ogbeide (1974) showed that in
mid-west Nigeria the animal protein intake of
children and of pregnant women was directly and
adversely influenced by food taboos and avoidances.
The temporary food avoidances of pregnant Tamilnad
women are based on a fear of abortion. Papaya, which
because of its shape may symbolise the female beast,
and sesame are commonly avoided (Ferro-Luzzi 1974).
After a woman has given birth there is a 41 day

pollution period during which ´impure´ foods are restricted (See Table 5.3). A similar 40 day laying-in period is prescribed for Malay women, who avoid ´cold´ fruit and vegetables, and ´toxic´ fish (Wilson 1973).

Table 5.2   Classification of food prohibitions

A. According to their length
      (i)   Temporary prohibitions
      (ii) Permament prohibitions

B. According to the size of human group they interest.
      (i)   a number of societies
      (ii)   a total society
      (iii) one of the kinship groups in a given society
      (iv)   a socio-professional group
      (v)   a social class
      (vi)   a masculine or feminine part of the society
      (vii) individuals according to specific individual experiences

C. Temporary Avoidances
      (i)   pregnant and lactating women
      (ii)   infant until weaning
      (iii) baby during weaning
      (iv)   infancy
      (v)   puberty and adolescence
      (vi)   sickness ...material or psychic.

Source: De Garine, I. Maroc. Med. 508: 764-7, 1967

Food avoidances and taboos can have the function of introducing social status differences between individuals and social groupings and of assigning people their place in society. Widespread prohibitions applied to women against the eating of flesh foods may have partly been derived from the male wish to keep the foods for themselves (Trant 1954). Bolton (1972) reports that the aboriginal Orang Asli in West Malaysia taboo many animal proteins - especially to women of child-bearing age and to children. Some foods are thought to contain spirits which may harm those who eat them; other

animals are rejected because they have a special
relationship to man - they are ´kindred spirits´.
Jelliffe and Jelliffe (1978) suggest that the
reservation of the best foods for males reflects the
ancient situation where it was imperative that the
hunters be well fed.

Table 5.3   Food avoidances amongst women of Tamilnad

Food	Avoidance period	Food	Avoidance period
´cold´ foods	C	´hot´ foods	C
meat in general	ABCD	chicken	ACD
chicken eggs	ABCD	sardines	D
crabs	C	cow´s milk	ABCD
butter	ABD	fruits in general	D
all vegetables	C	potato	CD
in quantity		yam	D
rice	CD	millet	A
dhals	ACD	cashew nuts	D
chillies	ABCD	onion	D
pickles in general	A	salt	A

A = puberty: B = menstruation: C = pregnancy:
D = puerperium & lactation

Source: Adapted from Ferro-Luzzi G.E., Food
Avoidances during the puerperium and lactation in
Tamilnad. Ecol.Food & Nutr. 3:7-15, 1974

Flesh Taboos
Most food taboos are of flesh foods and they are
often held with the strongest of convictions. The
Sepoy rebellion of 1857 was sparked by the
insensitiveness of British military officers who
issued rifle cartridges which were greased with pork
and cattle fat to Hindu and Moslem soldiers. The
sepoys would not bite these cartridges as was
necessary to uncap them. Simoons (1961) in a classic
work details the origin and diffusion of flesh
avoidance in the Old and New Worlds. Much of the
information presented here is based on Simoons, and
readers are encouraged to refer to his fascinating
and exhaustive account. Taboos against pork
consumption have already been discussed in Chapter 4

whilst avoidance of beef-eating is treated in detail in the following section on the Sacred Cow. Both of these taboos are relatively well-known; the avoidance of eggs and/or chickens is less well appreciated though it is indeed widespread in the Old World.

Simoons (op cit) suggests that the avoidance arose in the Orient though it is now most common in Africa. Originally, chickens were used for divination purposes and this role was only later usurped by their food potential. Many groups have associated eggs with fertility, childbirth and sex. Simoons quotes Hutton (1921) on the Sema Naga; ´...women must not eat chickens that lay here and there in different places lest they become unfaithful´. Most aboriginal Malays do not eat eggs because of fertility beliefs. Religious beliefs attached to Hinduism and Buddhism have also fostered chicken and egg avoidance. Hindus may have avoided these foods to distinguish themselves from Moslems and from aboriginal tribes, because of their vegetarian beliefs, or because chickens were seen to be unclean. In Buddhist India the prohibition is not strongly adhered to but in Tibet neither eggs nor chickens are widely used. Chickens are viewed as being unclean because of their dietary habits, and eggs are unclean because they come from fowl. Simoons gives numerous examples of egg avoidance in Africa, showing that in some areas breaking of the taboo is merely disapproved of whilst in others it is severely sanctioned. The prohibition is sometimes applied to a whole group, sometimes only to individuals within that group, commonly women of childbearing age. Such restrictions are based on fear of barrenness, lasciviousness or of injury to the unborn child. In the Caribbean it is believed that eggs will make the foetus too big and that the baby will cry like a fowl. Also, because they increase fertility, eggs can cause a child to become pregnant (Hope 1975).

Horseflesh is tabooed not only in most of Europe and the New World but in many parts of the Old World too. Nevertheless, horsemeat was consumed with relish by man in the early post-glacial period. Historically, horseflesh was eaten in northern Europe until the practice was suppressed by the spread of Christianity as described earlier. From a taboo with religious and sentimental connotations there evolved the notion that horsemeat was intrinsically unclean and then unhealthy (Gade

1976). However, the practice never fully died out and there are historical reports indicating that horse-eating continued through the Middle Ages in Ireland, Denmark and Switzerland. In general though it became a low status food and was largely avoided until the eighteenth century when widespread starvation conditions in France spurred a revival in its popularity. Horsemeat was popularised in France and Germany through banquets and specialist butcher shops and it gained a small degree of acceptance in both continental Europe and in Britain. Gade estimates that about one third of modern Frenchmen eat some horse meat, though the practice is largely urban centred and working-class orientated. This author suggests that consumption has probably reached its peak due to a combination of residual social disapproval and cost which limits availability. However, it is one of the few examples of an attitude change from aversion to qualified approval. Simoons comments that even this limited attempt at countering a food prejudice was only possible when religion was no longer involved in the matter (Simoons 1961, p86). As for the Old World situation, in areas such as the Mediterranean Basin, where the horse was a luxury animal, eating those animals was ecologically undesirable. Buddha outlawed the eating of horseflesh, and though Mohammed made no definite pronouncements most modern Moslems do not eat horseflesh. Others in Central Asia continue to do so. In India today, horseflesh is eaten by some lower caste groups and it is quite acceptable to the Ainu of Japan. Argentina is the leading exporter of horsemeat, half of it going to Japan for use in sukiyaki and in sausages (Gade 1976).

Fish avoidance is described in Chapter 4. Pariser & Hammerle (1966) draw attention to the widespread avoidance of fish as food, citing the dangerous nature of fishing, the sacredness of water and the perishability of fish itself as contributing factors. Fish is avoided in much of Asia, Africa and the S.W. United States.

New World Taboos
Much of the literature concerning prohibitions and taboos relates to traditional Old World societies. It is true though, that Western man holds equally irrational ideas regarding what is fit to be eaten. Because a Christian Englishman, say, does not eat insects or dogs or horses he tends to see these

171

practices as being deviant or abhorrent; however, he
will willingly eat the pig flesh which is forcefully
rejected by Moslems and Jews. In his examination of
dog-eating, Simoons sagely remarks that Western
anthropologists rarely comment on dog-flesh
avoidance because it is a prejudice which they
themselves share. Avoidance in this instance is
probably related to ideas of the dog as companion
and friend - the so-called ´rover complex´.
Obviously, no such qualms exist in mainland China.
Heisler (1981, p 48) cites a report from the London
Times of January 3rd, 1980.

> Peking, Jan 3 - A restaurant in Jilin,
> north-east China, was praised by the People´s
> Daily for capitalist-style enterprise in
> ensuring supplies of its most popular item -
> dogmeat. It appealed to people to bring in
> their own dogs to be eaten and it would buy
> them. The result: in under a month it bought
> 1,369 dogs - a year´s supply. - UPI

A valiant attempt to change attitudes toward a food
source was made by the Victorian Englishman, Vincent
M. Holt, who posed the challenge: ´Why not eat
insects?´ (Holt 1885). In building his case Holt
cites biblical precedents (´These ye may eat; the
locust after his kind, and the bald locust after his
kind, and the beetle after his kind, and the
grasshopper after his kind´. Leviticus 11:22) and
historical evidence of other races enjoying insects.

> We pride ourselves upon our imitation of the
> Greeks and Romans in their arts; we treasure
> their dead languages; why not then take a
> useful hint from their tables? We imitate the
> savage nations in their use of numberless
> drugs, spices and condiments; why not go a step
> further?
> (Holt 1885, p47)

Mr. Holt praises the virtues of insects as food not
only because he sees them as tasty delicacies (much
better than raw oysters and scavenging unclean
lobsters) but because they also offer a solution to
food shortages in England. He even provides recipes
- such as this one for grasshoppers, which he says
is based on a Moroccan locust recipe. ´Having
plucked off their heads, legs and wings, sprinkle
them with pepper and salt and chopped parsley; fry

in butter and add some vinegar.´ Finally, he
suggests menus which ´if unnaturally crowded with
insect items, serve as an illustration of what is
possible´ (Table 5.4).

Table 5.4   An insectivorous menu

Slug soup
Boiled cod with snail sauce

Wasp grubs fried in the comb
Moths sauteed in butter
Braized beef with caterpillars
New carrots with wireworm sauce

Gooseberry cream with sawflies
Devilled chafer grubs
Stag beetle larvae on toast

Source: Holt, V. Why not eat Insects? Classey, 1885

FOOD, SEX AND SYMBOLISM

Traditionally, hunger is seen as a basic drive for
survival of the individual whilst sex is a basic
drive for survival of the species. It might be
expected that there could be found some parallels
and interactions between these fundamental
activities. There are indeed some similarities
between food and sexual taboos. In a Thai village
ideas about proper human relations are pinned to
rules about the edibility of animals. Great
grandchildren may not intermarry; buffaloes reared
under the roof should not be sacrificed on behalf of
a member of the same house. Livestock and women are
not to be ´consumed´ at home but are reared for
exchange (Lindenbaum 1976, p141). The Massa of
Cameroon have rituals which allow an immigrant to
consume the food products of the community in which
he has established himself. As soon as he is
assimilated in this respect he develops a strong
avoidance towards getting married within the group
which has adopted him (de Garine 1976, p156).
Amongst the Kandya of Sri Lanka, cooking food for a
man and eating the food he provides, signifies
marriage (Yalman 1971). The woman who cooks a man´s
food is his sexual partner even though eating, as

173

well as many other activities, is done mostly apart.
Bleibtrau (1973) says there are masculine and
feminine foods. Meat may symbolise masculinity,
whilst salads are definitely feminine. Women are
expected to eat small dainty portions; men can tuck
into substantial helpings of heavy foods. Colour
supplements and best selling books telling us what
'real' men do or do not eat indicate that this is a
'real' phenomenon in contemporary Northern
societies. Cultural emphasis on body image
reinforces these sex-differentiated eating
practices. Females are supposed to be slender; young
men muscular. The dieting behaviour of young women
in particular reflects a concern with appearance
which far outweighs any consideration of health
(Fieldhouse 1981). Bruch's work on eating disorders
explores the role of psychosexual problems in the
aetiology of anorexia nervosa, a topic which is
considered further in Chapter 6 (Bruch 1974).

Food and sex may also be related through
symbolism. As an example, some of the many meanings
and uses of eggs in various cultures are briefly
described below. Eggs have commonly represented
fertility and fecundity in many cultures throughout
the world. The modern children's custom of hunting
for chocolate Easter eggs is itself a remnant of
fertility rites (Leach 1950). In seventeenth century
France a bride, on entering her new home, broke an
egg to assure her fecundity. In Morocco an egg is
used in magic rites or in medicine to encourage
female fecundity and male virility. Amongst the
Tamilnad too, eggs are recommended for their
strengthening and fertility increasing powers
(Ferro-Luzzi 1974). Bride and groom exchange eggs
after the wedding ceremony in Iran, and there is a
Chinese custom of feeding eggs to a new mother to
ensure that her fecundity continues. Eggs as a
symbol of life-to-come may have led to their
widespread use for divination purposes. The
symbolism of eggs in the Eastern Orthodox religion
was discussed in Chapter 4.

Eggs are not the only foods with symbolic
meanings. Bread is commonly referred to as 'the
staff of life'. Bread was broken because cutting it
represented the sacrificing of life; to break bread
with another symbolises trust, and of course,
breaking bread is an intrinsic part of the act of
Christian Communion (Hodgson 1977, Loeb 1951). Many
authors have pointed out that because food possesses
extensive symbolic values, nutritionists need to be

aware of potential social ramifications of changing
food supplies and dietary habits.

TABOOS - TWO EXAMPLES

The rest of this chapter is devoted to examination
of two prominent food prohibitions. The case of the
Sacred Cow of Hinduism is illustrative of a complex
interaction of religious and philosophical belief
with environmental pressures giving rise to a
prohibition which elevates the tabooed animal to a
symbol of an entire way of life. The account of
cannibalism shows how a practise universally reviled
as a mark of barbarism is continued on a symbolic
level and how even the most strongly sanctioned
prohibitions may be relaxed when human survival is
threatened.

The Sacred Cow
Earlier in this chapter it was suggested that
permanent avoidances had little effect on the
nutritional status of the group practising them.
Nutrition educators concerned with cross-cultural
studies have frequently commented that traditional
practices should not be interfered with unless they
are overwhelmingly negative in their effects. The
case of India's Sacred Cow provokes an intense
debate between interventionists and laissez-faire
nutritionists. India has an estimated 180 million
cattle - approximately one third of the total world
population (Lodrick 1981). The slaughter of these
beasts for human food is generally forbidden. Whilst
people starve to death cattle wander freely about
the streets untouched, and yet, in 1966, 120,000
people demonstrated in front of Indian Houses of
Parliament in support of the All-Party Cow
Protection Campaign Committee.

In India the cow is an especially revered
animal; it is a symbol of motherhood and fertility.
Cow calendars, carvings and posters attest to its
symbolic representation of health and abundance.
Prayers are offered for cows that are sick, and
garlands are hung around their necks on festival
days. Respect for cows has been incorporated in the
guiding principles of the constitution of India. The
1950 Constitution contains a section under the
'Directives of State Policy' which provides
guidelines for dealing with cow slaughter. However,
these guidelines are vaguely worded and there is no
national ban as such, the matter being left to

175

individual States - in some of which slaughter has
indeed been made illegal and subject to heavy
penalties. Groups opposed to the ban include
Moslems, who see butchering of cows as part of their
constitutional right to make a living, and
Communists; as well as economists who see that the
love of ´mother cow´ is slowly strangling the
country. Devout Hindus will touch a passing cow and
then touch their own foreheads; feeding cows brings
great merit. Cows wander at will through villages
and towns; they are often old and infirm. There are
even government run homes for aged cows. With his
usual political astuteness, Mahatma Gandhi used the
cow as a symbol around which he could rally his
people. Vinoba Bhave - spiritual heir to Gandhi -
went on hunger strike in 1979 in support of a
national ban on cow slaughter. Prime Minister Desai
had to provide an assurance that the government
would push for the ban before Bhave would break his
five-day old strike (Lodrick 1981).
    The taboo is often cited as the supreme example
of irrationality, and there is an ongoing debate as
to whether it is fundamentally ideological or
utilitarian in origin and effect. Does it have an
overall negative or dysfunctional impact on Indian
society or is it in fact a functionally positive
belief? Brown (1957) presents a widely accepted
account of the origins of cow sanctity. He says that
there are five contributing factors:

* role of the cow in Vedic ritual
* literal interpretation of words for cow used
  figuratively in Veda
* Vedic prohibitions against doing harm to
  Brahmans´ cows
* the ahimsa concept
* association of the cow with the Mother Goddess
  cult.

Alternative explanations have been proposed which
draw on political and economic factors. Countering
the impact of Buddhism and Islam is one such
suggested reason; an attempt on the part of rising
urban states to keep more animals for their own use
is another theory, proposed By Diener, Nonini &
Robkin (1978) - who favour a similar explanation for
the Moslem prohibition on pork. (See Chapter 4). A
detailed analysis of the cow in the Rigveda is
provided by Srinivasan, a pupil of Brown´s, who
comments that references to the cow appear nearly

700 times in the hymns. She points out that the cow is mentioned in ritual and mythological contexts far more often than in relation to economics (Srinivasan 1979). Thus, the first explanation usually offered for the taboo is the religious one.

The cow was created by Brahma on the same day as were the Brahmins and so is to be venerated above all others. ´All that kill cows rot in hell for as many years as there are hairs on the body of the cow ´ say the early scriptures. However, the earliest Vedas, the Hindu sacred texts from the second millenium B.C., do not prohibit the slaughter of cattle but instead ordain it as a part of sacrificial rites (Harris 1978). Amongst the Aryans who invaded North-West India about 1500 B.C. cattle were a general expression for wealth. A high value was placed upon the cow due to its many uses in providing food, drink, fuel and leather - as well as being a draught animal (Srinivasan 1979). Early Hindus ate the flesh of cows at ceremonial feasts presided over by Brahmin priests who acted, in a sense, as agents of the new Aryan overlords. Harris (1977) speculates that with growth in population it would have become increasingly difficult for the priests to provide sufficient meat for all at redistributive feasts. Therefore meat-eating was gradually restricted to become the privilege of a select group - the Brahmins themselves. Buddhism and Jainism may have arisen partly as protests against such an elitist system. Later, Hinduism was to adopt some of the reforms which had made Buddhism politically successful, and thus the Brahmins gradually came to see it as their sacred duty to prevent the slaughter and consumption of domestic animals (Harris 1977). Indeed the later Vedas began to contain contradictory passages, some permitting, some tabooing the slaughter of cattle. Bose suggests that many sacred cow passages were added by later priests.

Even in 250 B.C. when he made Buddhism the state religion King Asoka did not outrightly forbid the killing of cows; but by the beginning of the Christian era a ban on cow slaughter had become widespread. The Code of Manu prescribed penances for the slaughter of cattle, and by about the seventh century the situation was essentially the modern one (Simoons 1961). Thus cow worship is a relatively recent development evolving with changes in religious ideas. The rise of Islam may also have helped to entrench cow sanctity as a mark of

religious separateness. Some non-Hindu groups
continued to eat beef and today slaughter of cows by
Moslems is still a source of friction between
religous groups, though many Moslems and Sikhs forgo
beef in deference to their Hindu neighbours. At the
same time, some low caste Hindus do eat beef despite
the social stigma attached to that action. (For a
fuller discussion of the origins of the taboo see
Simoons 1961.)

An alternative view of the development of the
taboo is advanced by cultural ecologists foremost
amongst whom is Marvin Harris. The cultural ecology
thesis suggests that practices which are maladaptive
do not flourish. Therefore it follows that the
introduction of the cow prohibition must have had
some rational function. Farb and Armelagos (1980)
point to a population increase in India two
centuries ago which necessitated massive cultivation
of land to provide food. Subsequent deforestation
and erosion had fatal consequences; droughts became
commonplace and domestic animals became harder to
maintain. Only those domestic animals which were
essential could be allowed to share the diminishing
amount of available land, and cows were essential as
a source of traction animals for working the land.
Farmers who maintained their cows during times of
natural disasters survived, whilst those who ate
their cows lost their tools of production. Over the
centuries more and more farmers avoided eating their
cows until an unwritten taboo came into existence.
Only later was the taboo codified by the priesthood.
Thus religious sanctions forbade the villagers to
kill the cattle which were needed for other purposes
than as a supply of meat (Harris 1965, 1977).

Harris developed this line of argument to fit
in with his functional ecology theories. It is
criticised by Simoons (1979) and by Diener & Robkin
(1978). Simoons argues that the environmental
degradation was man-induced through overgrazing; he
says it does not make sense that farmers would ban
slaughter and thus increase cattle numbers and
thereby intensify pressures on the environment. He
also cites evidence from early literature which
indicates that cow sanctity was imposed from above
and not evolved by the farmers themselves. Simoons
also criticises Harris for ignoring or dismissing
religio-political factors. For example, Harris
claims that the concept of ahimsa has positive
functions in that it confers material rewards;
whereas Simoons points out that ahimsa operates in

circumstances where there is no possibility of
material reward.

The cultural ecologists press their case by
referring to the importance of the cow in modern
Indian economy. With deforestation in India, dung
has become an important source of fuel. Cow dung is
a good fuel as it burns slowly and cleanly, and
allows for food to be cooked whilst the family is in
the fields. From 40 to 70 per cent of all manure
produced by Indian cattle is used as fuel for
cooking. The rest is returned to the fields as
fertiliser, forestalling the need for expensive
chemical fertilisers. The energy equivalent of the
dung used for cooking fuel is estimated at 43
million tons of coal, and is an important saving on
foreign exchange needed for other sources of fuel.
The National Council of Applied Economic Research
report that over 25 per cent of all energy used in
rural India comes from dung (India 1965). More
important even than this is the draught function.
Oxen are still needed in huge numbers for farm work,
and of course cows are needed to produce these work
animals. 'What makes the cow essential to the Indian
farmer, therefore, is not the need for meat or milk
or for an object of veneration, but as the only
source for producing oxen ' (Farb & Armelagos 1980,
p121). During the dry season cows may become barren,
so the temptation to sacrifice them becomes greater.
The prohibition against beef eating is thus a kind
of insurance that farmers will not slaughter their
cattle during this difficult time and that the
agricultural system will recover when the rains come
(Harris 1974, 1978). Local governments maintain
homes for barren cows; farmers reclaim, with a small
fine, any cow that has calves or begins to lactate.
Thus Harris and Farb both argue that ownership of
cows is crucial to the well-being of rural peasants,
for a farmer who loses a cow loses everything.
Sharing of oxen is not practicable - because of
seasonality and monsoons everyone needs them at the
same time - and so every farmer ideally needs his
own team. On this basis it is possible to calculate
that there are too few rather than too many cattle
in India.

Although cows provide less than half the milk
produced in India - most of them are not dairy
breeds - their products, milk, curd, butter, dung
and urine are regarded as having purifying
properties. But despite its sacredness the cow is
not treated particularly well by most Indians. Cows

are left to scavenge whilst limited food will go to
the oxen (though the cows will not be allowed to
die). When they are sick they are worried over like
sick children; decrepit beasts may just recover,
whilst those that die from natural causes are in
fact eaten by lower caste Hindus. Thus even after
death, cows continue to be useful (Harris 1978).
Whilst high caste Hindus revile the lower caste
beef-eaters, the latter do get access to protein
sources which supplement their largely vegetarian
diet. The hide of the cow is also used in the
extensive leather trade - again plied by the lower
caste Hindus. Even the bones may be processed for
fertiliser. Given this economic usefulness, it may
be thought that a better breed of cow could be
introduced. Western agronomists claim that breeding
programmes could produce stronger, healthier beasts
capable of better work and of producing more milk.
But the land that this would require is needed to
produce food for people. In the U.S huge amounts of
arable land are used to grow food for cattle and the
energy inputs are enormous, whereas in India the
cattle basically consume what is inedible for
humans. By being allowed to wander freely, cows can
scavenge, thus relieving the pressure on human food
supplies. Also the Zebu cattle have adapted to their
erratic climate; they can survive drought and are
highly resistant to diseases. Like camels, they
store water and food in their humps. An economic
observer points out that 17 per cent of the energy
consumed by zebus is returned in the form of milk,
traction and dung. American cattle raised on Western
style ranges return only 4 per cent (Odend´hal
1972).
     Some Indian authorities agree with received
Western opinion that the refusal to kill ´useless´
cattle is inimical to the wellbeing of the people.
These beasts consume or destroy food which could be
used for feeding people. The Supreme Court of India
took the position that the sacred cow concept was
detrimental to Indian life and well-being, noting
that more money was spent per capita to maintain an
old cow than to educate a child (Simoons 1976).
Harris commments that Indians do adjust their
religious restrictions to accomodate ecological
realities. This is in line with the theory of
prohibitions arising as products of ecological
necessity. Cows cannot be killed - but they are
tethered and left to starve; they cannot be
slaughtered - but they are sold to Moslems, who will

slaughter them. A study of the sex ratios of cattle
in different parts of the country reveals marked
differences which implies that some culling does
take place. Famine in the drought-stricken area of
Bihar in the 1960s led some Hindus to break the
taboo, as happened also in Bengal during the Second
World War (Harris 1974, p21). Harris argues that
with an appreciation of the economic importance of
the cow we can see that the taboo is not irrational
and ignorant.

> Practices and beliefs can be rational or
> irrational, but a society that fails to adapt
> to its environment is doomed to extinction.
> Only those societies that draw the necessities
> of life from their surroundings without
> destroying those surrounding, inherit the
> earth.
> (Harris 1978)

Harris' cultural ecology approach, then, views
the cow complex as being the outcome of positive
functioned adaptations to ecological and
technological conditions rather than to the negative
influence of religious concepts. It is a cultural
mechanism to ensure that economic resources are
protected. His rejection of the social and religious
aspects of cow keeping, however, weaken his thesis,
for such functions have been amply demonstrated by
other scholars. Lodrick, for example, emphasises the
central role of the ahimsa concept in Jaina and
Hindu philosophy and the effect this has on
attitudes to the sanctity of life (Lodrick 1981).
Cow preservation is an intrinsic part of religious
values. After a close study of goshalas and
pinjrapoles (animal homes), Lodrick concludes that
they are primarily religious institutions and cannot
be justified in purely economic terms. Upkeep of old
and infirm cows costs more than any potential
returns in the form of hides or dung. In addition,
fodder used for decrepit cattle is not then
available for healthy productive beasts; this
situation is exacerbated during periods of shortage,
when animal homes can outbid local farmers for
supplies of fodder (Lodrick, op cit). In any case,
the economic role of animal houses in providing
milk, dung and hides did not really develop until
the population explosion of the twentieth century
placed increased demands on agricultural resources,
thus confirming the primary religious nature of the

institution.

Max Weber noted that economic development was impeded in India because of the effects of Hinduism and the ´traditional and anti-rational nature of the caste system´ (Weber 1958). He believed that the values of Hinduism acted as a retarding force in economic development. Several modern writers agree that Hinduism is on the whole a negative force on economic behaviour - even if it has had value in the past. Lodrick is able to cite Kapp (1963) as an example of this line of thought:

> It can hardly be doubted that Hindu culture and Hindu social organisation are determining forces in India´s slow rate of development. It is not only the lack of capital resources or skilled manpower which impedes the processs of economic growth but non-secular and pre-technological institutions and values such as the hierarchically-organised caste system, the limited or static levels of aspirations, moral aloofness, casteism and factionalism - to name only a few of the major barriers.

Others, however, are not convinced of this explanation and point to the irrationality of many Northern practices which are also rooted in cultural bias and which have not prevented economic development in that part of the world. Harris points out that we have the ´sacred dog´ and the ´sacred car´ in our own society. Sahlins (1976) discussed the American clothing system in similar terms. If irrationality is a barrier to material economic development then why are we in the North able and willing to divert so much of our resources into feeding pets? Lodrick concludes that instead of asking how Hindu beliefs have interfered with economic progress, we should instead ask what impact these beliefs have had on cultural evolution and what role they have in future social and economic change. For we are dealing in a cultural context which emphasises values other than efficiency and material gain.

Cannibalism
Cannibalism is a term used to describe the eating of humans, or parts of them, by other humans. It is derived from ´Carib´, the name of a West Indian tribe, mispronounced by Spanish explorers as Canib. Anthropophagy or ´man eating´ is the term used by

anthropologists though, of course, the practice
existed long before the coining of the word.
Columbus reported that New World natives ate their
prisoners; brutish rumours steadily grew and were
embellished by later explorers and missionaries.
Hogg (1961) presents a survey of anecdotal evidence
collected by early travellers. The halting of this
´barbarous practice´ was often used as an excuse by
would-be conquistadors to subdue native peoples. In
expressing their pious horror they conveniently
overlooked the fact that cannibalism was rife in
Europe in the early Middle Ages and there is some
justification in the suspicion that their
accusations against native groups were sometimes
fabricated as excuses for invasion. It reflected a
not-uncommon historical pattern where unpopular or
minority groups were frequently accused of deviant
behaviours. The Romans accused Christians of
cannibalism; the Christians so accused the
Non-Conformists. In the sixteenth and seventeenth
centuries it was the turn of the witches to become
the scapegoats of righteousness.

Two forms of cannibalism are defined which are
motivated by quite different concerns; exogamy -
eating one´s enemies and endogamy - eating one´s
friends. Endocannibalism has always been the rarer
of the two - being practised by some South American
tribes, and in New Guinea. Though members of the
same tribe would not generally be killed for food,
when they died through natural causes or accident
the eating of their bodies was part of normal
funeral rites and was done with reverence and
affection. New Guinean cannibals ate relatives and
enemies with no distinction though there were
certain restrictions in force. A woman did not eat
her own children and a man did not eat his
parents-in-law, and vice versa; a husband did not
eat his deceased wife though she would have no
qualms in eating him; a man would not eat his
grandchildren, but he was entitled to a piece of
flesh of a deceased nephew or niece. When a child
died the mother usually sent word to her brother who
could come to her husband´s village and obtain meat
from the body (Farb & Armelagos 1980, p137). In
contrast, the Jale of New Guinea believed that
´people whose face is known must not be eaten ´
(Koch 1970). When outsiders were killed passions of
aggression and revenge were involved. The corpses of
enemies were frequently sexually abused and used for
venting hostility. By eating one´s enemy one could

take possession of his life essence and vitality, and through this act cannibalism could fulfil the desire for total vengeance (Sagan 1974).

Levi-Strauss, in the development of his culinary triangle theory, suggested that methods of cooking reflected social structure. Boiled foods were everyday foods whilst roasted foods were more prestigious and were served to guests. With regards to cannibalism he claimed that in endocannibalism the victim would be boiled, whilst in exocannibalism roasting would be used. This claim was completely refuted by the studies of Shankman (1969) who found that only 6 out of 60 societies boiled their victims exclusively, whilst only 17 boiled at all. Both roasting and boiling were used irrespective of the source of human flesh, thus strongly disconfirming Levi-Strauss´ hypothesis.

Motives for Anthropophagy
Anthropologists have ascribed several possible functions to the practice of cannibalism. These are not necessarily mutually exclusive though one or other may have been dominant in a given society at a particular period of history. Religious, magical and dietetical motivations are interwoven in the explanations offered.

Dietary Source of Protein. The nutritional value of cannibalism is a favourite theory used to lend rational weight to the practice, the claim being made that it provided at least a partial answer to the problem of scarce animal protein supplies. Tannahill remarks that people-eating can never have been a regular dietary feature for prehistoric man as there would not have been a sufficient population to provide meat (Tannahill 1976, p7). Nevertheless, there is some evidence that hunter-gatherers had to supplement diet with human flesh. With the advent of settled cultivation food supplies became more reliable and human flesh was reserved for solemn ceremonial occasions. As settlements grew, the practical ban on eating family (they were needed for working the land) had to be extended to a wider network. Reinforced by evolving ideas of law and religion, a climate of opinion was created which was opposed to casual eating of human flesh (Op cit, p18).

Walens and Wagner (1971) support the idea that human flesh contributed other nutrients besides protein to the diet of primitive man and was a

valuable emergency supply of meat. On the other
hand, Garn and Block (1970) dismiss the nutritional
importance of cannibalism, saying that while it
might usefully supplement a one-cereal diet, the
numbers of bodies needed would be too great for it
to be major source of food. They calculated that one
body would provide daily 9g. protein servings to
about 60 people for a week, and that a group would
have to be willing to consume the equivalent of its
own number in a year. Farb and Armelagos (1980)
claim that for tribes in New Guinea human flesh
provided a major source of animal protein - perhaps
10 to 35% of their needs. Following the success of
the Australian government in eradicating the
practice of anthropophagy, animal meat must now be
imported into New Guinea to make up the deficiency.
    Cannibalism has been observed to have certain
negative physiological consequences. The condition
known as Kuru was first observed by Australians when
they entered villages of the Fore tribe in New
Guinea in the 1950s. The Fore word ´kuru´ signifies
trembling, and describes accurately the loss of
co-ordination characteristic of this degenerative
disease. The victim is eventually unable to stand;
death results from an inability to eat, from
pneumonia or even simply from rolling into the fire
(Farb and Armelagos 1980, p138). About 1400 deaths
were recorded between 1957 and 1964. It was found to
be rare in adult males, who did not practice
cannibalism, and with the subsequent decrease of
cannibalism kuru also decreased in incidence. The
disease was eventually found to be caused by a virus
with a long incubation period which was spread
through the eating of brain tissue.

Taste. Apparently a number of peoples ate their
brethren simply because they enjoyed the taste,
which is reputed to be similar to pork. Perhaps this
is more properly seen as ´an added bonus´ where the
primary purpose was usually ritual or practical in
nature. In Western Australia there was an aboriginal
tribe which ate every tenth baby born to keep the
population from expanding beyond the capacity of the
territory to provide sustenance (Tannahill 1976,
p8). Population control was also at least a
by-product of Aztec practices, according to Harner
(1977). Where a practice becomes perceived to be a
utilitarian necessity it is not surprising that it
also comes to be enjoyed for its own sake.

<u>Vengeance.</u> Tannahill says that Caribs practised cannibalism purely from vengeance motives. They did not need human bodies as dietary supplements for animal proteins were plentiful. Koch´s account of the Jale tribe of New Guinea reveals their obsession with revenge and warfare. The victims bought back by raiders were steam cooked in a ground oven; special rituals were enacted to prevent retribution and the body was then butchered and cooked. The meat was given mostly to the family of the person whose death has been avenged by the killing. Afterwards, more rituals were performed, this time to banish the victim´s ghost. Koch adds that there was no religious connotation to the practice; it was purely one of vengeance and a wish to eat tasty meat (Koch 1970). A modern example of the desire for total vengeance and scorn occurred as recently as 1977, when a member of the Black September organisation responsible for assassinating Mr Wasfi Tal, Prime Minister of Jordan, said: ´I am satisfied now. I drank from Tal´s blood´. Witnesses confirmed that this was a literal statement (Tannahill 1976, p9).

<u>Ritual.</u> Amongst several groups who practised cannibalism there was a belief that by swallowing the dead one could reabsorb the power or life essence that would otherwise be lost. A tribe could thereby retain the skills of members who had died or could take possession of an enemy´s vitality. Sometimes this supernatural function was combined with a gastronomic one, as with the Panoans of South America who:

> regarded eating the flesh of relatives as a duty, in order to banish the spirit of the deceased, preventing it from reoccupying the body. But some Panoans also roasted the dead body like a piece of game, drinking the blood like wine, and even hastening the death of the old and sick so they could be eaten while some nutrition was left.
> (Farb & Armelagos, p136)

New Guineans did not practise ritual cannibalism in order to absorb power or to kill the enemy´s spirit, but they did believe human flesh to have magical qualities, particularly in increasing fertility. For example, flesh might be placed in trees to encourage the garden to grow, a practice reminiscent of other sacrificial and fertility rites.

Macabre. In the twentieth century, examples of
cannibalistic practices sometimes come to light most
often as a response to stressful situations,
although sometimes explainable only as psychological
aberrations. There was, for instance, the case of
Fritz Haarmann - the so-called ´Hanover Vampire´ -
who, in 1924, was found guilty of biting to death at
least twenty seven people and converting them into
sausage meat (Tannahill 1976, p170). A psychiatrist,
Friedman, concluded from his case studies that some
individuals practising true or intermittant
vegetarianism did so because of oral impulses which,
if satisfied, would have been cannibalistic in
nature (Friedman 1975).

Cannabalism in History
It is fairly easy to show that cannibalism has been
practised by different peoples for different reasons
throughout recorded history. There is, in addition,
early evidence of prehistoric practices of
anthropophagy. The charred bone fragments of human
beings discovered at a Neanderthal site in
Yugoslavia suggest that cannibalism had been
practised. In Choukoutien cave were found roasted
Homo Erectus skulls, smashed at the base ´presumably
to enable the cave occupants to remove and eat the
brains´ Williams (1973). During the early centuries
of human civilisation the idea of cannibalism
gradually came to be thought of as largely
impractical and somewhat reprehensible morally. But
it was not until the second century B.C. when
visions of Heaven and Hell, and of damnation and
salvation, emerged that the view prevailed that man
needed his body after death. This effectively placed
a taboo on anthropophagy amongst Jews and, later,
Christians which has no real parallel in the other
great religions of the world. Although most
societies condemn murder only Jews and Christians
are fundamentally dedicated to the proposition that
eating people is worse than murder (Tannahill 1976,
p34).
    It was to take more than the rise of a powerful
religious movement to halt the reviled practice.
(Indeed, the Christian Church itself was to endorse
a form of cannibalism with the propounding of the
Doctrine of Transubstantiation.) Adverse
circumstances bought about through war, famine or
drought led desperate people to turn to cannibalism
as a means of survival during the Dark Ages of

Medieval Europe. Tannahill´s exhaustive account of
the ´cannibal complex´ describes harsh conditions
and widespread famine in the first thousand years of
the Christian era. Tales of cannibalism are drawn
from histories of the Crusades; of the Tartars,
Chinese, and Europeans; as well as from Greek
legend. Tannahill also includes a long account by
Abd al-Latif, of an Egyptian famine of 1201 A.D.,
which gives a harrowing recital of cannibalistic
practices.

Aztec Sacrifice
The fact that the Aztecs sacrificed thousands of
victims, some of whom were undoubtedly eaten,
contradicts the view that cannibalism was
essentially a trait of primitive civilisations. The
Spanish conquistadors were appalled at the savagery
and scale of the Aztec sacrifices. Farb and
Armelagos (1980) quote a sixteenth century
eye-witness report from Bernal Diaz. After the
victims hearts had been cut out and offered to the
Gods: ´The feet, arms and legs of the victims were
cut off and eaten, just as we eat beef from the
butcher´s in our country´. Three of the four limbs
became the property of the warrior who had captured
the prisoner, and with them he gave a feast of human
stew.
    Resorting to a cultural ecological approach,
Farb explains that the Aztecs suffered severe
famines and shortages of animal protein as cattle,
sheep and pigs had never been domesticated and wild
animals were overhunted. Human flesh was therefore a
necessary protein supplement (although there is
evidence that a protein-rich alga was commonly
consumed as part of the diet). Farb supports his
functionalist theories by pointing out that bravery
in combat was the means by which an Aztec could
attain status and power. Warriors received certain
privileges - including the eating of human flesh -
and they and their families were therefore better
off nutritionally. This provided an incentive for
others to become warriors and thus the numbers of
victims inexorably increased.
    Like the Spanish invaders four centuries
before, the cultural ecologists seem to have assumed
that the purpose of Aztec sacrifice was gastronomic
and to have largely ignored its primary religious
purpose. The Aztecs believed that the sun had been
created by the self-sacrifice of the Gods and was
thus born in sacrifice and blood. In order to ensure

that it continued to rise each day and thus preserve
the world from the monsters of the twilight who has
destroyed four previous worlds, it was necessary to
sustain the sun with continuing sacrifices of blood
(Tannahill 1976, p82). This author comments that:
´Aztec sacrifice was an extreme form of "substitute
theophagy". Kings were often seen as earthly
incarnations of the Gods responsible for the
country´s well-being. They were expected to
sacrifice themselves before their powers waned.
Being reluctant to do this they substituted the
blood of thousands of lesser men for their own
lives´. Prisoners-of-war, slaves and youths and
maidens specifically chosen to impersonate the Gods
and Goddesses were offered on the sacrificial
altars.
    Animal sacrifice did not, as it did elsewhere,
replace human sacrifice for there was not a ready
supply of suitable animals. Hogg (1961) comments
that the Aztecs practised cannibalism because the
consumption of human flesh had come to be a small
[!] but integral part of an elaborate system of
sacrificial ceremonial that was aimed primarily at
propitiating the Gods. Outside of ritual sacrifice,
the Aztecs did not consume human flesh. Harris
(1977) insists that ritual slaughter was geared to
the production and redistributon of substantial
amounts of animal protein in the form of human
flesh, and that political control was maintained by
rewarding warriors with concentrated packages of
meat. The eventual decline of the practice has been
ascribed to the realisation that the eating of one´s
prisoners was a waste of potential manpower. The
very need for prisoners perpetuates war with
neighbouring states creating a chaotic and
unpredictable situation not commensurate with empire
building. In the case of the Aztecs, systematic
slaughter by the Spanish invaders may also have had
something to with it.

Modern Anthropophagy
In modern times incidents of cannibalism have
usually been connected with questions of survival.
In conditions of severe hardship survival becomes an
overall priority, and when the only hope of survival
lies in anthropophagy the practice is generally
sanctioned. The bitter retreat of Napoleon´s army
from Moscow; the famines which swept the Ukraine in
the thirties and forties; the Siege of Leningrad
during the Second World War; all provide examples of

humans overcoming their revulsions and breaking the
taboo. In the late nineteenth century the pioneering
Donner party, who were caught in a snow storm in the
Sierra Nevada mountains, kept half their number
alive to see California through the expediency of
cannibalism. Nikita Khruschev recalled an incident
from the Ukrainian famine of 1947 which left a
lasting impression on his mind.

> The woman had a corpse of her own child on the
> table and was cutting it up. She was chattering
> away as she worked. "We´ve already eaten
> Marechka (little Maria). Now we´ll salt down
> Vanechka (little Ivan). This will keep us for
> some time." Can you imagine? This woman had
> gone crazy with hunger and butchered her own
> children!
> (Kruschev 1970)

A celebrated case in 1972 involved the crash of an
aeroplane in the Andes, whereby members of the
Uruguayan rugby team were stranded for over ten
weeks. This incident is fully described in Piers
Paul Read´s book, ´Alive´ (Read 1974). Following the
rescue of the Uruguayans from their ordeal there
were of course many questions to be asked. Faced
with a press conference in Montevideo the survivors
were unsure as to how to tackle the topic of
cannibalism - the means by which they had endured.
In the end, their spokeman made a speech in which he
claimed that their actions had been inspired by the
fact that Jesus had shared His flesh and blood at
the Last Supper and that eating of the dead had
represented an intimate communion between them all.
Whilst some people thought that the men should have
chosen to die, the Roman Catholic Church supported
their action, saying that in a matter of survival
there was no sin in incorporating the substance of
another in one´s own flesh. On the other hand the
idea that a kind of communion had occurred was
rejected by the theologians.
    In the same year, 1972, a Canadian Arctic
pilot, Martin Hartwell, ate the flesh of a dead
nurse when his plane crashed in the wastes of the
Northwest Territories (Tannahill 1976, p177). In
1979, another plane accident led Brent Dyer and
Donna Johnson of Saskatchewan, to eat parts of their
dead father´s body.
    Taboo is usually acknowledged to fulfil some
function - whether it is religious, social, economic

or ecological - and whether or not it is perceived
as being effective or useful. However, there is a
continuing debate between those who claim that
cannibalism is a natural practice and that aversion
to it has been culturally learned, and those who say
there is an instinctive repugnance to it so that it
is only practised in circumstances of dire need.
Whichever viewpoint is taken it is true to say that
anthropophagy, once widespread, has largely
disappeared from the face of the earth. Hogg
confirms that true cannibalism, motivated by ritual
and sacrifice, is rarely practised now; but he does
cite as an extant example the brutish initiation
ceremonies of the Mau Mau of East Africa (Hogg 1961,
p206). Whilst reviling ritualised cannibalism,
society has normally regarded it as being acceptable
when performed through necessity of survival.

SUMMARY

There is no society where people are permitted to
eat everything, everywhere, with everyone and in all
situations (Cohen 1968). Prohibitions vary in
cultural importance and hence in the vigour with
which they are enforced. Persons breaking cultural
taboos are liable to some sort of punishment ranging
from disapproval, scorn, a fine, ostracism or
prison, to death (Gifft, Washbon & Harrison 1972,
p11). The more severe sanctions are reserved for
breaking of taboos involving flesh foods. Usually,
compulsion is not necessary to maintain dietary
taboos. 'Most individuals feel more secure when they
are conforming to the standards of their own
cultural system, which they view as being superior
to all other...more rational, more logical, more
practical, more noble.' (Op cit).
   Sometimes the reasons why particular foods are
circumscribed are obvious pragmatic ones related to
questions of availability or of potential danger. In
many cases though the rationale for food
prohibitions, taboos and superstitions is far from
clear and it is easy then to make the assumption
that no good rationale ever existed. Historical
analysis of taboos such as that of the Sacred Cow
reveal the error of making these kind of
assumptions. There is a tendency for us to want to
explain every phenomenenon in terms acceptable to
objective science and because of this we often
impose our own materialistic interpretations on
cultural behaviours which defy our notions of

191

commonsense. It is difficult of course, when looking
in on a culture from the outside, to understand the
practices of that culture, and so much more
difficult to comprehend the value of those practices
in the context of an earlier epoch. To compound the
difficulty, we find that often earlier practices
have been adopted and adapted by subsequent
generations and invested with new meanings. If we
look merely at the current manifestation of a given
prohibition we see only a snapshot in time; taken
out of the context of the entire album it is not
surprising that that snapshot is incomplete and thus
often misleading. In saying this, I am arguing the
merits of the culture-history approach to
anthropology outlined in Chapter 1, and so ably
expoused by Frederick Simoons.

Perhaps though, instead of trying to choose
between religious or ecological, political, health
or economic explanations for taboos and prohibitions
we should recognise that each of these have had
their part to play in the gradual evolution of the
food practices we see today. Thus we can acknowledge
that even seemingly irrational practices are
cultural products, and that dietary change is
inseparable from cultural change.

REFERENCES

Bleibtrau, H.K. ´An Anthropologist Views the
    Nutrition Profession.´ J. Nutr. Ed. , 5:11,
    1973
Bolton, J.M. ´Food Taboos Among The Orang Asli in
    West Malaysia: A Potential Nutritional Hazard.´
    Am. J. Clin. Nutr. , 25:789-799, 1972
Bose, A.N. Social and Rural Economy of Northern
    India 600 B.C. - 200 A.D. Firma K.L.
    Mukhopadhyay, Calcutta 1961
Bringeus, N.A. ´Food and Folk Beliefs: On Boiling
    Blood Sausage.´ In. M. Arnott (ed.),
    Gastronomy: the Anthropology of Food and Food
    Habits. Mouton Publ., The Hague 1975
Brown, W.N. ´The Sanctity of the Cow in Hinduism.´
    The Madras University Journal , 28:29-49, 1957.
    (Cited in Lodrick 1981.)
Bruch, H. Eating Disorders. Obesity, Anorexia
    Nervosa and the Person Within. Routledge &
    Kegan Paul, London 1974
Cassel, J. ´Social and Cultural Implications of Food
    and Food Habits.´ Am. J. Publ. Hlth. ,
    47:732-740, 1957

Cohen, Y.A. 'Food Consumption Patterns.' In Sills
    (ed.), International Encyclopedia of the
    Social Sciences. Vol. 5. pp508-13. MacMillan
    Co. & The Free Press, 1968
Concise Oxford Dictionary. 6th Ed. Clarendon Pr.,
    Oxford 1976
de Garine, I.L. 'Aspects Socio-culturals des
    Comportements Alimentaires. Essai de
    Classification des Interdits Alimentaires.'
    Maroc. Med. , 508: 764-773, 1967 (Cited in de
    Garine 1970).
de Garine, I.L. 'The Social and Cultural Background
    of Food Habits in Developing Countries
    (Traditional Societies).' In G. Blix (ed.),
    Symposium on Food Cultism and Nutritional
    Quackery , Swedish Nutr. Found., Almqvist &
    Wiksells, Uppsala 1970
de Garine, I.L. 'Food, Tradition and Prestige.' In
    D.N. Walcher, N. Kretchmer and H.L. Barnett
    (eds.), Food, Man and Society. Plenum Pr.,
    New York 1976
Diener, P., D. Nonini and E.E. Robkin. 'The
    Dialectics of the Sacred Cow: Ecological
    Adaptation vs. Political Appropriation in the
    Origins of India's Cattle Complex.'
    Dialectical Anthropology , 3:221-241, 1978
Farb, P.& G. Armelagos. Consuming Passions: The
    Anthropology of Eating. Houghton Mifflin,
    Boston 1980
Ferro-Luzzi, G.E. 'Food Avoidances at Puberty and
    Menstruation in Tamilnad.' Ecol. Food & Nutr.
    2:165-172, 1973
Ferro-Luzzi, G.E. 'Food Avoidances of Pregnant Women
    in Tamilnad.' Ecol. Food & Nutr. , 2:259-266,
    1973
Ferro-Luzzi, G.E. 'Food Avoidances During the
    Puerperium and Lactation in Tamilnad.' Ecol.
    Food & Nutr. , 3:7-15, 1974
Fieldhouse, P. 'Slimming Beliefs of Adolescent
    Girls', Paper presented to the Canadian
    Dietetic Association, Vancouver 1981
Freidl, J. and J.E. Pfeiffer. Anthropology: The
    Study of People. Harper's College Pr., New
    York 1977
Friedman, S. 'On Vegetarianism.' J. Am. Psychoanal.
    Assn. , 23:396-406, 1975
Gade, D.W. 'Horsemeat as Human Food in France.'
    Ecol. Food & Nutr. , 5:1-11, 1976

Garn, S.M. and W.D. Block. ´The Limited Nutritional Value of Cannibalism.´ Am. Anthrop. , 72:106, 1970

Gifft, H.H., M.B. Washbon and G.G. Harrison. Nutrition, Behaviour and Change. Prentice Hall, New Jersey 1972

Harner, M. ´The Ecological Basis for Aztec Sacrifice.´ Am. Ethnol. , 4:117-135, 1977

Harris, M. ´The Myth of the Sacred Cow.´ In Leeds & Vadya (eds.), Man, Culture and Animals. Am. Ass. for the Advancement of Sci., Publ. No 78, Washington D.C. 1965

Harris, M. Cows, Pigs, Wars and Witches. Random House, New York 1974

Harris, M. Cannibals and Kings. Random House New York 1977

Harris, M. ´India´s Sacred Cow.´ Human Nature , 1(2):28-36, 1978

Heisler, C.B. Jr. Seed to Civilisation. 2nd ed. W.H.Freeman & Co., San Francisco 1981

Hodgson, P.A. ´The Many Faces of Food - As Seen Through the Eyes of the Artist.´ J. Am. Diet. Ass. , 71:248-252, 1977

Hogg, G. Cannibalism and Human Sacrifice. Pan Books, London 1961

Holt, V.M. Why Not Eat Insects? E.W.Classey Ltd., Middx. 1885 (reprinted 1969)

Hope, M. ´Food Taboos and Nutrition in the Caribbean.´ Cajanus , 8:190-193, 1975

Hutton, J.H. The Sema Nagas. Macmillan, London 1921

India (Republic). Domestic Fuel Consumption in Rural India. Nat. Coun. App. Ec. Res., New Delhi 1965

Jelliffe, D.B., and E.F.P. Jelliffe. ´Food Habits and Taboos: How Have They Protected Man in His Evolution?´ Prog. Human Nutr. , 2:67-76, 1978

Kapp, K.W. Hindu Culture, Economic Development and Economic Planning. Asia Publ. House, Bombay 1963

Khruschev, N. Khruschev Remembers. Little, Brown & Co., Boston 1970

Koch, K.F. ´Cannibalistic Revenge in Jale Warfare.´ Natural History , Feb., 1970

Leach, M. (ed.), Standard Dictionary of Folklore. Funk & Wagnalls, New York 1950

Levi-Strauss, C. The Raw and the Cooked. Harper & Row, New York 1969

Lindenbaum, S. 'The Last Course: Nutrition and
    Anthropology in Asia.' In T.K. Fitzgerald
    (ed.), Nutrition and Anthropology in Action.
    van Gorcum, Amsterdam 1977
Lodrick, D.O. Sacred Cows, Sacred Places.
    University of California Pr., Berkeley 1981
Loeb, M.B. 'The Social Functions of Food Habits.'
    J. Appl. Nutr. , 4:227-429, 1951
Malinowski B. Sex, Culture and Myth. Harcourt
    Brace & World, New York 1962
Newman, L.F. 'Folklore of Pregnancy: Wive's Tales in
    Contra Costa County, California.' West.
    Folklore , 28:112-135, 1969
Odend'hal, S. 'Gross Energetic Efficiency of Indian
    Cattle in Their Environment.' J. Human Ecol. ,
    1:1-27, 1972
Ogbeide, O. 'Nutritional Hazards of Food Taboos and
    Preferences in Mid West Nigeria.' Am. J. Clin.
    Nutr. , 27:213-216, 1974
Pariser, E.R. and O.A. Hammerle. 'Some Cultural and
    Economic Limitations on the Use of Fish as
    Food.' Food Tech. , 20(5):61-64, 1966
Pumpian-Mindlin, E. 'The Meaning of Food.' J. Am.
    Diet. Ass. , 30:576-580, 1954
Pyke, M. 'The Development of Food Myths.' In G. Blix
    (ed.), Symposium on Food Cultism and
    Nutritional Quackery. Swedish Nutr. Found.,
    Almqvist & Wiksells, Uppsala 1970
Read, P.P. Alive. J.P. Lippincott Co., New York
    1974
Sagan, E. Human Aggression and Cultural Form.
    Harper & Row, New York 1974
Sahlins, M. Culture and Practical Reason.
    University of Chicago Pr., Chicago 1976
Shankman, P. 'Le Roti et Le Bouille: Levi-Strauss'
    Theory of Cannibalism.' Am. Anthrop. ,
    71:54-69, 1969
Shifflet, P.A. 'Folklore and Food Habits.' J. Am.
    Diet. Ass. , 68:347-50, 1976
Shifflet, P.A. and Noel. 1979

Simoons, F.J. Eat Not This Flesh. University of
    Wisconsin Pr., Madison 1961
Simoons, F.J. 'Geographic Perspectives on Man's Food
    Quest.' In D.N. Walcher, N. Kretchmer and H.L.
    Barnett (eds.), Food, Man and Society. Plenum
    Pr., New York 1976
Simoons, F.J. 'Questions in the Sacred Cow
    Controversy.' Current Anthropology ,
    20:467-493, 1979

Snow, L.F. and S.M. Johnson. ´Folklore, Food, Female Reproductive Cycle.´ Ecol. Food & Nutr. , 7:41-49, 1978

Srinivasan, D. Concept of Cow in the Rigveda. Motilal Banarsidass, Delhi 1979

Strodtbeck, F.L. Malnutrition, Learning and Behaviour. MIT Pr., Cambridge Mass. 1968

Tannahill, R. Flesh and Blood. Sphere Books, London 1976

Trant, H. ´Food Taboos in East Africa.´ Lancet , 2:703-705, 1954

Walens, S. and R. Wagner. ´Pigs, Proteins and People-eaters.´ Am. Anthrop. , 73:269-270, 1971

Weber, M. The Religion of India: The sociology of Hinduism and Buddhism. Free Pr., New York 1958

Williams, B.J. Evolution and Human Origins: An Introduction to Physical Anthropology. Harper, New York 1973

Wilson, C.S. ´Food Taboos of Childbirth: The Malay example.´ Ecol. Food & Nutr. , 2:267-74, 1973

Wodehouse, P.G. Very Good, Jeeves! Penguin, Middx. 1957 (Reprinted 1978)

Yalman, N. Under the Bo Tree: Studies in Caste, Kinship and Marriage in the Interior of Ceylon. University of Calif. Pr., Berkeley 1967

Young, J.H. ´Historical Aspects of Food Cultism and Nutrition Quackery.´ In G. Blix (ed.), Symposium on Food Cultism and Nutritional Quackery. Swedish Nutr. Found., Almqvist & Wiksells, Uppsala 1970

Chapter 6

PSYCHOLOGICAL ASPECTS OF FOOD CHOICE

We have already seen that people eat not only to
meet physiological needs but also in response to
social needs and pressures. To these we can now add
the third dimension of psychological needs. Hunger
and appetite are intimately connected to emotional
needs. Emotional sensations such as yearning,
craving, and compulsion give rise to patterns of
eating behaviour which are gauged to relieve anxiety
or tension, to provide security and comfort, or to
provoke anger and frustration in others. Emotional
responses to food develop early in childhood and are
long-lasting; indeed, an infant´s earliest
pleasurable associations are with food, for rooting
and sucking reflexes which are associated with
food-getting provide emotional contentment as well
as physical nourishment. Feeding relieves unpleasant
hunger pangs and produces feelings of well-being and
satiety; thus babies quickly learn to equate eating
with comfort. Food gratification is important in
shaping an infant´s future attitudes to food and
sharing, and the foundations for healthy eating
habits may be laid by provision of positive food
experiences early in life.
     Thus the biological necessity to eat is readily
turned into a highly emotionalised activity. Food
not only sustains the corporeal man but also elicits
feelings of pleasure and emotional gratification or,
in other circumstances, of anxiety and guilt.
Because food is rich in symbolic meanings the act of
eating can also be a way of expressing or reflecting
emotions; furthermore, because the meanings are
largely internalised, this is often done without
conscious deliberate decision. Foods acquire
particular associations through the circumstances in
which they are commonly offered or eaten; for
example, children quickly learn that sweetness

equals love. When a new food is tasted it evokes an
emotional response along the attraction/repulsion
continuum which will influence its immediate and
future acceptability. The nature of a foodstuff -
its sweetness or bitterness for example - gives rise
to physical sensations of pleasure or pain by direct
sensory stimulation. Later recall of these
sensations also contributes to the ultimate
labelling of a food as being pleasant or unpleasant.
Such judgements regarding acceptability may be made
merely from the look or smell of the food or even
from pictures and photographs; actual consumption is
not essential in order for pleasant or unpleasant
associations to be made. Repeated experiences with a
food fix its position in the constellation of
feelings; thereafter, that food has the power to
provoke emotional responses through the recall of
particular or accumulated experiences of it.

Eckstein (1980) suggests that historically, due
largely to the influence of religion and its
teachings regarding self discipline and temptation,
people were more aware of these responses to food,
but that now they are rarely conscious of emotions
elicited by food contacts. Nevertheless, that such
associations are made is uncontestable. Eckstein
examines the large number of words in the English
language which have meanings that can be applied to
foods, showing how attitudes and feeling are
expressed through the use of food words.

Figure 6.1   Food Metaphors

        Sweetheart
        Sourpuss
        Apple of my eye
        Peaches and cream complexion
        Bad egg
        Cool as a cucumber
        (Hot as) mustard
        Cheesed off
        Salt of the earth

The primary tastes - sweet, bitter, sour and salty
- are all used to describe personalities or
temperaments; sweet has positive connotations whilst
bitter and sour have definite negative connotations;
salty is a less commonly used descriptor and its
associations are not as obvious, though in some

parts of Britain it denotes wit. Some common food
metaphors and phrases are listed in Figure 6.1.

FOOD AND EMOTIONS

There was once an advertisement on British TV which
depicted a family at the breakfast table. Although
everyone else was smiling and happy, the teenage
daughter moodily pushed her bowl of cereal aside,
untouched, whilst the voice-over pronounced: ´Susan?
Well, Susan´s in love.´ This vignette of family life
exemplified certain emotional uses and meanings of
food in order to sell a product; happiness and
laughter were associated with consumption of the
product whilst a touch of humour was added by
recognising the effect of ´love´ on teenage eating
behaviour. It is perhaps useful to note that eating
behaviour can be used actively, to express a
particular feeling or state of mind, or passively as
a reflection of an emotional state. In the first
instance the behaviour is usually quite deliberate
and its effect is calculated; in the latter case it
is a subconscious response to internal needs.

Boredom
Eating may be used as a way to avoid or to stave off
boredom especially, it seems, by adolescent girls.
When there is ´nothing to do´ the refrigerator
beckons and the larder stocks seem to take on a
peculiar attraction. Food may be picked at or eaten
in quantity, not because of hunger or appetite but
simply for the sake of keeping occupied. Perhaps
related to this is the idea of eating as a
displacement activity. When studying gets just too
tedious for words the answer is to make a cup of tea
or a sandwich; when the lecturer drones on and on,
or the car journey seems interminable, a packet of
mints quickly disappears.

Loneliness
An emotionally insecure person may eat as a
substitute activity for seeking love and affection.
The idea that ´nobody loves me´ leads naturally to
the thought that ´it doesn´t matter what I look
like´. If nobody cares what does it matter if
appearance suffers; hence whole cakes and chocolate
bars are consumed yet hardly tasted. Repetitive
behaviour of this kind triggers off feelings of
guilt which in turn produces conditioned food
responses. Eating can be a way to ward off

199

depression, of cheering oneself up after a bad
experience or a hard day. Often too, alcohol fulfils
this function. Food and drink relieve frustration by
substituting for desired love or affection. Butler
(1968) comments that old people capture symbolically
through food, the rewarding and nurturing
experiences of earlier life.

Anxiety

Anxiety also leads to compensatory eating for
comfort. Changed patterns of eating by students
during exam week are related to anxiety and have
both physical and emotional components. Butterfly
stomachs leading to reduced appetite make large
meals seeem unappealing, so that commonly, sweet
high-calorie chocolate bars and soft drinks are
substituted as they are more readily digestable. The
emotional associations of these foods also connote
comfort and reassurance. Adolescents often use food
to restore emotional balance after a crisis; food
provides transitory gratification until life settles
down again. Chronic anxiety or depression may lead
to obsession with a problem and food is then eaten
compulsively. Whatever is chosen is defined as good
because it leads to immediate gratification and the
food retains this association even when the problem
or crisis no longer exists. This type of behaviour
can contribute to eating disorders such as obesity.

An example from another culture - that of the
Gurage people of Ethiopia - illustrates connections
between food and anxiety. During early milk feeding
and weaning Gurage children are exposed to a pattern
of alternating glut and want; this, combined with
the emotional detachment shown by parents toward
their children, may explain the extreme anxiety
exhibited by adults toward their food supply (Farb
1980, p377).

Guilt

The hardships of therapeutic diets may sometimes
produce guilt reactions which are ultimately
counter-productive. A large proportion of would-be
slimmers cheat on their diets. Usually the cheating
is clandestine and is not readily admitted to; the
dieter continues to protest to not understanding why
there is no weight loss and maintains that he or she
is following the diet faithfully. Guilty feelings
over such deception may lead to identification of
the ´forbidden´ sweets and treats as ´good´ and
´desirable´, and thereby their consumption is

justified. In another type of therapeutic situation a mother may feel guilty at depriving her diet-bound child of a favourite food and in an effort to compensate puts the whole family on the diet.

Guilt feelings may be related to a failure to adhere to parental expectations. Immigrant Jewish mothers in New York in the 1930s implored their children to eat and become fat as they reasoned that fat children would not get tuberculosis. These children, as adults, then felt guilty if they did not overeat (Bruch 1974).

Food is sometimes offered as a gift to assuage guilt. Thus a box of chocolates is offered to redress a wrongdoing; food parcels substitute for personal visits; ice-cream treats follow childhood chastisements. Is it possible to see in the fruit basket brought to the bedside of the sick an element of guilt, analogous to the guilt felt by survivors towards those who die?

Weapons and crutches
Food can be used as an emotional weapon by children who quickly learn to wield the power gained from unco-operative eating behaviour. Not-eating is a certain way of getting attention; by being overly fussy a child may learn to expect a reward as a bribe for desired behaviour. Food wars are a source of ill-feelings, anger and frustration. To the child they represent attempts to achieve control of the environment; the thwarting of his wishes confirms the dominance of adults and builds a sense of impotence and dependence. To the adult, the child´s rejection of food symbolises rejection of love and of parental authority. By not eating what he is told is ´good for you´ the child questions the adult´s competency and knowledge of ´what is best´. Adolescents too can show defiance and assert independence by rejecting previously accepted foods.

The authors of a major book on food and behaviour sum up the emotional importance of food in the following passage.

Adults too frequently use food as an emotional outlet - a crutch to help them handle and to live with anxiety, tension, frustration, unhappiness, irritability, disappointment, loneliness or boredom. No human can escape such emotions as these and thus he must find ways to cope with them. Using food as a compensation

201

mechanism to help one get rid of these emotions
or accept their inevitability and learn to live
with them may seem a bit ridiculous at first
glance - but consider the alternatives. Few
people are self-disciplined enough to make no
alteration in their behaviour when under
emotional stress except to keep an unusually
stiff upper lip. Thus they resort to some kind
of protective mechanism. They drink or take
drugs; they whine or complain to elicit
sympathy; they take it out on someone else by
being cross or disagreeable; they wallow in
self-pity. Compared to these destructive
mechanisms, altering one's eating patterns
would seem to be fairly innocuous.
(Gifft, Washbon and Harrison 1972, p38)

WEIGHT DISTURBANCES

The point made above is an interesting one to keep
in mind when discussing the concept of poor eating
habits. All too often only physical parameters and
consequences are used to judge the value and
desirability of eating habits. This is certainly
almost always the case with the current medical
opinion on being overweight. Although the
considerable effort which is devoted to treatment
and prevention of obesity is predicated largely on
the desirability of preventing physical health
problems, it is at least partly a reflection of
current norms of slimness in society. In other
cultures, and at other times when obesity has been
positively valued, such rigorous efforts have been
absent. For many people who face the daily ordeal of
diet and exercise health is merely an acceptable
by-product of a fashionable body image rather than
an end in itself. Whatever the motivation though,
the maintainance of a body weight which conforms to
fairly narrowly defined limits is generally seen to
be desirable. Inappropriate food choices may lead in
the long term to physiological body states which are
considered to be abnormal. Obesity and anorexia
nervosa are conditions which result from, or lead
to, food consumption patterns which are divorced
from actual physiological need. It is not within the
scope of this book to extensively discuss either of
these conditions but it is perhaps worth noting that
psychological mechanisms, some of which have been
already alluded to, play an integral part in the
genesis or maintenance of abnormal body weight. The

short discussion which follows identifies some
common themes.

Obesity
The aetiology of obesity is complex and, despite
extensive research studies and experimentation, is
only poorly understood. Explanations commonly
offered range from the deterministic role of
genetics, through social expectation theories, to
psychological responses to personal needs.
Deterministic theories, which view obesity as being
a product of genetic inheritance and biochemical
make-up (eg. the brown fat theory) tend to induce a
fatalistic attitude whereby obese persons see
themselves as the hapless, and helpless, victims of
body chemistry. Such an outlook not only destroys
feelings of personal control but also provides a
ready-made excuse for failure in weight control
efforts. At the other end of the spectrum, obesity
is conceived of as a deliberately chosen condition
to be used psychologically as a means of defence in
a hostile world. Susie Orbach represents the latter
view; claiming that fat is a feminist issue she
interprets obesity in women as a kind of defence
mechanism. Fat females are not pestered by men; they
are not objects of aggressive sexual attention
(Orbach 1980). Other authors have commented that
obesity can be used as a way to avoid the stresses
of adult sexuality, particularly when it arises
during the turbulent years of adolescence (Crisp
1977, Lacey 1978).
     Hilde Bruch suggests that there are two
distinct types of obesity which have psychological
components: developmental and reactive (Bruch 1974).
Developmental obesity stems from childhood and is
associated with many other personality disturbances.
Lacey comments that patients seen in obesity
clinics, who have developmental origins to their
obesity, are almost exclusively female and
demonstrate high levels of anxiety, depression,
social avoidance and somatic complaints as well as
often declaring reduced interest in sexual activity
(Lacey 1978). Reactive obesity occurs in more mature
individuals as a response to some traumatic event in
their lives, for example, a family bereavement.
Bruch says that obesity can have important positive
functions; for many people it is a compensatory
mechanism in a frustrating and stressful life.
     Most commonly though, obesity is viewed as
being a negative trait. There is no doubt that the

cultural norm of slimness is so entrenched that for
many, deviation from this norm provokes feelings of
guilt, unworthiness or rejection. By creating a
strict stereotype of cultural acceptability we also
create discontent and anxiety amongst those who do
not fall within its narrow limits. Consequently,
thousands of people devote substantial time, money
and effort to achieve and maintain an ´acceptable´
weight. Their behaviour is reinforced by a medical
establishment which emphasises the negative health
consequences of obesity and which chides overweight
patients for lack of willpower and self-control.
Paradoxically, our consumer-oriented society is
constantly providing us with messages telling us to
eat; we are exhorted to consume - but are punished
for consuming. And still the answer to our problem
is not to consume less - but more, of a myriad magic
potions and slimming aids.

The motivation necessary for an obese
individual to successfully lose weight must be
provided by internal rather than external stimuli.
Relaxation of the cultural demand for slimness would
allow individuals to determine if they truly wished
to lose weight or if they were in fact more
psychologically, and perhaps even physically,
comfortable at a higher weight. It would also, by
the way, largely wipe out an entire sector of
commercial food marketing.

Anorexia Nervosa
Anorexia Nervosa is an extreme example of the
potential effect of psychological disturbances on
eating behaviour. Although it has long been known
and there are a number of historical accounts of the
condition, Anorexia Nervosa has been reported with
greatly increased frequency over the past decade.
This may reflect a real increase in incidence - some
would relate it to the stressfulness of modern life
- or it may be the result of more accurate diagnosis
and better documentation and reporting procedures.
There is also some evidence, to judge by articles in
the popular press, that it has gained the status of
being a ´fashionable´ ailment.

Although the results of anorexia nervosa are
manifested as extreme inanition and emaciation, and
are thus of vital concern to nutritionists, the
aetiology of the disorder is rooted in psychological
disturbances. Most common amongst adolescent
females, primary anorexia nervosa is interpreted as
a struggle for self-identity; non-eating and the

subsequent drastic weight loss are late features of
the disorder and are only secondary to underlying
personality conflicts. Bruch (1974), in her seminal
work on the subject, identified three areas of
disturbed psychological functions. The first of
these concerns delusions regarding body image.
Anorexics deny the abnormality of their emaciated
state believing that their extreme thinness is
desirable and normal, and they thus reject the need
to eat. (This contrasts with a second group who
recognise the undesirability of their physical
condition but feel powerless to do anything about
it.) Anorexics become very knowledgeable about the
energy value of foods and are careful not to eat
anything which might increase their weight. They
resort to strategies such as lying, concealment of
food, and self-induced vomiting to avoid food
consumption and subsequent weight gain. The second
disturbance is manifested as distorted perception or
interpretation of internal body stimuli. Thus hunger
pains are denied and there is a failure to recognise
physiological need for food. Subsequently there are
changes in food preferences, tastes, eating habits
and manners (Bruch 1974); in addition, anorexics
exhibit hyperactivity and denial of fatigue.
Thirdly, there is an overwhelming sense of
incompetence and ineffectiveness; anorexics perceive
themselves as being reactive rather than proactive.
    Some of common elements which emerge in case
history studies of anorexics indicate that they
often are well-educated and come from middle-class
homes; as children they are responsible and
dependable, and parental expectations of them are
high. Perfectionist attitudes and a desire to please
are common, resulting in a subordination of self.
Control is exercised by a dominant and
overprotective mother, producing excessive
dependency and unquestioning obedience. Anorexia
nervosa may then be seen as an act of parental
defiance; it is a way of asserting control over
one's own body and thus over one's own life. Bruch
gives central importance to this struggle for
control. There is also a psycho-sexual element in
the anorexic's behaviour which can be interpreted as
a rejection of adult womanhood. Severe loss of
weight results in amenorrhoea and retardation in
development of secondary sex characteristics. By
retaining a childlike figure the anorexic denies
adult sexuality - which is challenging and a threat
to maintenance of self-control.

Anorexia nervosa is an alarming condition because of the associated mortality rate if treatment is not successful. Although probably the majority of adolescent girls try to ´slim´ at some time or other they are not at risk of becoming anorexic unless they have a previous history of psychological conflict. The dangers of slimming in response to peer pressures may thus be somewhat exaggerated. However, Bruch adds a note of caution:

> It may be objected that Anorexia nervosa is a rare disease. This is true: but for every youngster who declines to the woeful state of cachexia, there are dozens, if not hundreds who waste their efforts and energies in trying to be thinner and slimmer than is natural for their body build or compatible with a healthy effective life. Our whole society is so preoccupied with slimness that there is a need to draw attention to the fact that many can achieve it only at a great sacrifice to health and competence.
> (Bruch 1974, p384)

FOOD AND PSYCHOLOGICAL SECURITY

In examining Maslow´s hierarchy of human needs it was earlier noted that food security followed basic survival as the next rung on the upward ladder of need-achievement. Security implies a lack of anxiety over where the next meal is coming from. Maslow (1970) pointed out the need for an infant to have an undisrupted routine for proper emotional growth; thus regular meals are necessary for a happy child. Early lack of security may give rise to fussiness and eating difficulties in later life (Babcock 1948). It has even been suggested that the antisocial behaviour of hungry slum children is largely due to lack of satisfaction of this basic need for regular pleasurable feeding experiences (Lowenberg et al 1982, p129). Food is one of the major gratifications one receives on entering the world. It relieves bodily discomfort and provides comforting body contact. A mother´s treatment of the feeding process, be it relaxed, fidgety or fearful will determine the infant´s first impressions of the world. The anthropologist, Margaret Mead, has said:

> It is possible to associate a background of generous, ungrudging child feeding with an

206

adult´s emotional security regarding food
whereby he can go for a long time without.
Conversely, a child who experiences a rigidly
austere or very meagre diet throughout infancy
may have a conditioning which produces the same
adult strength.
(Mead 1953)

In times of crisis, familiar foods are highly
valued. Certain foods commonly represent comfort and
security. Milk - being the universal first food of
humans - often takes on this role, and people have
strong emotional attitudes to milk (Pumpian-Mindlin
1954) (Cussler & DeGive 1952). Harriet Bruce Moore
(1952) talks of: ´the unhappy, suffering, far from
home and loved ones, soldier [who] looks back to
milk as in many ways expressing the comfort security
and contentedness of life as it was at home´. For
other groups, different foods symbolise this
security. In the last century early missionaries to
Hawaii waited impatiently for sailing vessels to
arrive from their native Massachusetts, bringing
more supplies of their familiar wheat flour and salt
pork. After a six month trip around the Horn the
flour was often weevily and the pork rancid...but it
was consumed with relish whilst the Heathenish diet
of Taro, fresh fruit and fish eaten by native
Hawiians was rejected (Gifft, Washbon & Harrison
1969, p39). Familiarity often makes a food more
acceptable and sought after.Perhaps historically,
familiarity served as a protective device to guard
against poisoning with unfamiliar substances,
though, as we shall see, variety in the diet could
only be obtained by experimenting with unfamiliar
foods. Young children much prefer familiar foods
when they are in strange surroundings. Immigrants
use familiar foods as a means of feeling secure and
not losing their identity in a foreign land. Often
they set up food stores to import items from the
homeland, and are willing to pay high prices for
these familiar symbols of home. Whilst changes in
language and clothing may come fairly readily, food
habits change slowly, if at all.

Hoarding
After survival needs have been met, ensuring
security of food supply is an important human
activity. Hoarding behaviour is a reflection of
anxiety about security of the future food supply.
Shack (1971) in his account of the Gurage of

Ethiopa, refers to their hoarding of the food crop, ensete, during times of plenty. This, he suggests, is in response to their memories of fear during times of shortage and is a reflection of food insecurity. Similar hoarding behaviour has been observed in other societies which have a glut and famine existence. Food is stored against potential disaster and to this extent it is an adaptive behaviour, though when carried to excess it has negative repercussions.

The typically excessive storage of food by modern Europeans and Americans, which is usually done for overt reasons of cost-effectiveness and convenience, may contain an element of security-anxiety. Certainly when food shortages threaten people are easily panicked into buying and hoarding commodities. For example, a sugar shortage in Britain in the 1970s resulted in thousands of perfectly normal and reasonable housewives fighting openly in supermarkets to obtain the limited supplies available. Staff were abused for rationing what was available, and generally people acted with complete lack of consideration for the needs of others. This kind of reaction to shortages may occur even when the shortage is imaginary or overplayed by reporting in the mass media. Film footage in news reports provides visible evidence that a product is not readily available and thus increases the panic demand even further. It is not unknown for food corporations to withhold supplies for short periods in an attempt to deliberately induce panic buying. Certainly, it is common practice for powerful corporations to withhold staple commodities from the market until the price is judged to be right. (For examples of this phenomenon see Susan George (1976) - particularly the section entitled ´Planned Scarcity´. Also, Don Mitchell (1975) provides examples of the manipulation of food supply and prices in a Canadian context.)

Overfeeding of children may be in some instances a security response by parents who have themselves experienced food shortages. They are determined that their children will not suffer the same privations. The concept of obesity as a form of personal hoarding may sound strange - but we know that overeating is often linked to feelings of unhappinesss and anxiety, and is a source of comfort and solace. Cohen (1961) comments that in a society where the young are not fed on demand, adults will tend to hoard food and wealth. Early food

gratification creates an emotional predisposition to
share food. Food symbolises social interactions and
serves to meet the psychological need for
interchange. Weinberg (1972) sees hoarding by the
elderly as an attempt to hold on to things
previously shared in intimacy with others, through
the symbolism of food.

Stress and Food Selection
Animals under conditions of stress may substitute
one instinctual behaviour for another. Similarly, it
is possible that humans utilise eating as an
alternative response to fight or flight when
threatened (Hamilton & Whitney 1982, p225).
Emotional stress generates production of the same
hormones as does physical stress; this results in
fuel being made available to the body which, if not
used, is turned into fat. Lowered blood glucose
levels signal hunger, and food is eaten to relieve
this feeling. Emotional stress may have marked
effects on biological parameters of nutrition.
Everson (1960) cites the example of three young
single pregnant women, two of whom were emotionally
upset and the other who was emotionally secure. The
first two exhibited negative calcium balances whilst
the third maintained normal mineral levels. Other
examples of such physiological effects can be found
in the literature. Scrimshaw (1969) discusses at
length some of the interactions of stress and
nutrition.
       Dieting may itself be a source of stress.
Attempts to maintain a lower body weight and the
constant worry over gaining a pound or two results
in anxiety and tension and a lessened ability to
cope emotionally. Increased irritability as a
side-effect of dieting is familiar to all those who
have suffered the martyrdom of family or friends who
decide to ´slim down´. Any change in eating
patterns, in that it upsets familiar practices,
produces at least some emotional tension. Where the
change is imposed or made in response to external
motivators, the resulting stress will be greater
than when changes are made deliberately to meet
personal goals.

Personality and Food Choice
The stereotype of the fat jolly person is a
persistent one, and it lends popular credence to the
idea that personality is somehow related to food
consumption. If one were to investigate the basis

for the stereotype it might be found that fat people assume jolliness as a defence or as a social integration mechanisation; or it may be that people who are jolly indulge in more social eating events and therefore tend to become fat. Alternatively, study may reveal that there is really no basis for the stereotype after all. The effect of personality on food behaviour, or vice versa, has not been well studied. Murray and Watson (1978) used the Eysenck Personality Inventory to investigate food preferences of introverts and extroverts. They found that introverts had significantly more food dislikes than did extroverts. There was no relationship found between neuroticism and food dislikes, though other studies have reported an association of neuroticism with thinness. Thinness is also associated with schizophrenia, and Crisp & Stonehill (1976) have reported a relationship between thinness and sadness or tension states. Whilst fatness may be linked to lower levels of anxiety and depression, there is little evidence of clear relationships between obesity and psychiatric status (Lacey 1978).

I have suggested elsewhere that internal versus external locus of control may affect a mother´s choice of infant feeding method (Fieldhouse 1984). A mother with external locus of control will be more responsive to the normative influences of family, friends and community, and thus in a non-supportive culture will be less likely to breast feed than to bottle feed. Personal preference overrides normative influences in mothers with strong internal loci of control, who tend to do what they think is best rather than what they think is most acceptable to society. It is reasonable to speculate that creativity and self-actualisation in food selection and preparation is related to locus of control - though the hypothesis remains to be tested.

Food may be used as a way of demonstrating mood either through the care taken over food preparation or by the refusal to eat food prepared by others. The latter behaviour is an obvious sign of anger or annoyance. Older children will sometimes refuse previously liked foods as a means of regaining the attention they feel has been usurped by the arrival of a younger sibling. In adolescence and in adulthood food choice can be a reflection of one´s self image; conformity or individualism can be displayed through eating behaviour. As previously noted, the consumption of ´health foods´ or the practice of vegetarianism may be expressions of

210

certain values regarding the world. Back (1976)
comments that because the reaction to the hunger
drive is so visible in its effects it is bound to
have some social significance in assignment of
identity to an individual. Advertisers play on this
social need by encouraging identification with a
product or particular brand. What you buy and what
you eat tells others that you are discerning,
thrifty or extravagant, modern or old-fashioned. In
this way food choice becomes a manifestation of
personality.

FOOD PREFERENCES

> However, this bottle was not marked ´poison´,
> so Alice ventured to taste it, and, finding it
> very nice (it had, in fact, a sort of mixed
> flavour of cherry-tart, custard, pine-apple,
> roast turkey, toffy, and hot buttered toast),
> she very soon finished it off.
> (Alice in Wonderland)

Food preferences function as a means of assessing
the acceptability of foods, preference implying a
degree of like or dislike. Dickens (1965) identified
several factors as being determinants of food
preferences. These were itemised as: (1) cultural –
certain combinations of food ´go together´; (2)
social – other people´s influence; (3) personal –
older people are more habit-bound; (4) situational –
income. Such a view of food preferences would
indicate that they are conditioned responses to what
is available or expected. Preference though implies
an expressed choice rather than merely a willingness
to eat a food, and preferences may indeed differ
from actual consumption patterns. Foods may be
accepted even though they are not preferred – for
reasons of availability, cost or social courtesy.
When our favourite fruit – fresh strawberries – are
out of season, we buy frozen ones or choose
different fruits; when prime cuts of meat cost more
than the wallet can bear we settle for chops or
stew; when our new-found friends invite us to dinner
and serve up lasagna, we don´t admit that we loathe
pasta, but take the smallest portion and comment on
how nice it is (at the same time politely but firmly
declining second helpings). The rarity with which
people bother to enquire about specific food
dislikes of others suggests that either they see
their own tastes as reflecting majority tastes or

that they are more concerned with what the dish says
about themselves than with their guest's pleasure.
(On numerous occasions I have been expected to enjoy
elaborate meat dishes when no-one had the foresight
to ascertain that I was a vegetarian.)

It is sometimes argued that the body knows what
is good for it, and that given a free choice, humans
would automatically select nutritionally adequate
diets. To test this idea in conditions where
cultural learning was minimal, Davis (1928, 1939)
experimented with allowing newly weaned infants to
choose their own diets from a selection of offered
foods. He found that definite preferences were shown
which changed unpredictably from time to time;
appetite was the guiding factor and the diets
consumed were nutritionally adequate - but probably
only because the selection of nutritious foods
offered made it difficult for this not to happen.
There are of course ethical problems with this type
of study, but it is unlikely that, given a
completely free choice of foods, an infant would
select a nutritionally adequate diet; the role of
the family in providing suitable food experiences is
therefore paramount.

Dickens suggested that food preferences are
largely determined in early life by culturally
determined patterns in which foods are consumed in
specific combinations. Undoubtedly, many preferences
are developed in childhood years and reflect
experiences and associations made largely within the
sphere of influence of the family. Bass, Wakefield
and Kolassa (1979) review studies on food likes and
dislikes amongst various American groups, including
schoolchildren, students, armed forces and general
public. Vegetables commonly figured amongst the
least liked foods, whilst meat and desserts were
generally liked. Brown (1967) attempted to trace the
source of students' food likes and dislikes.
Variables uncovered included: variety of foods
served at home; likes and dislikes of family
members; appearance of foods; and parental policies
concerning foods. These findings again emphasise the
importance of the family in shaping food
preferences.

Pilgrim (1961) carried out extensive studies on
food preferences of men in the U.S. armed forces.
Amongst other things he was interested in the
practical question of whether or not food
preferences could be used to predict actual food
consumption, and thus help to reduce food wastage.

Despite the reservations noted earlier preference
and actual choice do seem to be positively related;
where food choice is not limited by income it seems
logical to assume that people will choose the foods
they prefer. Randall (1982) declares that food
preferences are affected by three sets of factors;
those associated with the food itself, with the
individual, and with the environment. Whilst these
must certainly be to some extent interactive they
are for convenience of discussion treated separately
below.

Characteristics of the Food

The sensory qualities of food are important in
determining what is preferred though, as previously
indicated, highly preferred foods will sometimes be
avoided if there is an unpleasant visceral
experience associated with their consumption. Thus
it is not uncommon to hear someone say something
along the lines of: 'Oh yes, I like it - but it
doesn't like me'. According to Bryan and Lowenberg
(1958) children's preferences are influenced by
taste, texture and temperature; adults also list
odour, appearance, method of preparation,
digestibility, ease of eating, and familiarity as
being of importance. The organoleptic or inherent
sensory properties of a food such as its visual
appearance, smell and taste, shape individual
preferences. Foods are often prejudged by their
appearance.

Figure 6.2   Organoleptic properties influencing
              preference for apples.

	COLOUR	FLAVOUR/ODOUR	TEXTURE
Appropriate	Red	Sweet	Crisp
Non-appropriate	Yellow	Sour	Soft
Fresh	Green	Sweet	Firm
Deteriorated	Brown	Sour	Mushy
Cooked properly	Clear	Sweet	Smooth
Improperly cooked	Brown	Burnt	Bitty

For example, appropriate colour is used as an index
of normality, of maturity, of purity and of quality.
Texture, flavour and odour are other indexes of
appropriateness, of deterioration and of proper
cooking technique (Figure 6.2). Most people have a
mental construct of what constitutes perfection in
any given food or dish; when offered these foods
they match them against the ideal in order to
determine their acceptability. Thus a food may be
quite edible, but, because it falls short of
perfection it is rejected and labelled as
´undesirable´ and ´unfit´. Children commonly refuse
to eat even preferred foods because they don´t ´look
right´, or because they are ´not cooked properly´.
Ironically, we often accept lower standards of
´perfection´ when we are paying more for food; ie.
in restaurants. Perhaps cognitive dissonance
dictates that in order to justify high expenditures
on a restaurant meal we have to convince ourselves
mentally that the food was really worth it -
whatever our taste buds tell us. Or perhaps we just
lower our expectations. Fortunately, children
usually do not make such compromises and reject
unsatisfactory dishes whether eating at home, Aunty
Mary´s, or the poshest restaurant in town.
    Sensory evaluation of foods has become a huge
area of interest for researchers and food
manufacturers, much effort and money being expended
on taste testing with consumer panels. Whatever the
organoleptic merits of a single foodstuff, it is
true that most foods are eaten in combination.
Eckstein (1982) discusses the aesthetic effects of
meal composition on acceptability and degree of
preference. She says that a high quality mixed dish
has the following attributes.
  * topography - some large and small pieces so that
    when it is served it forms a pile.
  * neatness   - pieces are cut uniformly and any
    sauce is not runny; no part extends beyond the
    edge of the dish.
  * quantity   - reasonable in proportion to the dish
    - neither skimpy nor too much.
  * harmony   - a pleasing integration and arrangement
    of items; colours, textures, shapes, flavours,
    and odours are compatible.
  * emphasis   - pleasing contrasts of colour, shape,
    texture, flavour and odour.

Eckstein applies the same criteria to the judgement

214

of a complete meal (p318-19). High preference foods may be avoided if served with inappropriate accompaniments; hence the importance of pleasing menu combinations.

Characteristics of individual
As mentioned above, F.E. Pilgrim carried out much of the early research work on food preferences in his studies of food acceptance amongst service men in the U.S. army. Pilgrim's model of food acceptance incorporated the triple factors of individual, food and environment in developing food preferences and shaping food consumption, though particular emphasis was placed on physiological parameters. This same author, using hedonic scales of like-dislike, found that people tended to like or dislike groups of foods. Individuals of similar background gave similar responses. Age influenced food-class preference, though educational level was less important (Pilgrim 1961). Food dislikes are common in young children; taste sensitivity decreases in later years as numbers of taste buds decline, and this may have the effect of enhancing the acceptability of foods. Korslund and Eppright (1967) discovered that children with the lowest taste sensitivities tended to accept more foods, though evidence that taste acuity and preference are strongly related is lacking. There appears to be some sex-difference regarding food preferences; for example, women have a greater preference for sour tastes - but it is not certain if apparent differences are real or culturally induced (Bender 1976). It also seems that women have more food aversions than do men. Randall (1982) comments that there is a difficulty in designing studies to measure such differences and in interpreting the results, as familiar foods are more readily accepted, and women are familiar with more foods than are men. By the same token, greater experience with foods increases the likelihood that some will be disliked. Reliable research methodologies are needed before any worthwhile conclusions can be drawn.

Characteristics of environment
Although it is well recognised that environmental factors play a large part in determining food availability and, indirectly therefore, choice - possible direct effects on food preference have not been extensively studied. Seasonality, urbanisation

and geographical area of origin and habitation may exert measurable effects, as do situational factors such as immediate physical surroundings. Food retailers and restaurateurs have long recognised the importance of physical surroundings and ambience in providing customers with pleasant and appropriate eating experiences. Thus fast food chains often employ bright bold colours to signal their up-tempo brashness, whilst cosy candlelit restaurants make the most of dark warm colours which invite the customer to linger.

It seems then as though those individualistic likes and dislikes which we collectively call food preferences are a product of cultural and biological taste preferences. The question is still open as to whether we seek preferred foods or learn to like those foods which are available, though it would appear sensible to look for a way of reconciling the two. To this end, the next section is devoted to a discussion of the interplay of culture and biology.

INTERACTION OF BIOLOGY AND CULTURE

As tastes and acceptable food combinations are learnt early it is not surprising that in later life familiarity is an important factor in influencing preferences. However, as Rozin (1982) points out, there is also a desire for variety in the diet and thus new foods must be sampled - with the possibility that they will be unacceptable, repulsive or even dangerous. Competing desires for familiarity and novelty must somehow be reconciled. In different parts of the world there are characteristic flavour principles which are repetitively used in all basic food dishes: eg. curry, chili, oregano. Rozin (1978) suggests that these flavours may be used to provide a familiar and reassuring flavour and thus blunt fear of the unknown whilst at the same time promoting acceptance of new foods. Variety is increased because within the overall ´flavour scheme´ there are many graduations of taste, just as there are considerable differences in the class of beverages labelled ´wine´. Repeated experiences with wine consumption lead to greater discrimination and changes in palatability; a wine which is initially rejected as being too dry may eventually become more acceptable than previously preferred sweet wines. Similarly, Europeans who learn to like curries may graduate from mild dishes to searingly hot ones as they

become accustomed to the spicy taste sensations.
Immediately after birth the human infant
already prefers sweet tastes and has aversions to
bitter and sour solutions; this preference for sweet
flavours continues through adult life (Desor, Maller
and Greene 1977, Beidler 1982). Rozin (1982)
explores the preference for sweet substances
utilising a schema in which culture and biology
interact and build upon one another. He begins by
describing the innate biological preference for
sweetness which he explains as being an adaptive
behaviour for humans in their search for energy
sources in the food environment. Once found, these
sweet foods are immediately liked by individuals and
thus are widely used and accepted in the diet; ways
of increasing their availability are sought -
including the use of technological processes - and
thus the taste for sweetness becomes culturally
entrenched. From then on, individuals need only to
be exposed to the substance to accept it, as they
have an innate liking for it and it is culturally
endorsed (Rozin p228). Jerome (1977) points out that
in many cultures sweet foods are offered to infants
and young children. Thus the role of culture is to
increase availability and amplify the basic
biological preference for sweetness. However, as
Rozin himself notes, an adaptive biological
behaviour does not necessarily result in an adaptive
cultural practice; thus the adaptive liking for
sweets in nature becomes a maladaptive over-reliance
on sweets in sophisticated society.

In nearly every culture there is at least one
innately unpalatable substance which becomes an
important food or drink. Several authors have
commented on the widespread use of chili pepper as a
condiment and on the use of coffee, which is
universally served in N. America for adults but
which is disliked by children, who must be taught to
like it. Farb (1980) says that only humans persist
in the use of a substance which they find
distasteful on the first few occasions of use. Why
should this be? Unpalatability is often associated
with plants which contain toxins and which therefore
could be dangerous; a bitter taste may be a warning
not to eat the plant. Most animals do avoid bitter
or irritant foods thus suggesting that human
reactions are culturally influenced. Rozin takes up
the case of chili pepper as an innately unpleasant
substance which has become very widely consumed; he
suggests that people do not eat chili for any

ulterior motive or benefit but do actually come to
like the burning sensation it imparts. Initial
forced exposure to chili is followed by social
reinforcement, which, combined with flavour
enhancement gives rise to a real preference (Rozin
1982). Rozin also speculates on the operation of an
´emotional homeostasis´ system; the unpleasant taste
of chili is countered by an opposing affect reaction
which gives rise to a pleasant internal sensation.
With repeated exposures, this pleasurable opponent
becomes dominant and thus chili becomes liked. An
explanation which invokes beneficial effects as a
rationale for consumption is offered by Pangborn
(1975) who speculates that the widespread use of hot
spicy foods is related to their bacteriostatic
properties.

Another example is found in the practice of
beer drinking. Adolescents taking their first drink
of beer often find it distasteful and even
nauseating. However they persist with the practice,
perhaps because of the social meaning of alcohol and
the manly associations of beer drinking combined
with pleasantly intoxicating effects, and so they
eventually come to like the taste. The phrase
´acquired taste´ is frequently used to describe
something which does not elicit pleasant sensations
when it is first encountered. Persistence can often
be explained in terms of meeting sociocultural
needs. (A particular example of this is the
deliberate cultivation of a taste for exotic and
high status foods such as oysters and ´high´ game.)

FOOD AVERSIONS AND CRAVINGS

The opposite side of the coin to food preference is
food aversion. A term which implies something
stronger than mere avoidance, aversion suggests an
active distaste. This may begin merely as a food
avoidance resulting from religious or social
regulations, or simply as a personal dislike. A
shared dislike for a food may turn it into something
at first undesirable, then repellant, then
detestable. Such is the case with insects and
rodents, as far as most Europeans and North
Americans are concerned, though these same creatures
are important food sources in Africa and other parts
of the world (Bodenheimer 1951, den Hartog 1973).
Potential food substances are primarily rejected
because of:

* Distaste - disliked sensory characteristics
* Danger - anticipated negative consequences
* Disgust - offensiveness of idea of what
  something is
* Inappropriateness - substance is classified as
  not edible
(Fallon & Rozin 1983)

Garb & Stunkard (1974) reported that the majority of
people learn food aversions through the unpleasant
physical experience of illness - usually
gastrointestinal in nature. If stomach-upsets follow
chronologically the consumption of a particular
food, an association between the two events is
readily made which may lead to permanent abstention
from the food item concerned. Strong aversions may
be formed to foods which have not even been tasted,
as in the above examples of insects and rodents.
Even a generous chocolate coating was not sufficient
to induce students in one of my classes to try
grasshoppers, whilst in another food class samples
of squid were resolutely avoided in favour of
familiar white fish! The idea of eating horsemeat
and dogflesh provoke similar feelings of disgust in
many people and yet they are perfectly acceptable
foodstuffs to others. Patently, our ethnocentric
views on what is food are culturally rather than
biologically conditioned.
     Food aversions are most common in children,
being acquired between the ages of six and twelve
years and declining in older age groups. Sometimes
children´s food avoidances are blamed on the mother
eating too much of the food during pregnancy. If
there is any truth in this assertion it is probably
because the food in question is not offered
frequently at family mealtimes or because the mother
attaches negative connotations to its consumption by
recalling that she ate it until she was sick of it.
Conrad (1937) offers a psychiatrist´s point of view,
saying that children are taught disgust reactions
about the time they are being introduced to varied
foods. Substances normally judged to be
inappropriate as food may be consumed under
specialised circumstances. Wallpaper paste was eaten
by the desperately hungry victims of the Siege of
Leningrad; dandelion or marigold leaves may be used
in salads - for effect, or to demonstrate ´bush´
living. Cannibalism may be the only resort of those
isolated through natural or man-made catastrophe.
Inappropriateness is a cultural judgement which may

be set aside if necessity dictates, as in survival situations, or to avoid giving offence when dining with hosts from a different culture.

Just as simple food dislikes may develop into disgust aversions so in some circumstances can food preferences be elevated to the rank of intense longings, or cravings. Cravings are often associated with the physiological status of pregnancy. Dickens and Trethowan (1971) studied cravings and aversions in a group of pregnant young English women; aversions identified most frequently were to tea, coffee, cocoa, vegetables, meat, fish and eggs. Cravings were strongest for fruit, fruit drinks, sweets, ice-cream, milk and dairy products. The authors comment that these desires were more common in women who were orally fixated. Hook (1978) also found that sweets, ice-cream, milk and fruit were frequently craved during pregnancy and that meats and poultry were more frequently avoided than craved. Both authors suggest that cravings and aversions of pregnancy may be due to changes in taste thresholds and sensitivity of smell.

The ´Doctrine of Maternal Impression´ holds that any strong emotional state of the mother will be imprinted on the child. Wet nurses in Victorian England, were screened by their upper class employers for temper, sobriety and morality in the belief that temperament and passion could be passed through the milk during breast feeding, thus rendering the child vulnerable to immoral habits. Similarly, connections are readily made between a mother´s eating behaviour and real or supposed effects on the baby. Snow and Johnston (1978) studied a clinic population in Michigan and found a number of widespread folk beliefs concerning diet in pregnancy. Over two-thirds of the women in the study sample believed in the possibility of ´marking the child´: a third of these respondents specifically mentioned food cravings as the source of the mark. For example, cherries or strawberries eaten by the pregnant woman could produce red spots on the infant. Most women gave examples in which unsatisfied cravings resulted in marking; for example, a woman with a craving for strawberries, who touched her cheek, would cause a strawberry birthmark on the cheek of her infant. The authors offer a rationalisation for this belief which says, in effect, that because birthmarks are out of the ordinary they must be explained; food cravings are associated with pregnancy - in which the obvious

physiological difference from the non-pregnant,
non-craving state, is the presence of the foetus.
Therefore it is easy to make the connection that it
is the foetus which ´needs´ the desired food, and
which is then marked if its needs are unmet. Another
example from Snow and Johnston´s study was the
reported belief that if a woman did not satisfy a
craving for chicken then her baby would look like a
chicken. Amongst some Guatemalan women, spontaneous
abortion may be attributed to unsatisfied food
cravings (de Gonzalez 1964).

Pica
Pica is derived from the Latin word for Magpie, a
bird which eats anything, and is used to denote
compulsive eating, particularly of substances which
are non-nutritive such as dirt and clay. The term
´geophagy´, meaning ´dirt-eating´ is also used. Pica
is commonly seen in the form of unusual cravings
during pregnancy though it is by no means restricted
to this physiological state. Hochstein (1968) listed
six hypotheses to account for the practice of pica
by pregnant women:

1. Psychological   - to get attention.
2. Anthropological - traditional behaviour
   taught by mothers to daughters during process
   of gardening and food preparation - which
   were women´s tasks.
3. Sensory - clay eating decreases uterus
   movements and intestinal mobility and thus
   reduces nausea. It also reduces hunger.
4. Microbial - pica influences acidity of
   intestinal tract, favouring growth of normal
   organisms and discouraging that of pathogens.
5. Physiological - reduces amount of saliva in
   mouth which is a problem for some pregnant
   women.
6. Nutritional need - pica provides some
   nutrient missing from the diet.

The evidence to give widespread support to any of
these hypotheses is scanty. Various studies have
indicated that pica is a culturally determined
behaviour but there is disagreement as to its
possible nutritional value. Dickens and Ford (1942)
reported that clay-eating was common amongst
Mississippi Negro schoolchildren and was viewed by
them as a cultural practice. Vermeer and Frate
(1975) say that the tradition of clay-eating was so

engrained in African ancestors of Southern U.S.
Negroes that its continuation was necessary for
psychological well-being. Hunter (1973) also
suggests that the practice was transplanted, via the
slave trade, to the United States where cultural
substitutes for the clay were found. Laundry starch,
baking soda, wheat flour and dried powdered milks
may be used as replacements.

Several authors have postulated that
clay-eating has possible nutritional and medicinal
benefits. Hunter (1973) suggests that minerals in
clays eaten in Ghana act as dietary supplements,
although Vermeer (1971) reported only small amounts
of calcium in analysed clay samples from the same
area. In contrast, this same researcher found
considerable amounts of calcium and magnesium in
clays eaten by pregnant Tiv women in Nigeria
(Vermeer 1966). Some clays may impair iron
absorption and thus contribute to the development of
anaemia, though on the positive side Halstead (1968)
points out that clay has chelating properties which
could protect against heavy metal poisoning. Solien
(1954) rejects the idea that dirt-eating results
from the body´s recognition of a physiologic need
for certain nutrients. Instead an eco-cultural
explanation is offered; dirt quieted hunger pains
during times of famine; it became an acquired taste
and so the practice was continued even when food
became plentiful. It is also possible that earth was
seen as a source of life and power and that magical
thinking was involved in the deliberate consumption
of part of that earth.

Many studies of Pica have focused on low-income
Blacks. However the practice has also been noted
amongst low-income Whites in a study in Tennessee
(Lackey, Bass & Kolasa 1973), though higher
socioeconomic groups have not been extensively
studied. Reasons given by practitioners of pica
themselves, for their habits, include relief of
nausea, social approval, tradition and expected
physical effects on the baby (Bass, Wakefield,
Kolasa 1979, p47). In Snow and Johnson´s study
(1978) some women thought that craving starch and
clay indicated a dietary need but thought that
taking too much would cause the child to be born
covered with the excess as a caul. Finally, the idea
that pica is an attention-getting strategem is
undermined by the finding that many women are
reluctant and embarrassed to admit to the practice.

SUMMARY

Because eating is so often a social activity
involving interaction with others, it provides an
ideal way in which to demonstrate mood and reflect
emotions. Without having to say anything we can show
that we are angry, bored, or anxious; we can
demonstrate love and caring, disinterest or neglect.
In a sense, eating behaviour is a form of non-verbal
communication containing coded messages of great
complexity and subtlety. The child´s sudden refusal
to eat says ´Give me some attention´; the anorexic
teenager proclaims ´You cannot control me´; the
obese young woman says (perhaps) ´Keep away!´. The
same gesture might mean quite different things
according to circumstance; for example, the gift of
a box of chocolates could mean: ´I love you´, ´I´m
sorry´, or ´I´m feeling guilty for neglecting you´.
Caution is the watchword when attempting to
interpret the language of food!
     Psychological disturbances may sometimes be
physically manifested as loss of weight control.
Although it would be absurd to claim that all
overweight people had other problems in coping with
life, the possibility of psychological elements in
the genesis of obesity should not be overlooked in
the professional counselling and treatment of
overweight patients. It is much more clear though,
that the nutritional consequences of Anorexia
Nervosa are symptomatic of underlying psychological
disorders. Whilst dietary treatment alone may be
effective in treating obesity (though it rarely is)
it is certainly not an adequate response to the
serious condition of Anorexia Nervosa. Here we have
a preeminent example of psychological stress
producing changes in food choice behaviour - which
in turn affect nutritional status and physical
well-being.
     Even in the absence of pronounced
psychological aberrations food selection is a
function of the way we think. Far from it being a
rational activity designed to provide nutritional
satisfaction in as efficient a manner as possible,
choosing what to eat is a complex process governed
to a great extent by mental deliberations; for there
is ample evidence to show that we eat with our eyes
and minds as much as with our taste buds and
stomachs. There is some basis for claiming the
existence of an inherent liking or dislike for
certain tastes and flavour principles; sweetness is

generally liked and desired, whilst bitterness is
not. However it is obvious that tastes can be
acquired and thus that likes and dislikes are
products of cultural learning. As they are learned,
they confer acceptability on regularly consumed
foods which leads to long-term preferences for
familiar items. Thus even at the level of individual
food selection it is difficult to maintain the
illusion that objective free choice is likely. Of
course it is possible to argue that we could choose
to eat earthworms or goldfish if we really wanted
to, but the very fact that we don't so choose seems
to indicate that there are indeed restraints
operating. My contention, repeated throughout this
book, is that we understand very clearly that edible
substances may be culturally classified as either
food or non-food and we are careful to preserve this
distinction in our personal eating habits.

REFERENCES

Babcock, C. 'Food and its Emotional Significance.'
    J. Am. Diet. Ass. , 24:390-395, 1948
Bass, M.A., L.M. Wakefield, and K.M. Kolasa.
    Community Nutrition and Individual Food
    Behaviour. Burgess Publ., Minn. 1979
Beidler, L.M. 'Biological Basis of Food Selection.'
    In L. Barker (ed.), The Psychobiology of Human
    Food Selection. , AVI, Westport 1982
Bender, A. 'Food Preferences of Males and Females.'
    Proc. Nutr. Soc. , 35:181, 1976
Bodenheimer, F.S. Insects as Human Food: a Chapter
    of the Ecology of Man. Dr. W.Junk, The Hague
    1951
Brown, E.L. 'College Students Look at the Basis for
    their Food Habits.' J. Home Ec. , 59:784, 1967
Bruch, H. 'Role of the Emotions in Hunger and
    Appetite.' Ann. N.Y. Acad. Sci. , 63
    (1):68-75, 1955
Bruch, H. Eating Disorders. Obesity, Anorexia
    Nervosa and the Person Within. Routledge &
    Kegan Paul, London 1974
Bryan, M., and M. Lowenberg. 'The Father's Influence
    on Young Children's Food Preference.' J. Am.
    Diet. Ass. , 34:30, 1958
Cohen, Y.A. 'Food and it's Vicissitudes:a
    Cross-cultural Study of Sharing and
    Non-sharing.', In Y.A. Cohen (ed.), Social
    Structure and Personality. Holt, Rinehart &
    Winston, New York 1961

Conrad, A. ´The Attitude Toward Food.´ Am. J.
    Orthopsychiatry , 7:360-67, 1937
Cussler, M.T., and M.L. DeGive. Twixt the cup and
    the lip. Twayne Publ., New York 1952
Davis, C.M. ´Self-selection of Diets by Newly Weaned
    Infants:an Experimental Study.´ Am. J. Dis.
    Child. , 36:651-79, 1928
Davis, C.M. ´Results of the Self-selection of Diets
    by Young Children.´ Can. Med. Assn. ,
    41:257-261, 1939
de Gonzalez, N.L.S. ´Beliefs and Practices
    Concerning Medicine and Nutrition Among Lower
    Class Urban Guatemalans.´ Am. J. Publ. Health
    , 54:1726-34, 1964.
Desor, J.A., O. Maller, and L.S. Greene. ´Preference
    for Sweet in Humans: Infants, Children and
    Adults.´ In J.M. Weiffenbach (ed.), Taste and
    Development. The Genesis of Sweet Preference.
    Fogarty Int. Center Proc. No.32. NIH, Bethesda
    1977.
Dickens, G., and W.H. Trethowan. ´Cravings and
    Aversions During Pregnancy.´ J. Psychosomat.
    Res. , 15:259-68, 1971
Dickens, D. ´Factors Related to Food Preferences.´
    J. Home Econ. , 57:427-430, 1965
Dickins, D., and R.N. Ford. ´Geophagy (dirt eating)
    Among Mississippi Negro Schoolchildren.´ Am.
    Sociol. Rev. , 7:59-65, 1942
Du Bois, C. The People of Alor: A
    Social-Psychological Study of an East Indian
    Island. Harper & Row, New York 1961
Eckstein, E.F. Food, People and Nutrition. AVI,
    Westport 1980.
Everson, G.J. ´Bases for Concern about Teenagers
    Diets.´ J. Am. Diet. Ass. , 36:17, 1960
Farb, P., and G. Armelagos. Consuming Passsions:the
    Anthropology of Eating. Houghton Mifflin,
    Boston 1980
Garb, J.L., and A.J. Stunkard. ´Taste Aversions in
    Man.´ Am. J. Psych. , 13:1204-7, 1974
George, S. How the Other Half Dies. Penguin Books,
    Middx. 1976
Gifft, H.H., M.B. Washbon, and G.G. Harrison.
    Nutrition, Behaviour and Change. Prentice
    Hall, New Jersey 1972
Halstead, J.A. ´Geophagia in Man:It´s Nature and
    Nutritional Effects.´ Am. J. Clin. Nutr. ,
    21:1384-1393, 1968

Hamilton E.M.N., and E.N. Whitney. Nutrition: Concepts and Controversies. West Publ., St.Paul 1982

Hochstein, G. ´Pica:A Study in Medical and Anthropological Explanation.´ In T. Weaver (ed.), Essays on Medical Anthropology. Southern Anthropological Society Proceedings No.1:88-97, 1968

Hook, E.B. ´Dietary Cravings and Aversions During Pregnancy.´ Am. J. Clin. Nutr. , 31:1355-62, 1978

Hunter, J.M. ´Geophagy in Africa and the United States: A Culture-Nutrition Hypothesis.´ Geog. Rev. , 63:170-95, 1973

Jerome, N.W. ´Taste Experience and the Development of a Dietary Preference for Sweet in Humans: Ethnic and Cultural Variations in Early Taste Experience.´ In J.M. Weiffenbach (ed.), Taste and Development. The Genesis of Sweet Preference. Fogarty Int. Center Proc. No.32. NIH, Bethesda 1977

Korslund, M.K. and E.S. Eppright. ´Taste Sensitivity and Eating Behaviour of Preschool Children.´ J. Home Ec. , 59:169, 1967

Lackey, C., M.A. Bass, and K. Kolasa. ´Study of Pica Among Pregnant Women in East Tennessee.´ Paper presented to Am. Diet. Ass., Denver 1973

Lowenberg, M.E., E.N. Todhunter, E.D. Wilson, J.R. Savage, and J.L. Lubawski. Food and People. J. Wiley & Sons, New York 1979

Maslow, A.H. Motivation and Personality. Harper & Row, New York 1970.

McKenzie, J. ´The Impact of Economic and Social Status on Food Choice.´ Proc. Nutr. Soc. , 33 (1):67-74, 1974

Mead, M. ´Food and the Family.´ In Food and People. UNESCO, New York 1953

Mitchell, D. The Politics of Food. James Lorimer & Co., Toronto 1975

Murray, H.L., and R.H.J. Watson. ´Personality and Food Preference.´ Proc. Nutr. Soc. , 37:36A, 1978

Moore, H.B. ´Psychologic Facts and Dietary Fancies.´ J. Am. Diet. Ass. , 28:789, 1952

Pangborn, R.M. ´Cross-cultural Aspects of Flavour Preference.´ Food Tech. , 29 (6):34-36, 1975

Pilgrim, F.J. ´The Components of Food Acceptance and their Measurement.´ Am. J. Clin. Nutr. , 5:171, 1957

Pilgrim, F.J. ´What Foods do People Accept or
    Reject?´ J. Am. Diet. Ass. , 38: 439-443, 1961
Pumpian-Mindlin, E. ´The Meanings of Food.´ J. Am.
    Diet. Ass. , 30:576, 1954
Randall, E. ´Food Preferences as a Determinant of
    Food Behaviour.´ In D. Sanjur, Social and
    Cultural Perspectives in Nutrition. Prentice
    Hall, New Jersey 1982
Rozin, P. ´The Use of Characteristic Flavourings in
    Human Culinary Practice.´ In C.M. Apt. (ed.),
    Flavor: It´s Chemical, Behavioral and
    Commercial Aspects. Westview Pr., Colorado
    1978
Rozin, P. ´Human Food Selection: the Interaction of
    Biology, Culture and Individual Experience.´ In
    L. Barker (ed.), The Psychobiology of Human
    Food Selection. AVI, Westport 1982
Scrimshaw, N.S. ´The Effect of Stress on Nutrition
    in Adolescents and Young Adults.´ In F.P. Heald
    (ed.), Adolescent Nutrition and Growth.
    Appleton-Century-Crofts, New York 1969
Shack, W. ´Hunger, Anxiety and Ritual: Deprivation
    and Spirit Possession among the Gurage of
    Ethiopa.´ Man. 6:30-43, 1971
Simoons, F.J. Eat Not This Flesh. U. of Wisconsin
    Pr., Madison 1961
Simoons, F.J., B. Schonfeld-Leber, and H.L. Issel.
    ´Cultural Determinants to Use of Fish as Human
    Food.´ Oceanus. 22:67-71, 1979
Snow, L.F., and S.M. Johnson. ´Folklore, Food,
    Female Reproductive Cycle.´ Ecol. Food Nutr. ,
    7:41-49, 1978
Solien, N.L.A. ´A Cultural Explanation of Geophagy.´
    Florida Anthrop. , 7:1-9, 1954
Tannahill, R. Food in History. Stein & Day, New
    York 1973
Vermeer, D.E. ´Geophagy Among the Tiv of Nigeria.´
    Assn. Am. Geog. Ann. 56:197-204, 1966
Vermeer, D.E. ´Geophagy Among the Ewe of Ghana.´
    Ethnology. 10:56-72, 1971
Vermeer, D.E., and D.A. Frate. ´Geophagy in a
    Mississippi County.´ Assn. Am. Geog. Ann. ,
    65:414-424, 1975
Weinberg, J. ´Psychologic Implications of the
    Nutritional Needs of the Elderly.´ J. Am.
    Diet. Ass. , 60:293-96, 1972

231